# GARY

# RHODES

# GARY RHODES

*fabulous food*

photographs by Sandra Lane

Dorling  Kindersley

London, New York, Sydney, Dehli, Paris,
Munich, and Johannesburg

Publisher Sean Moore
Editorial director LaVonne Carlson
Project editor Barbara Minton
Editor Jane Perlmutter
Art director Dirk Kaufman
Art editor Gus Yoo
Production director David Proffit

US edition ISBN 0-7894-6809-3
First US edition published in 2000 by
Dorling Kindersley, Inc.
95 Madison Avenue
New York, New York, 10016

This is a companion book to the PBS TV television series Great Food
Presented by

**thirteen**
WNET NEW YORK
Sponsored by
**looksmart**
www.looksmart.com
Produced by

west 175
productions

wine com

Published by BBC Books,
an imprint of BBC Worldwide Publishing
80 Wood Lane, London W12 0TT

First published 1997 © Gary Rhodes
The moral right of the author has been asserted.

Designed by Isobel Gillan
Photographs by Sandra Lane, © BBC Books
Styling by Mary Norton
Food for photography prepared by Gary Rhodes

Set in Bembo and Gill Sans by BBC Books
Printed and bound in Great Britain by Butler & Tanner Ltd, Frome and London
Color separations by Radstock Reproductions Ltd, Midsomer Norton
Jacket printed by Lawrence Allen Ltd, Weston-super-Mare

Permission to use the Wagon Wheel® name, a registered British trade mark, for the recipe on page 190 has been
kindly granted by Burton's Biscuits.

## For My Mother

## Acknowledgements
A special thank you to Borra Garson, Bill Toner, Wayne Tapsfield, Jane Huffer,
the kitchen team at city rhodes, Nicky Copeland, Khadija Manjlai, Frank Phillips,
Isobel Gillan, my wife Jenny and my sons Samuel and George for keeping me
sane (!) and ahead of everything.

*Previous page:* Green Tomato *Tarte Tatin* (page 130)

# contents

# notes on the recipes

1  Follow one set of measurements only; do not mix American Standard and metric.
2  Eggs are size large.
3  Wash fresh produce before preparation.
4  Spoon measurements are level.
5  A tablespoon is 15 ml; a teaspoon is 5 ml.
6  If you substitute dried for fresh herbs, use only half the amount specified.
7  Herbal tea bags are readily available and can be used as an alternative to bouquets garnis.
8  Unless otherwise stated, 'season' or 'seasoning' simply means seasoning with salt and pepper.
9  I recommend Lindt chocolate where recipes call for good quality semisweet chocolate.
10  When blind-baking pastry cases, it is best to leave the excess pastry hanging over the rim.  Once the pastry is cooked, simply trim off the edges to give a neat even finish.
11  Butane torches can be used to give a crispy sugar glaze to many desserts.  It is important to be fully aware of how to operate and use the torch since this is not a conventional kitchen utensil.  And, obviously, the torches should not be used by children.
12  Oven temperatures and cooking times are flexible and may vary according to the equipment and ingredients used.
13  Butter and cream may be reduced, if not excluded, in most savory recipes.
14  Where a pat of butter is stated, it may be used more than once in the recipe. The exact quantity of butter is left to your discretion – you can use 1 teaspoon or 1 tablespoon, or replace the butter with a small amount of vegetable oil.
15  *Mirepoix* is a term used to mean a general mixture of chopped carrots, onion, celery, and leeks.
16  Ingredients are listed with the main ingredient(s) first, followed by the other ingredients in order of use.
17  Always be careful when increasing quantities of ingredients to serve more people; quite often not all the ingredients will need to be increased by the same proportion. It is best to taste as you add.

# introduction

*i* am often asked where the ideas and recipes come from to put these books together. To be totally honest with you, I'm not quite sure! An idea for a 'new' dish (is there such a thing?) can often come from the oddest and strangest situations. Take Omelette Vesuvius or Baked Alaska as we know it. Was somebody skiing or mountaineering when they thought of this classic dish? The inspiration for the Jaffa Cake Pudding from *Open Rhodes* came from a Saturday-afternoon shopping trip; the Wagon Wheel® Pudding (page 190) came from memories of my school days, and to be honest, the Bourbon Biscuits (page 210) came purely from dunking one!

Working in a busy restaurant kitchen spreads thoughts among the whole team, and often young chefs approach me to say they have an idea for a new dish. This automatically inspires me and it pleases me to know that their minds are on the job and that they are also trying to look further than their everyday tastes to create something new. To encourage that inspiration, I want to listen, discuss, and then try the dish. Sometimes the idea isn't quite right, but it might have something that sparks off another idea, which then develops into something completely different, but is always credited to its originator.

Reading cookbooks is one of my favorite pastimes, not in an effort to find new dishes, but in the hope that reading them will encourage another new idea. I also find myself thinking up recipes when I'm driving, and as soon as I get to work, I scribble them down on paper. Some never develop any further, but I'm pleased to say, many of them do. I also have a golden rule for any new dishes: when I've had an afternoon with the sous-chef, and a brainstorming session for a menu change, all ideas are listed and put on hold for a few days. This is because, I'm sure you'll agree, the mind can get a little carried away and totally lose its initial track. Many times we've looked at our ideas three days later and said to each other "What is that?," pointing to a dish that's never going to work and looks like nonsense.

I remember visiting a smoked-salmon maker and dealer in northern Scotland. He has won many awards for the quality of his smoking, giving the salmon a flavor and texture that's an experience to try. One of the stages of his smoking was to marinate the salmon fillets in a mixture of water, black treacle (somewhat like molasses), sherry, black peppercorns, juniper berries, and thyme. The balance between those flavors worked so well and left a taste that I hadn't experienced before. The blend played on my mind for some time. I eventually took the majority of those ingredients and turned them into a dressing, but instead of serving smoked salmon with it, I chose fresh salmon. The flavor is immense and the recipe has been a great success on the menu.

I mentioned driving and ideas coming to me. Could it be the music I'm playing that's at work here? Does Soul give you a warm, sensual feeling towards eating, Jazz a delicate depth, and Country something hearty; and maybe heavy Funk just explodes in the mouth? (I think Pop is take-away and Punk, nouvelle cuisine!) All are part of communication and work together so well.

It's interesting and educational to read a dictionary, looking for the true meanings of words. Often, though, I feel the definitions are quite shallow and don't communicate enough real information to us. The biggest vehicle for communication, I believe, is food: it brings us all together. Restaurants and dining room tables are probably the most used meeting places in the world. We do all have to eat! There's so much more to it than that. One style of cooking and food communicates a totally different message to your friends and colleagues. I'm sure none of us 'popped the question' over a hot dog, french fries, and beans affair!

Chefs in the kitchen are not just putting flavors together for the sake of it. There's a link, a sense of communication, between tastes and textures. When dishes are being put together, they are formed with a meaning, to make sure every taste involved is going to be happily mingling with the others. There really should always be a purpose for any item being on the plate, and I mean in terms of flavor rather than just being decorative.

Looking up the word 'communicate' in the dictionary made interesting reading. It gives quite a few explanations. Speech, writing, gestures, imparting knowledge. One that stood out for me is 'to make or have a connecting passage,' that is, the kitchen 'communicating' with the dining room. What about the food communicating with the eater? The distance between the two rooms is purely a passageway, but, for me, the real communication comes from what you are carrying on plates from one to the other. When the plate is put in front of you, it's the food that is talking to you, leading me to another word that has a close relationship with cooking: 'expression.'

The first example and, being the first, it means it's the most important current meaning, is the act or instance of transferring ideas into words. How right that is – transferring ideas into words. The ideas are in the cooking; I'm always wanting to create ideas of dishes for the public – the eaters – with the food and flavors. Another explanation for the word expression is 'a look on the face that indicates a mood or emotion'. Cooking should be about trying to tell a story or communicating. When you look at the dish, it should be alive and talking to you.

I always check people's faces when dishes are presented to them; they are immediately inquisitive. Then, when all is right, their expressions turn into smiles of appreciation and, more importantly, the 'can't wait to taste it' look.

The biggest compliment a chef can receive is when his or her food has totally changed the direction of conversation. The only line you want to hear then is 'you've got to try some of this' or 'mmmm, delicious'.

In talking about communication and expression, I haven't been referring solely to restaurant and dinner party food; it applies to all food. The same strength of passion and feeling with me is featured in all the recipes in this book, from a humble bowl of pea soup through to the more sophisticated roasted *foie gras*. It's quite a strong message!

This book is about trying to take flavors even further and about continuing to express my passion for making British cooking among the best, if not the best, that can be found anywhere. I'm still looking at British classics and trying to put them on a new plane, with more refinement and more exact flavors. I also hope that, somewhere among all of these recipes, we'll find a new 'classic', a dish that will be cooked and talked about for years to come. Looking ahead means thinking ahead in place, time, and order, and for me, that implies never sitting back, but always trying to cook the next dish better than the last.

I hope you are going to enjoy the dishes and read the personal messages in them. I feel as though I've been writing a letter to a friend. Make sure you reply by trying them out.

The cooking in this book is definitely about expression and communication. Let's make sure we all keep talking.

Gary Rhodes

APPETIZERS

# appetizers

We'll start the meal with Warm Champagne Oysters (page 24), followed by a large bowl of Moules Marinière (page 22) and then how about Roast *Foie Gras* (page 42) or Confit of Bacon (page 38)? Sounds like a very tasty meal already and we haven't even looked at the main courses or desserts yet!

All of these dishes are featured in this first chapter, which shows the range of cooking and eating styles that you can achieve without looking much further (but I hope you do!).

I always say that we should never be too strict with our cooking from, or reading of, cookbooks. When I hunt for recipes, no matter what type, I look through the whole book and, quite often, have the pleasure of finding, for example, a simple appetizer that will stand up as a main course. Among all of these appetizer recipes you will find some interesting flavors, styles and combinations: Potato, Scallion, and Mozzarella Risotto (page 53), Smoked Haddock and Sorrel Omelette (page 25) and Mussels glazed with Cider Cream Sauce (page 21). There is one, though, that has really made an impact: Escalope of Salmon with Molasses, Juniper and Sherry Dressing (page 30). I'm sure you'll all be wondering how salmon and molasses can complement each another but, I promise you, they do. The molasses doesn't mask the flavor of the fish but helps to lift all the other flavors.

Here's a sample of some of the other dishes in this chapter: Tuna fish with lemon dressing, Asparagus and leeks, Scallops with a hot mustard sauce, Terrine of duck, pork and chicken liver and Escabeche of red mullet. I'm sure you'll notice the one common ingredient they all have – **TASTE!**

# Frozen Pea Soup

*Here's a really quick soup to make. After all, the peas only take about 3 minutes! The soup takes a little longer to finish, but only a few minutes more.*

---

**Serves 4–6**

1 lb (450 g) frozen peas
1 large onion, finely chopped
1 tablespoon butter
2 cups (450 ml) Vegetable
   or Chicken Stock (page 240)
   or alternative (page 243)

A pinch of sugar
⅔ cup (150 ml) light cream
   (optional)
Salt and pepper

Cook the onion in 1 tablespoon butter for a few minutes, without letting it brown, until softened. Add the stock and bring to a rapid simmer. Add the peas now and cook on a fast heat for 3 minutes. Once the peas are soft and tender, season with salt, pepper and sugar and then liquidize to a smooth consistency. For an even smoother finish, push the soup through a sieve. For a creamier consistency, add the light cream. The pea soup is now ready to eat, preferably with lots of crusty bread!

**Note:** A sprig or two of fresh mint can be added to the soup during the cooking of the onion for some extra taste. The soup can also be garnished with fried or toasted bread croutons and small, crisp strips of smoked or unsmoked bacon.

# Cauliflower Soup *with 'Harry's Bar' Toasties*

*Cauliflower soup is pretty self-explanatory, but what are 'Harry's Bar' toasties?*

*Harry's Bar is a very famous bar in Venice, Italy. It is renowned for its drinks and sandwiches, among many other foods. The toasties are really a Harry's Bar version of the French croque monsieur – a cheese and ham toasted sandwich. The Harry's Bar version is made with Swiss Gruyère, which is turned into a speedy rarebit mix, to give a creamier and more tasty finish. The sandwich is then fried in olive oil for a crispy warm finish.*

*Both flavors, ham and cheese, go very well with cauliflower, so I decided to make these sandwiches part of the dish. After all, we often sprinkle croutons over soups. Here, you'll be dipping your crouton into the soup!*

**Serves 4**

**For the Cauliflower Soup:**
1 small cauliflower, trimmed and
   roughly chopped
1 tablespoon butter
1 onion, chopped
1 small leek (white only), chopped
2 cups (450 ml) Vegetable
   or Chicken Stock (page 240)
   or alternative (page 243)
⅔ cup (150 ml) light cream or milk
Salt and pepper

**For the Filling:**
1 cup (225 g) Gruyère, grated
½ teaspoon English mustard
1 teaspoon Worcestershire sauce
A pinch of cayenne pepper
A pinch of salt
1 tablespoon light cream (optional)

**For the Toasties:**
8 slices of white bread
4 slices of ham
Olive oil, for frying

For the soup, melt the butter in a large saucepan and add the onion and leek. Cook for 3–4 minutes, without letting them brown, and then add the roughly chopped cauliflower with the stock. Season with salt and pepper and bring to a simmer. Cover and cook the soup for 15–20 minutes.

Check that the cauliflower is cooked and then add the cream or milk. Blend the soup to a smooth consistency and check the seasoning. If the consistency is a little grainy, simply push the soup through a sieve.

To make the filling for the toasties, the cheese must first be left to reach a warm room temperature. If you try to make this with cheese straight from the fridge, the flavors and textures will not emulsify.

Place all the filling ingredients, except the cream, in a food processor and mix to a smooth consistency. If the spread appears to be a little thick, add the light cream and mix again.

Spread the cheese mix onto all the slices of bread. Put a slice of ham on four slices and sandwich with the remaining four slices. Trim off the crusts. These sandwiches can be made well in advance to this point and refrigerated.

To finish the toasties, heat a frying pan with enough olive oil to coat the base. Once hot, pan fry the toasties to a crisp golden brown on both sides. This will warm the cheese spread and give it a melting consistency that goes well with the ham and crisp bread. Once all the sandwiches are fried, cut them into two-inch strips and offer one or two pieces per portion.

**Note:** These quantities are quite substantial enough for a main course, so if you just want a snack make half the quantity of toasties.

The soup can also be spiced up with a touch of English or Dijon mustard.

# Roast Mushroom Soup

*This is a basic recipe with only a handful of ingredients, but it certainly has lots of flavor. The twist in the taste comes from the roasting of the mushrooms. The soup could be made without roasting at all, by chopping the mushrooms and stewing them with the onion and potato instead. The mushrooms, however, become very watery without roasting and lose their good, strong taste.*

*I like to save one or two of the roasted mushrooms and chop them for the garnish, along with some chopped tarragon or parsley.*

---

**Serves 4–6**

1½ lb (750 g) cremini mushrooms
2 tablespoons cooking oil
2 onions, finely chopped
1 large potato, peeled and cut into
    a rough ½ in (1 cm) dice
1 tablespoon butter

2½ cups (600 ml) Vegetable
    or Chicken Stock (page 240)
    or alternative (page 243)
1¼ cups (300 ml) light cream
    or milk
Salt and pepper
Chopped fresh parsley or tarragon,
    to garnish (optional)

Preheat the oven to 425°F/220°C.

First wipe the mushrooms clean, rather than washing them. (If you wash them, they tend to absorb too much water.) Heat a roasting pan or an ovenproof frying pan and add the cooking oil. You can now season the mushrooms and then add them whole and fry them on a high heat to brown them well. Once they are browned on one side, turn the mushrooms over and brown again. They should now be placed in the oven for 8–10 minutes.

Cook the onions and potato in butter, without letting them brown, until softened. Add the stock and bring to a simmer.

Roughly cut up the mushrooms, saving one or two for garnishing, and add them to the soup, together with any residue left in the roasting or frying pan. Bring the soup back to a simmer and add the light cream. Season with salt and pepper.

Cook for 5–6 minutes and then remove from the heat.

Puree to a smooth finish. The soup can also be pushed through a sieve to give an even smoother consistency. Bring back to a simmer and add the sliced or chopped roasted mushrooms to garnish. Taste again for seasoning and add the chopped parsley or tarragon, if using.

**Note:** If you are using tarragon, add some leaves during the cooking process to give some extra taste. Adding a squeeze of lemon juice once the soup has been pureed will also enhance the other flavors.

# Roast Ham and Porcini Soup

*Porcinis are popular and grown all over Europe; they are known as* cèpes *in France and* porcini *in Italy. They are one of the best wild mushrooms, packed with flavor, and need very little else to help them. Cepes can be bought fresh or dried; the dried are a lot easier to find – the fresh ones are only available in season from summer through to early winter.*

*The roast ham flavor in this soup is quite powerful but the porcini stand their ground making a big impression. The raw ham does need to be soaked for 24 hours, to reduce its saltiness. If you buy hock of ham on the bone, buy 2½ lb (1.25 kg) to allow for the weight of the bone. Cooking the ham on the bone does give the stock a wonderfully powerful flavor.*

*This is a very hearty soup that can stand as a main course, especially with some good crusty bread.*

---

**Serves 6–8**

2 lb (900 g) piece of raw ham, knuckle or hock
4 oz (100 g) dried porcini
4 oz (100 g) fresh porcini, wiped and sliced
3 cups (225 g) button mushrooms, sliced
2–3 tablespoons cooking oil
Chicken Stock (page 240) or alternative (page 243) or water, if necessary
1 tablespoon butter

⅔ cup (150 ml) heavy cream
Salt and pepper
1 tablespoon chopped fresh flatleaf or curly parsley

**For the *Mirepoix*:**

1 onion, chopped
2 carrots, chopped
2 celery sticks, chopped,
1 leek, chopped
Fresh thyme sprig
1 tablespoon butter

Soak the ham in plenty of fresh water for 24 hours. Cover the dried porcini with 2 pints (1.2 liters) of cold water and leave them to soak for 3–4 hours. Then preheat the oven to 375°F/190°C.

Heat the oil in a roasting pan and add the ham. Cook it on top of the stove, until golden, turning it from time to time. Then transfer to the oven and roast for 45–50 minutes. This gives you a half-cooked or perhaps three-quarters-cooked roast ham, having all of the roasted flavors.

While the ham is roasting, soften the *mirepoix* of vegetables and thyme with butter in a large, deep saucepan. Add the roasted ham and strain the water from the soaked porcini into the pan. Top up the pan with more water or some chicken stock, for extra flavor, so that it virtually covers the ham. Bring to a simmer and cook for a further 45 minutes and then remove from the heat. The ham will now be totally cooked and flake easily.

Leave to rest for 15–20 minutes.

Remove the ham from the stock. The stock can now be reduced by simmering to about a third to a half to give you a richer, tastier stock.

Add the soaked mushrooms to the finished stock. Fry the fresh porcini and button mushrooms in the butter and also add to the stock with all their cooking juices. Add the cream and bring to a simmer. Taste and reduce, if necessary, to increase the depth of flavor.

Season with salt and pepper. Remove any skin from the ham, shred the meat and add it to the soup. You may find you have too much ham: if so, I suggest you use it for some delicious ham and cheese 'toasties' (page 14)!

Add the chopped parsley and the soup is ready.

**Note:** If fresh or dried porcini are unavailable, simply replace with an extra 8 oz (225 g) button mushrooms.

# 'Main Course' Whole Chicken and Vegetable Soup

*This soup is entitled main course because that's exactly what it could be. It could also become a creamy casserole. What I love about this dish is the way in which it creates its own stock — packed with flavor from the chicken and the vegetables.*

*Many other ingredients can also be added — spaghetti, macaroni, rice, tomatoes, basil, and more!*

---

**Serves 6–8**

3 lb (1.5 kg) oven-ready chicken
2 large onions, cut in large dice
3 carrots, diced
4 celery sticks, diced
1 large potato, diced
1 medium leek, diced
A handful of frozen peas
2–4 tbs. (25–50 g) butter
⅓–⅔ cups (85–150 ml) cream
  (optional)
Salt and pepper

Season the chicken and place it in a deep saucepan; cover it with cold water. Bring to a simmer and skim any impurities from the surface. Cover the pot loosely and leave to simmer for an hour, skimming from time to time.

Add the onions, carrots, celery and potato. Return to a simmer and continue to cook for 20 minutes until all the vegetables are cooked and tender. Remove the chicken from the stock and, when it is cool enough to handle, break it into pieces and pull the meat into strips (remove and discard the skin and bones).

Bring the soup base to a boil and allow it to reduce to increase the flavor. Once a good strong flavor has been reached, add the leek and cook for 2 minutes before adding the frozen peas. Return the soup to a boil and cook for a further 3 minutes. Now add the butter with the cream, if using. Add the strips of chicken and check for seasoning. It is now ready to serve.

# Mussels glazed with Cider Cream Sauce

*These mussels are served out of their shells. Glazed in a nice, small appetizer bowl or serving dish, what you'll have are fresh mussels, lots of leeks and good cider-cream sauce glaze. Nothing could be a better accompaniment than a glass of good wine.*

*If you want to turn this into a main course, take a fillet of cod or salmon, poach it, sit it on a bed of spinach, and then glaze it with the mussel and cider sauce.*

---

**Serves 2**

1½ lb (750 g) live mussels, scrubbed, washed and 'beards' removed

2 small leeks, 1 cut in ½ in (1 cm) dice, 1 roughly chopped

1¼ cups (300 ml) Fish Stock (page 241) or alternative (page 243) or water

1 tablespoon butter

½ onion, roughly chopped

A few fresh tarragon leaves (optional)

1 star anise (optional)

1¼ cups (300 ml) apple cider

⅔ cup (150 ml) heavy cream

1 egg yolk

Salt and pepper

Blanch one diced leek in the fish stock or water for a minute until tender. Strain, saving the stock, and leave the leeks to cool.

Melt the pat of butter in a saucepan big enough to cook the mussels in. Add the onion, the other roughly chopped leek, tarragon (if using) and star anise. Cook for a few minutes until the onion is tender. Increase the heat and add the mussels. Stir the mussels in the pan and then add the cider and reserved stock. Bring to a boil, while stirring the mussels. After a few minutes, the mussels will begin to open. Discard any that don't open. Strain the mussels through a sieve into a large, clean pan, saving only the cider and mussel stock. Bring the stock to a boil and reduce by two-thirds by simmering gently. While the stock is reducing, take the mussels from their shells and keep them warm in a little of the stock.

Add half the heavy cream and return to a boil. The sauce may well need to reduce further by a quarter in volume. It is ready when it just coats the back of a spoon. Add the reserved cooked leeks and mussels and warm through.

Lightly whip the remaining cream. Preheat the broiler to hot.

Add 1 tablespoon butter to the sauce with the egg yolk. Do not allow the sauce to boil or the egg will 'scramble.' Fold in the whipped cream and check the seasoning. Spoon the mussels, leeks and sauce into serving bowls or plates and glaze under a preheated broiler. After a minute or two, the cider sauce will have glazed to a lovely golden brown.

**Note:** For the ultimate glaze, the sauce is better bound with a tablespoon of Quick Hollandaise Sauce (page 235) or a whisked *sabayon* of egg yolk and cider, both folded in with the whipped cream.

# Moules Marinière

*I love eating large bowls of mussels, with some good bread to mop up any juices.* Moules Marinière *is a French classic that, for me, stands as a complete dish. I have added one or two extra flavors but they are optional, so you can keep this dish as simple as possible.*

**Serves 2–3**

2¼ lb (1 kg) live mussels, washed, scrubbed and 'beards' (the threads that hang from the shells) removed

4 tbs (50 g) butter

2 heaping tablespoons chopped fresh shallots or onions

1 heaping tablespoon finely diced carrots (optional)

1 heaping tablespoon finely diced celery (optional)

1 garlic clove, crushed

1 heaping tablespoon finely diced leek (optional)

2 glasses of white wine

3 glasses of Fish Stock (page 241) or alternative (page 243) or water

1 star anise (optional)

⅓ cup (85 ml) heavy cream

A squeeze of lemon juice

Salt and pepper

1 tablespoon mixed chopped fresh herbs e.g. parsley, tarragon, chervil

Melt 1 tbs (15 g) of the butter in a saucepan and add the shallots or onions, carrots, celery, and garlic. Cook for a few minutes, until beginning to soften, and then add the diced leek, if using. Cook for a minute more, remove from the heat and leave to one side.

Place the mussels in a large saucepan on a medium high heat and add the white wine and fish stock or water with the star anise, if using. Cover with a lid and cook for 30 seconds, then stir for 3–4 minutes. During this time, the mussels will open. Once all are opened (any that don't should be discarded) lift the mussels from the pan into serving dishes and keep warm. Strain the cooking liquor through a fine sieve onto the cooked vegetables. Bring to a boil and reduce by a third. Add the cream and whisk in the remaining butter with a squeeze of lemon. Season with salt and pepper and add the chopped mixed herbs. Pour the finished liquor over the mussels and serve.

**Note:** *Moules Marinière Royale* is another favorite, with a name I've taken from the famous Kir drink: Kir is a glass of white wine flavored with *cassis* (blackcurrant liqueur). *Kir Royale* is made with champagne. So, for *Moules Marinière Royale*, just replace the white wine with champagne.

# Warm Champagne Oysters *with*
## *Smokey Cabbage*

*Eating oysters the classic way, raw with a squeeze of lemon or Tabasco sauce, and accompanied with a glass of champagne is certainly a favorite of mine. But I also really enjoy eating warmed, cooked oysters, which take on an even more tender texture. All of the extras, champagne, lemon and Tabasco, are being used in this dish, so you are not missing a thing! The same idea can be used with other fish and shellfish – scallops, lobster, shrimp, or salmon, for example.*

**Serves 2**

10 rock oysters, opened and all
   juices saved
2 ½ cups (275 g) finely shredded
   savoy cabbage
Butter for frying, plus 2 tbs
   (25 g) butter
4 shallots or 1 onion, finely sliced
4 strips of bacon, very finely diced
1 glass of champagne

1 teaspoon white wine vinegar
A small pinch of sugar
2–3 tablespoons heavy cream
A squeeze of lemon juice
A drop or two of Tabasco sauce
Salt and pepper

Once all the oysters have been opened, wash the shells and save for serving the oysters.

The cabbage can be prepared in advance. Heat a frying pan and add butter. Fry the shallots or onion for 3–4 minutes until completely tender and beginning to caramelize. Season with salt and pepper and remove from the pan. Fry the bacon for 4–5 minutes, allowing its fat content to cook out, leaving you with fine, crisp bacon. Add the bacon to the shallots. Wipe the pan clean and melt another small pat of butter. Fry the cabbage (which can be blanched in boiling water for 1 minute to give a richer color) for 4–5 minutes, allowing a slight golden tinge among the deep green.

Mix together the cabbage, shallots and bacon and season with salt and pepper. You can do this beforehand and then fry to reheat all together, or cook it at the last minute.

To make the sauce, boil the champagne with the vinegar and sugar until reduced by three-quarters. Add the oyster juices and cream and bring to a simmer. Add the lemon and Tabasco and whisk in the 2 tbs (25 g) of butter. Season with salt and pepper. The sauce is now ready. If you have an electric blender, blitz the sauce for a few seconds, just before serving, to make it lighter in taste and consistency.

Warm the oysters in 1 tablespoon butter and season. To serve, divide the cabbage between the oyster shells, sit the oysters on top and spoon the sauce over.

**Note:** If making a larger quantity, some fish stock can be used to produce more sauce. If you're wondering why I'm working with five and not the traditional six oysters per portion, it is because the extra garnish more than makes up for the sixth oyster!

# Smoked Haddock and Sorrel Omelet

*Eggs and smoked haddock are a great combination but the eggs are normally in the form of poached eggs and not omelets. Here, the haddock is poached in a little water and butter. This creates a good smoky fish stock; the haddock is then broken into the omelet. The stock isn't wasted either – I make a cream sorrel sauce to go with the finished dish.*

*For another classic flavor, add a spoonful or two of cooked spinach to the sauce and mix it to a smooth cream to give a wonderful finish to this dish.*

---

**Serves 2**

6–8 eggs, depending on size

4–6 oz (100–175 g) natural
  smoked haddock

1 tablespoon butter

6 sorrel leaves

A squeeze of lemon juice

6 tablespoons heavy cream

⅓ cup (50 g) cooked spinach
  (optional)

Salt and pepper

Put the haddock fillet in a small, buttered pan with 1 tablespoon butter and half cover with water. Break and add 2–3 leaves of sorrel. Add a squeeze of lemon juice, cover with foil or a lid and bring to a simmer. Cook for a few minutes until tender. Leave to stand for 1–2 minutes. Remove the haddock and break it into flakes. Take one or two tablespoons of liquor and drizzle it over the fish. This will keep it moist and warm.

Reduce the cooking liquor by half and add the cream. Bring to a boil and cook for 1 minute. Check for seasoning and add salt, pepper and lemon juice to taste. If using spinach, add it to the sauce and return to a simmer. Purée in a blender or processor and strain through a sieve to give a green spinach-cream sauce.

To make the omelet, heat a 6 in (15 cm) omelet pan. Crack the eggs, enough for one portion at a time, and beat with a fork. Add a twist of pepper. It is very important never to add salt until the last second as salt breaks eggs down and they become watery.

Shred the remaining sorrel leaves and add half to the egg. Put 1 tablespoon butter in the pan and, once it begins to bubble, pour in the omelet mix. This can now be stirred in the pan with a fork, not allowing it to stick, set or turn golden on the base. A really good omelet, where the eggs are just set in a pan of butter, should not be browned at all!

Once the eggs are setting but still moist on top, stop stirring and sprinkle the haddock flakes over. Hold the pan at a slight angle and tap it so the omelet slides towards the front of the pan. Fold it over. Fold in the other side and turn the omelet onto a plate. Repeat to make the second omelet. The omelette will have an oval shape; make it neater by covering it with a clean cloth and shaping it. Pour the spinach sauce around and serve at once.

**Note:** If you are not using spinach in the sauce, add one or two extra shredded leaves of sorrel just before serving.

# Seared Scallops *with Hot Mustard Shallot Sauce*

*This dish is one of my favorites. The flavor from the scallops alone is sensational, with a hint of bitterness from the searing, and with the 'hot' sauce and a very creamy mashed potato to go with it, it's unbelievable. That's a pretty big statement to make and the only way to prove it is for you to try it!*

---

**Serves 4**

12 scallops, trimmed and
    cleaned of roe
3–4 cups (225–350 g) Mashed
    Potatoes (page 140)
¼–½cup (50–85 ml) light cream

1 quantity Hot Mustard Shallot
    Sauce (page 246)
1 tablespoon cooking or olive oil
1 tablespoon butter
Salt and pepper

The mashed potatoes should be loosened with light cream: the consistency should be very soft but still holding its own weight. If, after adding the cream, the mash still seems to be too firm, add either more cream or milk. Check the seasoning.

Warm the mustard shallot sauce.

Heat a frying pan with the tablespoon of oil. Once hot, sit the scallops in the pan, making sure the maximum heat is maintained, which will ensure the scallops are searing. Season the scallops in the pan and once a good, almost burned, tinge has caught on the edges, add the pat of butter. Leave for 30 seconds and turn the scallops over. They can now be cooked for a further 30 seconds–1 minute.

To present the dish, either spoon or pipe the potatoes, using a ½ in (1 cm) plain nozzle, at the top of the plate. Spoon 2–3 tablespoons of sauce in front and sit three scallops on top.

# Macaroni Cheesecake

*This must be the first cheesecake made without cream cheese! It is made the original way with a good cheddar sauce. So what makes it into a cheesecake? I'll leave you to read the recipe and find out!*

**Serves 6**
12 oz (350 g) dried macaroni
1 tablespoon butter
1 tablespoon olive oil
Salt and pepper

**For the Sauce:**
2 tbs (25 g) butter
¼ cup (25 g) all-purpose flour

1 onion, 1 bay leaf and 1 clove
  (optional)
2 ½ cups (600 ml) milk
⅔ cup (150 ml) heavy cream
  (optional)
1 teaspoon English mustard
  (optional)
2 cups (225 g) cheddar, grated
Salt and pepper

To make the sauce, melt the butter in a saucepan and add the flour. Cook on a low heat, stirring from time to time, for 8–10 minutes. While the 'roux' is cooking, stud the clove through the bay leaf onto the onion (if using) and place in the milk. Heat the milk slowly, so the flavor of the onion and aromatics will infuse into it. Add the milk to the roux, a spoonful at a time, stirring well and bubbling it before adding more. Once all the milk has been added, place the onion in the sauce and simmer gently for 30 minutes. The sauce will now have become very thick. Remove and discard the onion. Add the cream, if using, for a smoother finish.

Add the teaspoon of mustard (more or none if preferred). Sprinkle in the cheddar, tasting as you add and it melts. Once at the strength you prefer, drain the sauce through a sieve.

While the sauce is cooking, cook the macaroni according to the package instructions and then drain. Not all of the sauce will need to be mixed with the macaroni for this stage of the dish; add just a spoonful at a time until the macaroni feels completely bound. Set the rest of the sauce aside for later. Season the macaroni mixture with salt and pepper.

Butter 2½ x 2 in (6 x 5 cm) deep rings and place them on a tray covered in plastic wrap. Spoon the mix into the molds, pushing it down to pack it in, which will hold the mix together. Refrigerate for at least 30 minutes until completely set.

Preheat the oven to 400°F/200°C. Melt 1 tablespoon butter with a tablespoon of olive oil in an ovenproof frying pan. Place the cakes, still in the rings, in the pan and fry on a low–medium heat to a golden brown. During this cooking time the macaroni will become crisp. Then bake them for 10–12 minutes until heated through. Or remove the cakes from the pan and leave to cool. Once cooled, turn them over and remove the rings. The golden, crisp cakes can now be microwaved for a few minutes, when needed.

To serve the macaroni cakes, warm the remaining sauce (do not boil it or the cheese will separate). Spoon some onto the center of the plates and sit the cake on top.

The cheesecakes can be served in many different ways. Here are two ideas that both go very well with the cheesecakes and make it complete.

APPETIZERS

# Macaroni Cheesecake *with Roasted Tomatoes and Olive and Chive Dressing*

**Serves 4**

1½ tomatoes per portion
1 tablespoon butter
4 tablespoons olive oil
2 teaspoons balsamic vinegar (optional)

A few black olives, pitted and
  quartered
1 teaspoon chopped fresh chives
Salt and pepper

Halve and seed the tomatoes; cut each half into three. Melt 1 tablespoon butter in a hot pan and add the tomatoes. Season with salt and pepper and fry on high heat until golden and softened. Remove from the heat. Mix the olive oil with the vinegar, if using. Season with salt and pepper. Add the black olives and chives. Spoon the tomatoes around the cheesecake or sit them side by side and finish by spooning the black olive and chive dressing around.

# Mixed Mushroom Cheesecake

*The mushrooms in this dish can be porcini, shiitake, or cremini. If none of these is available, replace them with button mushrooms.*

**Serves 4**

4–5 cups (275–350 g) wild or
  cultivated mushrooms, washed
2–3 tablespoons olive oil
2 tablespoons sliced scallions
1 tablespoon mushroom ketchup
  or essence

3 tablespoons peanut oil
A squeeze of lemon juice
1 tablespoon sherry or
  red wine vinegar
Salt and pepper
½ teaspoon chopped fresh parsley
½ teaspoon chopped fresh marjoram

If using cultivated mushrooms, they should all be quartered. Porcini will need to be sliced, *trompettes* halved and shiitake left whole or halved if large.

Heat a frying pan with the olive oil. Add the mushrooms and scallions and sauté for a few minutes. Mix the mushroom ketchup or essence with the peanut oil, a squeeze of lemon and the vinegar. Season with salt and pepper and add the chopped herbs. Spoon the mushrooms and scallions around the plate and finish with the herbed dressing.

**Note:**  Cooked lentils also go very well with the mushroom dressing.

# Escalope of Salmon *with Molasses, Juniper, and Sherry Dressing*

*This recipe came to me after a visit to a small town, very far north in Scotland, called Achiltibuie, where I was shown the stages of preparation for Scottish salmon before it's smoked. The inspiration for this recipe comes from the early stages when the salmon are soaked in a marinade made from shallots, juniper berries, black peppercorns, garlic, thyme, sherry, molasses, and water. Once the fish has been marinated and smoked, it takes on an amazing flavor. This recipe uses fresh (not smoked) salmon, with one or two changes to the marinade, giving us, instead, a rich dressing. The bitter-sweet flavor of molasses lifts all of the other tastes.*

---

**Serves 4**

½ in (4 x 1 cm) thick (4–6 oz/
   100–175 g) slices of fresh salmon
1 tablespoon butter
8 oz (225 g) mixed green salad
   leaves e.g. arugula, baby spinach
1 teaspoon olive oil, mixed with a
   few drops of lemon juice
Salt and pepper

**For the Dressing:**

2 heaping tablespoons finely
   chopped shallots or onions
10–12 black peppercorns, crushed
15–20 juniper berries,
   finely chopped
1 garlic clove, crushed
4 tablespoons sherry vinegar
⅓ tablespoon molasses
3 tablespoons walnut oil
3 tablespoons peanut or
   safflower oil
A pinch of salt

To make the dressing, mix together the shallots or onions, crushed peppercorns, finely chopped juniper berries, garlic and sherry vinegar. Bring to a simmer and cook until the vinegar has almost completely evaporated. Add the molasses and oils and bring back to a simmer. Cook for 1–2 minutes and season with a pinch of salt. This dressing can be made hours or even days in advance. It's best kept refrigerated – the flavors will become more dominant as it relaxes – and brought back to a warm temperature before serving.

To cook the salmon, and finish the dish, first heat a frying pan and season the salmon with salt and pepper. Add the butter to the pan and lay the salmon slices, presentation side down, in the sizzling butter. Cook for 2–3 minutes on one side only, keeping the fish pink. While the salmon is cooking, spoon the dressing onto four plates. Season and add the olive oil and lemon juice to the green leaves, sitting them on top of the dressing. Place the salmon, presentation side up, on top of the leaves. The dish is now ready to serve.

**Note:** This dressing also works well with smoked salmon, trout, mackerel or herrings. Pan fried scallops sitting on the molasses dressing are also very good.

# Spiced Tuna *with Lemon and Tomato Dressing*

*For this recipe, I use fresh tuna fillets. The best size fillet is about 2½–3 in (6–7.5 cm) diameter, giving enough texture and actual fish to balance the spice paste.*

*Small tuna fillets can also be used, but they should be cut at a fairly acute angle to give the right quantity of 'meat' to spice.*

*I am also giving a recipe for homemade curry oil, which is an optional extra. This has a warm flavor that works well with this dish and could also be used to spice up salads, vegetables, risottos and more.*

---

**Serves 4**
1 lb (450 g) fresh tuna fillet,
  skinned and trimmed
1 tablespoon butter

**For the Spice Paste:**
2 teaspoons yellow mustard seeds
½ green chili, finely diced
½ teaspoon cumin seeds
¼ teaspoon ground turmeric

**For the Dressing:**
8 plum or salad tomatoes, blanched,
  skinned and seeded
2 lemons, peeled and segmented
4 tablespoons olive oil
Salt and pepper
1 tablespoon shredded fresh cilantro

First make the spice paste. Grind the yellow mustard seeds, chili, cumin, and turmeric in a coffee grinder or mortar and pestle to a spreadable paste (you may need to add a teaspoon of water). Spread the paste over the tuna fillet, covering it completely.

Wrap the fish in plastic wrap and refrigerate for 1 hour to help set and firm the paste. Unwrap and fry the fish in the butter on all sides for 4–5 minutes, which seals the fish and also cooks the spices. It is important not to cook the fish for too long; it should be served raw, with the cooked spices around the outside. Obviously, if you would prefer the fish to be rare or medium-rare, simply cook for 5–6 minutes, turning it to brown all sides.

The small tuna fillets, being thinner, will need very little time in the pan. Remove the fish and leave to rest at room temperature.

To make the tomato and lemon dressing, first cut the tomato flesh into ½ in (1 cm) dice. The lemon segments can also be sliced thinly. Warm 2 tablespoons of the olive oil and add the tomatoes and lemon. Season with salt and pepper and warm through, allowing the tomatoes just to soften. Add the remaining olive oil with the shredded cilantro. Divide the tomato mixture between four plates or bowls. Carve the tuna fish into ⅛–¼ in (3–5 mm) slices and set them, overlapping, on top, allowing two or three slices per portion. The dish is now ready to serve or it can be finished with a tablespoon of curry oil poured around the plate.

**Note:** It is very important that the tuna used is absolutely fresh.

To make a curry oil to accompany the fish, cook 4 tablespoons chopped onion, 4 tablespoons chopped apple, 1 tablespoon medium–hot curry powder, 2 teaspoons ground cumin and salt and pepper in 12 tablespoons safflower or peanut oil, without letting them brown, until softened and translucent. Purée in a blender or food processor. Either tie up and hang the purée in muslin or pour into a fine strainer; in either case, set over a bowl. The flavored oil will begin to drain. If you leave it for an hour or two, you will be left with about ⅔ cup (150 ml) of curry oil.

# Red Mullet Escabeche *with Shallots, Orange, and Capers*

*Escabeche is a Spanish way of preparing fish and meat. The word itself literally means 'pickled' but, before pickling, the main ingredient is cooked. This dish will suit most fish, especially trout, herrings and mackerel, and will take on a lot more flavor if this dish is prepared a few hours in advance.*

---

**Serves 4**

8–10 oz (4 x 225–275 g) red mullet, scaled, filleted and all pin bones removed

½ cucumber, peeled and seeded

2 shallots, cut into thin rings

1 tablespoon fine capers or chopped large ones

3 tablespoons white wine vinegar

3 tablespoons water

The juice of 2 large oranges, plus one curl of zest

2 fresh tarragon sprigs

4 tablespoons olive oil

1 tablespoon butter

Salt and pepper

Mix the shallot rings with the capers in a small pan and add the vinegar and water. Bring to a simmer and cook for 1–2 minutes. Drain off the vinegar liquor into another small pan, reduce by a third and reserve. Reserve the shallots and capers to finish the dish. Boil the two juices with their zests and one sprig of tarragon in a third small pan. Reduce by half. Once reduced, drain through a sieve onto the reserved reduced vinegar and mix with the olive oil. Preheat the broiler to hot.

Lay the red mullet fillets (skin side up) on a buttered and seasoned baking pan. Brush the fillets with butter, season and place under the broiler. The fish will take 2–3 minutes, leaving a good, crisp skin. Transfer the hot cooked fish to a shallow, clean dish and pour the orange-lemon marinade over it. The fish will start to take on the marinade's flavors. For maximum taste, leave the fish for 3 hours at room temperature. Half an hour before serving, cut the cucumber into thin julienne strips, approximately 3 in (7.5 cm) in length. Mix with ½ teaspoon of salt and leave to soak and drain in a colander for 30 minutes. Taste it for excess salt flavor. If it tastes too salty, quickly rinse it under cold water and dry it well.

To serve the fish, add 2 tablespoons of the marinade liquor to the cucumber and season with a twist of pepper. Tear the remaining tarragon leaves. Put a pile of cucumber towards the top of the plate and set two red mullet fillets either side. Sprinkle the shallot rings, capers, and torn tarragon leaves over the fish and around the plate. Finish by drizzling with the marinade.

**Note:** The dressing can be rewarmed to bring the fish back to room temperature.
Use 3 oranges and 3 lemons to give an even stronger flavor to the dish.

APPETIZERERS

34

# Duck, Pork, and Chicken-Liver Terrine

*This terrine recipe is quite something. The ingredient list might appear to be quite frightening as well! It uses four duck breasts, 1½ lb (750 g) chicken livers, a pork fillet, and veal kidneys – just to start!*

*The terrine will in fact feed 12 people or maybe even 15. It is the sort of dish that you will make for a large dinner party or, perhaps, at Christmas time when you have lots of visitors.*

*I felt I had to share it with you because it is very easy to make; you don't have to create mousses, but more or less just stack the ingredients in the mold. It is exciting to eat, having such a variety of textures and flavors in one slice. The watercress salad, with a port and red-wine dressing to go with it, makes a perfectly rounded dish.*

*The terrine mould I use for this recipe is a 6–7 cups (1.5–75 liter) size.*

---

**Serves 12–15**

4 small duck breasts, skinned
1 pork fillet, taken from behind the
    loin, trimmed of all sinew, weighing
    10–12 oz (275–350 g)
1½ lb (750 g) chicken livers, trimmed
2 veal kidneys, trimmed of all fat
    and sinew
½ cup (120 ml) Madeira
¼ cup (50 ml) port
¼ cup (50 ml) brandy
Milk, enough to soak livers
20 thin, rindless strips of bacon
Salt, pepper, and ground mace

**For the Red-wine Dressing:**

2 teaspoons Dijon mustard
2 tablespoons red wine vinegar
4 tablespoons walnut oil
4 tablespoons peanut oil
1 tablespoon red 0currant jelly
4 tablespoons port
Salt and pepper
1 bunch watercress, picked and
    washed, or a 3 oz (75 g) bag

Begin two or three days before you want to cook the terrine. It is best to buy the veal kidneys already cleaned – you can even ask your butcher to grind them for you, using a medium cutter. If you have a meat grinder, just cut the kidneys into small pieces for now and pour over the Madeira. Stir, cover and refrigerate.

Pour the port over the pork fillet and leave it in the refrigerator. Flavor the duck breasts with the brandy and refrigerate them.

Fresh chicken livers have a slightly bitter flavor. If they are soaked in milk and refrigerated for 2–3 days, along with the other meats, they will be less bitter and simply sweeter to eat.

Turn all the meats in their marinades from time to time.

After 2–3 days, drain the chicken livers from the milk. Preheat the oven to 300°F/150°C. Remove all of the marinated meats from the fridge. If necessary, mince the kidneys through a medium cutter. Line the terrine mold with buttered wax paper and then with the strips of bacon, making sure to leave the ends overhanging so you can cover the top surface once it's filled.

Season all of the meats and livers with salt, pepper, and ground mace.

Spoon half the minced kidneys into the base of the terrine, smoothing them out. Sit two duck breasts on top. Put half the chicken livers close together in the mold. Place the pork fillet along the center and then continue to lay the chicken livers on top. Sit the two remaining duck breasts over the livers and spoon on the remaining minced kidneys. Fold over the overhanging bacon, to cover the terrine.

Place the terrine in a deep roasting tray and half fill with hot water. Bake for 35 minutes. Reduce the oven temperature to 265˚F/130˚C and continue to cook for another hour.

The terrine should now be cooked, but still slightly pink inside. Check by inserting a skewer or thin, sharp knife: if it's warm when removed, the terrine should be ready. Cook the terrine for another 20–30 minutes if you feel it needs a little longer or you like it less pink. Once cooked, remove from the oven, lift out of the roasting tray and leave to rest for 20 minutes. Now you can weigh down the terrine to press all of the cooked meats together. Either use another empty terrine dish or wrap a rectangle of firm cardboard, cut to fit the terrine top, in foil and plastic wrap and put directly on top of the terrine's surface. Put some weights, for example, two 1 lb (500 g) bags of sugar or cans of baked beans inside the empty terrine or on top of the cardboard and leave to cool.

Once cold, refrigerate the terrine overnight with the weights in place. In the morning, you have the duck, pork and chicken liver terrine. This can now be turned out and carefully sliced.

For the dressing, whisk together the mustard and red wine vinegar. Mix the two oils together and gradually whisk them into the mustard and vinegar, like for mayonnaise. Once the ingredients are blended, season with salt and pepper. Warm the redcurrant jelly with the port, melting the jelly to a liquid. Whisk it into the red wine sauce and adjust the seasoning.

Separate the watercress into generous sprigs. Add two tablespoons of the finished dressing and gently fold in. Arrange the watercress on the slices of terrine. Trickle a further tablespoon or two of dressing around the plate before serving.

**Note:** To achieve the absolute maximum flavor, the 'meats' should be marinated for 2–3 days in advance.

I like to finish the terrine presentation with a small twist of pepper and a few coarse seasalt granules sprinkled on top.

# Confit of Bacon *with Apple and Celery Salad*

*Confit is the French word for preserving. The most usual use is for a confit of duck – duck cooked and then set in its own fat – which allows it to keep almost indefinitely. I'm not exactly looking to do that with this bacon. Once you've cooked it, you'll want to eat it – not save it!*

*This piece of bacon (unsmoked bacon can also be used) could just be roasted, instead of cooked in a confit, but it will not have the same succulence.*

*This dish is a good appetizer or will work very well as a summer main course. The horseradish dressing is my choice, but you can of course improvise or simply use a basic salad dressing. The confit and the horseradish oil can be made well ahead.*

---

**Serves 4–6**

1½ lb (750 g) unsliced piece of
    bacon
2 ½–3 ¾ cups (600–900 ml) cooking
    oil or pork fat

**For the Dressing:**

6 tbs (100 g) fresh horseradish,
    grated
½ fresh green chili, finely chopped
¾ cup (175 ml) peanut oil
A squeeze of lemon juice
Salt and pepper

**For the Dressing Garnish
  (optional):**

2 tablespoons horseradish-chilli oil
6 radishes, finely diced
6–8 marinated anchovies
    (not canned), diced

**For the Salad:**

2 apples, peeled, cored and
    quartered
4 celery sticks, peeled and
    thinly diced
2–3 handfuls of mixed green
    salad leaves

The cut of bacon must first be skinned and trimmed, leaving a clean piece. This is best soaked for 24 hours in cold water, removing excess salt flavor.

Preheat the oven to 350°F/180°C. In a small, hot roasting pan, put a drop of the cooking oil or fat and heat on top of the stove. Fry the bacon, fat side down, to a golden brown. Turn the bacon in the pan and pour on the remaining oil/fat just to cover the bacon, and bring to a gentle simmer. Cover and cook in the oven for about 1–1½ hours.

After an hour, check the tenderness of the meat by piercing with a knife or carefully removing it from the fat and pressing it between thumb and forefinger. The meat should feel totally tender; if it's slightly firm, continue to cook for the remaining ½ hour.

Once cooked, if you're using it immediately, remove the bacon; a lot of excess fat will drain off.

Carve it when it's just warm.

The bacon can be preserved in the fat and refrigerated until needed. When ready to use, remove the bacon from the fat and bring back to its original 'just-cooked' status by roasting in the oven (fat side down) for 15–20 minutes.

To make the dressing, mix all of the ingredients together in a small pan, except the lemon juice, and bring to a simmer. This can now be left to stand until cool. The oil will take on a horseradish flavor – that's quite a classic combination, working well with the bacon.

Once cool, the horseradish can be left in the oil and kept refrigerated until it is needed; the flavor just gets stronger. Or, if using immediately, strain it and finish with salt, pepper, and a squeeze of lemon.

If you're making the dressing garnish, add enough horseradish-chili oil to flavor and moisten the radishes and anchovies.

For the salad, cut the apple quarters into thin slices. Mix with the celery and green salad leaves and flavor with a trickle of the horseradish-chili oil.

To serve, spoon some of the radish and anchovy garnish around the plate. Carve the bacon into thin slices and lay them, overlapping, across the middle; five or six slices per portion is plenty. Put the salad on top, drizzle some extra dressing around and serve.

**Note:** All of the salad oils, garnishes, etc. will work very well with simple, crisp bacon strips in place of the confit.

# Peppered Chicken Livers
## *on Watercress Toasts*

*The pepper on the livers and sweet brandied shallots in the dressing are flavors that work so well together.*

---

**Serves 4**

3–4 chicken livers per portion, previously soaked for 24–48 hours in milk

4 tablespoons fine fresh breadcrumbs

2 level teaspoons crushed black peppercorns

Salt and pepper

4 thick slices of bread

½ garlic clove

1 large bunch watercress, picked, or a 3 oz (75 g) bag

2 tablespoons olive oil

1 tablespoon butter

1 quantity Gravlax Sauce (page 74), omitting the chopped dill

Remove the chicken livers from the milk. Mix the breadcrumbs with the crushed peppercorns. Season with salt. Cut the slices of bread into discs with a plain cookie cutter and toast them. Rub each slice with garlic. Season the watercress and add a tablespoon of olive oil.

Heat a frying pan with the remaining tablespoon of oil and the butter. Roll the livers in the peppered crumbs and pan fry them until crisp and golden brown. The total cooking time of the livers will be between 3–5 minutes, depending on the size of the livers.

Sit the toasts in the center of the plates and top with the watercress and chicken livers. Finish by spooning the gravlax sauce liberally around.

# Roast *Foie Gras* on Potato Pancakes with *Macerated Grapes*

*Goose and duck* foie gras *are both the most luxurious of livers. They are expensive to buy and not that easy to get hold of, but I want to share this recipe with you because it is a dream to eat.*

*The other reason I am including it is that other livers can be used for this recipe: pan-fried chicken livers or broiled calves' or lambs' liver will all work very well.*

*The pancake recipe will give you approximately 8 pancakes: 4 for this recipe and the remaining 4 to enjoy the following day! Other ingredients, such as corn, or ratatouille, or shrimp, or herbs, can also be added to the remaining pancake mixture to give you a completely new dish.*

---

**Serves 4**

12 oz (350 g) duck *foie gras,*
  cut into 3 oz (75 g) lobes
Cooking oil
6 tablespoons Macerated Grapes
  (page 239)
6 tablespoons *Jus*/Gravy (page 242)
  or alternative (page 243)
Salt and pepper

**For the Potato Pancakes:**

1 ¼ cups (150 g) plain mashed
  potatoes
1 tablespoon milk
1 tablespoon all-purpose flour
1 tablespoon heavy cream
  (or extra milk)
1 egg
1 egg white
Salt and pepper

Preheat the oven to 400°F/200°C. To make the potato pancakes, simply beat all the ingredients together and season with salt and pepper. You will now have a thick batter.

Heat a frying pan with a trickle of cooking oil. Season the *foie gras* with salt and pepper and place the lobes in the pan. The livers will brown very quickly so, once they are browned on one side, turn over and finish cooking in the oven. They will take 3–4 minutes to become tender.

The pancakes should be started while the *foie gras* is frying to ensure everything is cooked together. The pancakes can even be made 10–15 minutes beforehand and kept warm.

To cook the pancakes, heat a tablespoon of oil in another frying pan and ladle the batter into four discs – they should be about 3 in (7.5 cm) diameter each. Cook on a medium heat for 1–2 minutes until golden and then turn each one over carefully with a spatula. Continue to cook for 1–2 minutes.

Bring the grapes to a boil with 2–3 tablespoons of the macerating liquor. Add the thick *jus* or gravy. Continue to boil and reduce, if necessary, to a rich, glossy consistency. Check for seasoning and add salt and pepper as necessary.

Sit two pancakes in the center of the plates with the *foie gras* on top. Spoon the macerated grapes and their sauce around and serve.

APPETIZERS

# Spaghettini or Tagliolini *with Roast Tomato Sauce*

*A bowl of pasta just bound with a great tomato sauce is easy to make and great to eat. There is no end to the flavors that you can add. I like to use broad beans and black olives in this dish, with a drizzle of olive oil and freshly grated Parmesan.*

*Spaghettini and tagliolini are both quite fine pastas. Spaghettini is just a thinner spaghetti and tagliolini a thinner noodle. If you've never made pasta, try it, but if you're pressed for time use bought – either fresh or dried. And, of course, everyday spaghetti and noodles can also be used.*

---

**Serves 4**

**For the Roast Tomato Sauce:**

2 lb (900 g) ripe plum
   or salad tomatoes
2 tablespoons olive oil
1 tablespoon butter
2 garlic cloves, sliced
10 fresh basil leaves (optional)
Coarse sea salt and black pepper

**For the Pasta:**

2 quantities Homemade Pasta (page
   234) or 1 lb (450 g) fresh or dried
   spaghettini or tagliolini
Olive oil
Salt and pepper
A squeeze of lemon juice (optional)
Grated Parmesan (optional),
   to serve

If using homemade pasta, roll it out thinly on a floured or semolina covered surface. Cut the pasta into 4 in (10 cm) thick strips and roll it through a hand-cranked pasta machine several times. If you do not have a pasta machine, simply roll the pasta on a floured work surface with a rolling pin until you have a ⅛ in (3 mm) thickness. Roll the sheet of pasta carefully into a cylinder and cut into very thin strips with a sharp knife to give you spaghettini, or into ⅛ in (3 mm) wide strips to give you tagliolini. Unroll each slice into strands as you cut, otherwise the pasta will stick together. Dry on a cloth.

Preheat the oven to 425°F/220°C. Halve the tomatoes. Heat the olive oil in a flameproof roasting pan or large ovenproof frying pan. Place the tomatoes in the pan, flesh side down, and cook to a golden brown with slightly burned tinges. (You may need to do this in two batches.) Add the butter and turn the tomatoes. Season with a sprinkling of sea salt and black pepper and add the garlic slices. Cook for a few more minutes and then add the basil leaves, if using.

Roast the tomatoes for 15–20 minutes. The tomatoes will have cooked completely and should have a mushy texture. These can now be pureed in a food processor or blender, to make a smooth sauce. Taste for seasoning. For an even smoother finish, push the sauce through a sieve.

Cook the pasta in boiling, salted water. Fresh spaghettini takes 3–4 minutes, dried 5–6 minutes, fresh tagliolini 2 minutes, dried 5–6 minutes. Drain, once cooked, and season with salt and pepper. Drizzle with olive oil and lemon juice, if using. Mix with the tomato sauce, divide into portions and serve, offering grated Parmesan as well, if you like.

**Note:**  Any of the following extra flavors can also be added: fava beans, black or green olives, onions or shallots, chopped fresh tarragon, wild or button mushrooms, bacon or prosciutto, chilies, fresh peas.

**1** Cook the leeks until tender. Drain and separate the leaves. Line the mold with them, leaving enough overhanging to fold over at the end.

**2** Cook the potatoes and pencil-thin leeks separately until slightly overcooked. Drain and season. Put a third of the leeks into the pan, then totally cover with half the potatoes.

**3** Add the shallots and parsley to the stock. Spoon over half the stock and repeat with more leeks, stock, and potatoes.

# Potato and Leek Terrine

*Here's a vegetarian dish that tastes and looks spectacular, using just two very basic ingredients, lifted with a shiny, glossy dressing. I am using a basic Le Creuset terrine mold. This will give 10–12 portions. If you have a smaller terrine mold, simply halve the ingredients.*

### Serves 12–15

#### For the Herb Oil:
⅔ cup (150 ml) olive oil
2 bay leaves
1 garlic clove, chopped
A few sprigs of fresh thyme, basil, sage, tarragon and marjoram

#### For the Saffron Vinegar:
2 tablespoons white wine vinegar
A pinch of saffron strands
6 tablespoons water
2 teaspoons salt
2 teaspoons sugar
1 teaspoon pepper

#### For the Terrine:
2 large leeks, split lengthwize
2 lb (900 g) new potatoes, unpeeled
1 lemon
30 pencil-thin leeks
2 ½ cups (600 ml) Vegetable Stock (page 240; good-quality bouillon cubes can be used)
½ oz (15 g) leaf gelatin (approximately 4 leaves), soaked in cold water, or 1 x 11.7 g sachet powdered gelatine
8 shallots or 2 onions, finely chopped
2 tablespoons chopped fresh parsley
Salt and pepper

**4** Finish with a final layer of leeks and fold over the overhanging leek leaves. Put a weight on top and refrigerate for 2 hours.

Make the herb oil in advance (a minimum of 24–48 hours will give you a stronger taste). Heat all of the ingredients together and then leave to infuse. Strain before using.

To make the saffron vinegar, heat all of the ingredients together. Leave to stand for 15–20 minutes. Reheat and then strain through a sieve.

To make the terrine, first line the terrine mold with plastic wrap.

Cook the large leeks in salted, boiling water for 4–5 minutes until absolutely tender. Refresh in ice water. Drain on paper towels and separate the layers. Line the terrine mold with these leek leaves, making sure there is enough left overhanging to fold over the filling at the end.

Cook the new potatoes in salted, boiling water with the peel of 1 lemon until slightly overcooked. Once cooked, drain and start to peel while still warm.

While the potatoes are cooking, cook the pencil leeks in salted, boiling water until completely tender. Drain and keep warm.

Reduce the vegetable stock by a third to increase its flavor. Let it cool slightly and then add the gelatin and half the chopped shallots or onions. When just at room temperature, add half of the chopped parsley.

Halve the potatoes lengthwise, using a fork to give a more natural break. Season the leeks and potatoes, adding a squeeze of lemon to the softened potatoes. Line the bottom of the terrine with a third of the leeks. Now place half the new potatoes on top, totally covering the leeks. Spoon half of the vegetable, shallot and parsley stock on top and repeat with more leeks and then the remaining stock and potatoes. Finish with a final layer of leeks and fold over the large leek leaves. Put another terrine, or some form of weight, the same shape, on top. This will press all of the vegetables together to give a proper terrine texture. Refrigerate for 2 hours.

To finish the dressing, mix the herb oil and the saffron vinegar together (they will not emulsify totally, but the combination of flavors and colors does work well). Stir 3–4 tablespoons of this into the remaining shallots and parsley and check for seasoning.

Turn out the terrine; this should happen quite easily because of the plastic wrap. It is now best to serve it at room temperature. The terrine can be sliced into about ½ in (1 cm) thick portions.

Place the slices on plates and spoon around a border of the shallots and parsley. To finish, drizzle the remaining dressing over the terrine to lift the shine and heighten the flavor.

**Note:** Once completed, the terrine will keep refrigerated for at least 3–4 days.

# Skate, Potato, and Leek Terrine

*The recipe is more or less identical to the Potato and Leek Terrine with the same dressing and the same quantity of leeks and potatoes. The vegetable stock, however, should be replaced with fish stock or water.*

---

**Serves 12**

Ingredients for Potato and Leek
   Terrine (page 46), but replacing
   the Vegetable Stock with Fish
   Stock (page 241) or alternative
   (page 243) or water, and using

only 2 leaves gelatine or $\frac{1}{2}$ × 11.7 g
   sachet powdered gelatin
1$\frac{1}{2}$–2 lb (750–900 g) skate wings on
   the bone
$\frac{1}{2}$ onion, chopped
1 star anise

Poach the skate in the stock or water with the chopped onion and star anise. The fish will only take 8–10 minutes. Remove the skate and strain the stock. Reduce the stock by two-thirds and then add the gelatin leaves. This can now be mixed with the shallots and parsley as for the vegetarian recipe. Carefully remove the skate fillets from the bone.

Line the terrine with plastic wrap and large leeks as for the vegetarian terrine.

Line the base with one-third of the pencil leeks, follow with a layer of half the potatoes, spooning some of the fish stock, shallot, and parsley mix over. Now carefully place half the skate fillet on top with a drop more stock. Sit more leeks on top, more stock, the remaining fish, more stock, the rest of the potatoes and then a final layer of leeks. Fold over the large leek leaves. Press gently and refrigerate.

The terrine is best eaten at room temperature, presented in the same way as the potato and leek terrine.

# Broiled Asparagus and Leeks *with*
## *Parsley Eggs*

*Leeks are known as 'poor man's asparagus,' a vegetable to stand in for or replace the lovely green spears. I think leeks are a wonderful vegetable, so I thought I would treat them as equals.*

*It's not necessary to broil the leeks; simply boil them and roll them in butter or dressing and they will be delicious. The parsley eggs are hard or soft boiled eggs, chopped, and flavored with olive oil, parsley, and lemon. A grinding of pepper and a sprinkling of sea salt and you have a complete dish. Another flavor I like to add is Parmesan shavings melted over the spears.*

**Serves 4**

16–20 thin asparagus spears
16–20 thin baby leeks
3 hard boiled eggs (boiled for
    6–7 minutes, so slightly soft)
6 tablespoons olive oil
A squeeze of fresh lemon juice

1 tablespoon butter, melted
1 tablespoon chopped freshly cut
    flat leaf parsley
Salt and pepper
Coarsely ground black pepper and
    coarse sea salt granules, to garnish
Fresh Parmesan shavings (optional)

The first job is to prepare the asparagus and leeks. The asparagus should be lightly peeled from halfway down to the base of the spear. Cut about 1 in (2.5 cm) of the base stalk away as this will be tough and stringy. It may be enough to cut off the bases of the leeks and remove one layer; wash away any grit.

Both need to be cooked separately in salted, boiling water. The asparagus will take only 2–3 minutes, still leaving a 'bite'. The leeks will take 4–5 minutes to cook completely. If you are serving them broiled, refresh both in iced cold water. If not, they are ready to serve.

Shell and roughly chop the eggs. Season the olive oil with salt, pepper, and lemon juice.

The leek and asparagus spears can now be broiled. This is best done on a ridged cast-iron grill pan or a barbecue, but they can also be pan fried or browned under the broiler for 3–4 minutes. Heat the grill pan until really hot and brush with oil. Place the asparagus and leeks on top and brush with butter. The grilling will take only a couple of minutes, leaving good grill lines on the vegetables.

To serve, arrange the asparagus and leeks in the classic asparagus fashion, close together in line across the plate (alternating with the leeks) or just dotted about, rustic style. Both can be halved and mixed all over the plate (which makes it look like a lot more!). Add the parsley and chopped egg to the olive oil and lemon dressing and spoon on top. Finish with a twist of black pepper, coarse sea salt, and Parmesan shavings, if using.

**Note:** The Parmesan can be placed over the asparagus and leeks before the dressing and melted under the broiler.

If thin baby leeks are unavailable, simply use 3 larger ones per serving.

# Red Wine Caramelized Lamb's Kidneys
## with Creamy Scrambled Eggs

*Scrambled eggs are normally just beaten eggs, cooked in melted butter. These, however, take on a different texture. Cream and butter are boiled together before the eggs are added, giving a good creamy finish.*

*The lamb's kidneys are pan fried and caramelized at the same time. The flavor is powerful and immense but gently calmed when eaten with the eggs. I like to serve the eggs on crisp toast.*

*This eats well as a appetizer, snack, or a main course. The scrambled eggs on toast go just as well with bacon for breakfast. If serving as a main course, then a rich jus/gravy/red wine sauce just drizzled around adds an extra flavor to the dish.*

---

**Serves 4**

8 lamb's kidneys, skinned, trimmed
   and quartered
¼ lb (100 g) butter
3 tablespoons red-wine vinegar

1 teaspoon light brown
   granulated sugar
⅔ cup (150 ml) heavy cream
8 eggs, beaten
4 thick slices of crusty bread
Salt and pepper

---

Season the kidneys with salt and pepper. Heat a frying pan with 2 tbs (25 g) of butter and pan fry the kidneys quickly on a good, high heat for 2–3 minutes until they're slightly browned. This will seal all the juices in the kidneys. Add the vinegar and sugar and allow to reduce for a minute. This will very quickly caramelize around the kidneys, giving them a rich shiny glaze.

While the kidneys are cooking, make the creamy scrambled eggs. In a separate pan, boil the cream with the remaining butter and pour in the seasoned, beaten eggs. Stir the eggs, for an even scrambling. Meanwhile, toast the bread. Check the eggs for seasoning before serving on the toast. The kidneys can be spooned over or around the toast.

The dish is now ready to serve.

# Potato, Scallion, and Mozzarella Risotto

*The book just wouldn't be right without a risotto somewhere! Risottos in general have become so popular, with almost unlimited flavors and variations to choose from. This one is slightly different, having mashed potato added to create a more than creamy texture.*

---

**Serves 8 as a starter or 4 as a main course**

1 ¼ cup (225 g) arborio risotto rice

2 bunches of scallions

4 tbs (50 g) butter

1 onion, finely chopped

2 ¼ cups (1.2 liters) Vegetable or Chicken Stock (page 240) or alternative (page 243)

2 large potatoes, cut in ¼ in (5 mm) dice

1 ⅓ cups (100 g) Mashed Potatoes (page 140)

2–3 tablespoons grated Parmesan (optional)

¼ cup (25 g) per portion coarsely grated mozzarella

Salt and pepper

Virgin olive oil, to serve

---

Shred the scallions finely, separating the white from the green. Blanch the green scallion in boiling water until tender, then strain.

Melt the butter in a saucepan and add the chopped onion with the shredded whites of scallion. Cook without letting them brown for a few minutes until softened. Add the rice and continue to cook for a few minutes. While the onions and rice are cooking, heat the stock. Add the stock, a ladle at a time, stirring the rice continuously. Once the rice has absorbed the stock, add another ladleful and continue to cook and stir; repeat until the rice is tender. This process will take 20–30 minutes.

While the rice is cooking, boil the diced potatoes until tender.

To finish the risotto, add the mashed potatoes and Parmesan, if using, to lift all the flavors, with the diced potatoes and greens of scallions. Check the seasoning and add salt and pepper to taste; add a little more stock, if necessary, to give a looser, creamier consistency.

Add the mozzarella and let it melt into the risotto or – as I like to do – serve the risotto in bowls and sprinkle the mozzarella on top. Put the bowls under the broiler to melt the cheese for a few seconds. Now just drizzle with olive oil and serve.

**Note:** You could add half the mozzarella to the risotto and use the remainder to sprinkle over the top.

You can also add an extra 2–4 tablespoons (25–50 g) butter to enrich the dish.

MAIN COURSES

# MAIN
# COURSES

Welcome to main courses, often seen as the most important part of the meal. I've broken this chapter down into sections: fish, poultry and meat, and vegetarian dishes and vegetables. With all of the dishes featured in these categories there's room for your interpretation. You should not be too strict in keeping to the recipes, especially if you feel like mixing, changing, and swapping! And if the results are better – send me the recipe!

There are also lots of main courses that don't really need an accompaniment, such as a vegetable served, out of habit, to fill the plate. Vegetables also stand as complete dishes on their own – sitting proudly on the table, with flavor simply oozing out of the dish.

I'll leave you to read on. Enjoy your meal and don't forget to leave some space for dessert – coming up next!

# fish

ish is such a wonderful food to cook: nothing in terms of flavor or time needs to be extensive. I think of anything that is served with fish as the tomato that goes in your grilled cheese sandwich: it's there to spice up the flavor and excite the tastebuds, but the taste of the cheddar should always shine through.

Different ways of cooking fish also give, obviously, a different feel and taste. Scallops, for example, just can't taste any better than when seared in a hot pan and allowed almost to burn at the edges, while ensuring they have a moist medium-rare center. They can also be steamed and poached, but then the meat has a totally different texture and won't give off that caramelized, natural sweetness that is just sensational to eat.

Among all of these recipes you'll find almost every cooking method possible for fish; deep-frying, pan-frying, poaching, steaming, roasting and griddling, all of which means there are plenty of fish for you to try and taste, and I'm sure you'll find one of them, for once, will catch you!

Happy fishing!

# Steamed Smoked Haddock on Spinach
## *with a Warm Poached Egg, glazed with a Sweet Pepper Béarnaise Sauce*

*Smoked haddock on spinach, with a warm poached egg, is a great dish well known in Britain. Finishing it with the sweet pepper béarnaise sauce lifts it to entirely new heights.*

*Béarnaise sauce is similar to hollandaise, which is made with egg yolks, clarified butter, vinegar and seasoning. The béarnaise version is flavored with tarragon, which gives it a more powerful finish. To speed things up, you could use a package of béarnaise or hollandaise sauce.*

*The sweet red peppers are cooked and then puréed. This purée, added to the béarnaise, is delicious. Peppers and tarragon have always worked well together and, when glazed over the poached egg and smoked haddock, they are even better!*

---

**Serves 4**

4 x 6–8 oz (175–225 g) smoked
   haddock fillets, skinned (preferably
   naturally smoked)
1 lb (450 g) fresh spinach, stalks
   removed
1 tablespoon butter
2 tablespoons water
4 poached eggs (see Note)
Salt and pepper

**For the Pepper Purée**

2 red peppers, seeded and cut into
   ½ in (1 cm) rough dice
1 tablespoon olive oil
1 garlic clove
Salt and pepper

**For the Béarnaise Sauce:**

6 oz (175 g) butter, melted
3 shallots or 1 onion, roughly
   chopped
½ teaspoon crushed black
   peppercorns
3 tablespoons white wine vinegar
1 heaping tablespoon chopped fresh
   tarragon leaves, stalks reserved
3 egg yolks
¼ cup (50 ml) heavy cream, lightly
   whipped
Salt and pepper

First make the béarnaise sauce. To make a reduction for the sauce, mix together the shallots or onion, black peppercorns and vinegar (plus any tarragon stalks) in a small pan and bring to a simmer. Reduce by three-quarters, which takes 1–2 minutes. Add a tablespoon of water, strain and leave the liquid to cool. The butter should be left to stand after it has melted. This separates the solids from the butter oils, leaving you with clarified butter.

Mix the egg yolks with the reduced liquid in a bowl over simmering water. Whisk together until a 'sabayon' is achieved. This is the stage when the yolks are thickening and approaching a softly whipped, creamy consistency.

Remove from the heat and continue to whisk until at room temperature. The warm clarified butter can now be ladled in very slowly, whisking continuously until you have a thick sauce and all the butter has been added. Season with salt and pepper and then strain through a sieve. Add the chopped tarragon and keep in a warm place.

To cook the peppers, heat the olive oil in a pan. Add the peppers and garlic and cook on medium heat for 8–10 minutes until the peppers have softened. Season and purée in a food processor. Push the purée through a sieve to remove any skin.

Melt a small pat of butter with the water and bring to a fast simmer. Add the spinach and cook for a few minutes until softened and tender. Season with salt and pepper and pour off any excess liquid.

Put the four portions of haddock on buttered and peppered wax paper. Steam them over a pan of boiling water covered with a lid for 5–6 minutes. The cooking time will differ, depending on the thickness of the fillets. The maximum time will be no more than 10 minutes.

To serve, mix the béarnaise sauce with the sweet pepper purée. Gently fold in the whipped cream. Divide the spinach between four bowls or plates. Sit the steamed fillets of smoked haddock on top.

Preheat the broiler. Warm the poached eggs for 1 minute in boiling water. Sit one on top of each haddock portion. Spoon over the sweet pepper béarnaise sauce, covering the egg and fish, and then glaze under the broiler to a golden brown. The dish is now ready to serve. Any remaining sauce can be offered separately.

**Note:** For the perfect poached egg, fill a small saucepan with two-thirds water and one-third malt vinegar. The vinegar reacts with the egg white and draws it around the yolk. Salt should not be added because this tends to break down the egg white consistency. Bring the water and vinegar mixture to the boil and stir. Now crack 1 egg at a time into the center of the water and poach for 3–3½ minutes. The eggs can be poached in advance and plunged into iced water immediately. To reheat, simply plunge into boiling water for 1 minute.

A hint of Dijon mustard in the béarnaise sauce will fire up the flavors even more.

# Crispy Salmon *with Sweet pepper and Tomato Sauce*

*I normally use a homemade tomato coulis sauce for this, which is simple enough to make, but for this recipe I'm making it even simpler. For the base I'm using passata, a strained tomato sauce. It's just pure tomatoes and easily available in all supermarkets. Mixing it with all of the other flavors and lots of fresh tomatoes gives you a powerful tomato flavor. The salmon is cooked using a method that will give a crackling finish to the salmon skin.*

*New potatoes with buttered spinach work very well with this dish.*

---

**Serves 4**

4 × 6–8 oz (175–225 g) salmon fillet portions, scaled, skin left on
2 tablespoons olive oil
4 large shallots or 1 onion, finely chopped
1 teaspoon green peppercorns
1¼ cup (300 ml) passata
4 tomatoes, blanched, peeled and seeded

½ × 14 oz (400 g) can or 7½ oz (210 g) jar of sweet red peppers
1 lemon, peeled, segmented and sliced
1 dessertspoon fine or ordinary capers, chopped
A pat of butter
Salt and pepper
1 teaspoon chopped fresh parsley
1 heaping teaspoon chopped fresh tarragon

For the sauce, warm a tablespoon of olive oil and add the chopped shallots or onion in a medium pan. Cook on a moderate heat for 1–2 minutes until softened. Add the green peppercorns with the passata. Bring the sauce to the simmer and cook for 2–3 minutes.

Cut the tomato flesh and canned peppers into ¼–½ in (5 mm–1 cm) dice. Add the sliced lemon segments, capers, diced tomato and sweet red pepper. Bring back to a simmer for 1 minute and season with salt and pepper. The sauce is now ready. Save the parsley and tarragon until just before serving (if added too early, the herbs will lose their color). Keep the sauce warm while you cook the salmon.

First, I like to score the skin of the salmon carefully, making 3–4 incisions. This helps to release any fat, leaving you with crispier skin. Season the salmon with salt and pepper.

Heat the remaining tablespoon of olive oil in a frying pan. Place the salmon, skin side down, in the oil on a moderate heat. Leave the fish for a good 5–6 minutes, not moving the pan around but checking the skin is not burning. The skin will now be just crisp and turning golden. Add the butter and turn the salmon and finish cooking for 2–3 minutes. The salmon will be lovely and tender with a pink finish.

Add the parsley and tarragon to the sauce. Spoon it onto the plates and put the crisp salmon, skin-side up, in the center.

**Note:** For a thicker, chunkier tomato pepper sauce, just use ⅔ cup (150 ml) passata.

# Parsley Cod *with Roasted Potatoes and Mustard Butter Sauce*

*I have changed this classic cod and parsley combination to give a purée of parsley mixed with spinach, which is spread over the fish, so that the parsley flavor comes through in every bite. This dish is a complete meal: the roasted potatoes and kale finish it off perfectly.*

*You can find the pork caul required by ordering from special meat markets. Caul works like a net to hold the parsley purée in place. If it's unavailable, wrap the cod in buttered foil and steam it instead of pan frying and roasting. Or leave the parsley purée off the cod, pan fry the cod and put it on top of the warm purée.*

*I use two varieties of parsley: the flat for flavor and the curly parsley for texture.*

---

**Serves 4**

4 x 6–8 oz (175–225 g) portions of
  cod fillets, skinned and boned
½ bunch of fresh flatleaf parsley
½ bunch of fresh parsley
1 cup (100 g) spinach, cooked
8 oz (225 g) pork caul (crépine)
1 tablespoon cooking oil

A pat of butter
Salt and pepper

**To serve:**
1 recipe of Kale (page 148)
1 recipe of Mustard Butter Sauce
  (page 237)
1 recipe of Banana Roast Potatoes
  (page 138)

Pre-heat the oven to 400°F/200°C. The two parsleys should be plunged into salted, boiling water for 2–3 minutes until tender. Drain in a colander and refresh with cold water. Once cold, squeeze out any excess water and purée in a food processor with the cooked spinach until smooth. Season with salt and pepper.

This purée can now be spread ⅛ in (3 mm) thick on the presentation (skinned) side of the cod. Then wrap in the pig's caul. Refrigerate to set and firm.

To cook the cod, warm a frying pan with a tablespoon of cooking oil. Put the cod portions in, parsley side down, and add the butter. Cook and brown for 3–4 minutes until golden with the rich green coming through. Turn the fish over and transfer to an ovenproof dish, if necessary. Complete by cooking in the oven for 8–10 minutes.

While the cod is cooking, warm the kale in a little butter and season it. Warm the mustard sauce and add one or two spoonfuls to the curly kale. The banana roast potatoes should be crisp and golden with tinges that are almost burned.

Once the cod is cooked, remove it from the pan and put it at the front of the plate. Make a small pile of roast potatoes, allowing four pieces per portion, and add a few spoonfuls of kale. Pour the mustard sauce over and around the kale and serve.

**Note:** I also like to serve a drizzle of fish *jus* (page 64), omitting the fennel, with this dish.

FISH

# Steamed Fillet of Cod *with a Cilantro Butter Sauce and Ratatouille Cake*

*Steaming cod gives you the pure, natural flavor of the fish, which in this dish is complemented by the cilantro butter sauce and the zesty flavors from the ratatouille cake.*

---

**Serves 4**

4 x 6–8 oz (175–225 g) cod fillet
    portions, skinned
all-purpose flour
Cooking oil, for deep-frying
Mashed Potatoes (page 140)
1 recipe of Cilantro Butter Sauce
    (page 237)
Salt and pepper

**For the Ratatouille Cake:**

½ small eggplant
1 medium zucchini
2 red onions, chopped,
    or 1 large Spanish onion
1 red pepper
3 tomatoes, blanched, skinned
    and seeded
Olive oil
A pat of butter
1 garlic clove, crushed
Salt and pepper

**For the Fennel *Jus*
    (optional):**

1 small fennel, diced
1 small onion, diced
A pat of butter
1 star-anise
1–2 teaspoons red-wine vinegar
    (cabernet sauvignon vinegar is
    preferable because it has a much
    thicker and richer consistency),
    (optional)
1 glass of red wine
⅔ cups (150 ml) Fish Stock (page
    241) or alternative (page 243)
Salt and pepper
A squeeze of lemon juice,
    if needed

For the ratatouille, all of the vegetables and tomatoes need to be cut into ¼ in (5 mm) dice and kept separate. Fry the onions in olive oil and butter with the crushed garlic and season with salt and pepper. Cook the onions for a few minutes until softened and slightly golden. Remove the onions from the pan. Return the pan to the heat and fry the zucchini, red pepper, and eggplant in the same manner, without the garlic. These can now all be mixed together and seasoned again.

If you don't want it immediately, let the cooked vegetables cool and keep them refrigerated until needed. If heating from cold, just warm it with the tomatoes in a drop of olive oil. If using immediately, add the tomatoes and heat through.

If you are making the *jus*, melt the butter with the onion and fennel in a saucepan and cook, without letting them color, with the star anise for a few minutes. Add the vinegar, if using, and reduce until almost dry. Add the red wine and reduce by three-quarters. Meanwhile also reduce the fish stock by three-quarters. (Using the fish stock will completely change the finished sauce, giving you a much fuller flavor.) Add this to the red wine mixture and cook for 5–10 minutes and then strain through a sieve. This fennel *jus* may well need more seasoning with salt, pepper and a squeeze of lemon juice to help lift all the flavors.

The cod fillets can be bought already skinned and boned if you wish, but I like to remove the skin myself and serve it as part of the dish. Lightly flour it and deep-fry until golden and crisp. Leave to drain on paper towels and sprinkle with salt.

Season the fillets with salt and pepper and place them on squares of buttered wax paper. Steam the fillets over a pan of boiling water covered with a lid for 8–12 minutes, depending on the size and thickness of the fish. The cod will begin to feel firm to the touch but it will still just 'give' in the center. This will give you beautifully cooked, translucent flakes.

To make the ratatouille cakes, I use small, buttered individual ring molds 2½–3 in (6–7.5 cm) in diameter and 2 in (5 cm) deep. Set them slightly to one side of the serving plates. Pipe some mashed potato approximately ½ in (1 cm) deep into each mold. Spoon some of the ratatouille into the top of the mold, pushing down to ensure the cake will keep its shape.

Lift off the molds and put the fried cod skins, if using, on top of each ratatouille cake. Place the cod next to the cake and spoon over some of the cilantro butter sauce. Pour a little fennel *jus*, if using, around the cake.

**Note:** You can make the cilantro butter sauce 20–30 minutes in advance and simply heat and whisk it (an electric hand blender works very well) at the last minute, adding the chopped fresh cilantro just before serving.

# Seared Scallops *with Homemade Pasta, Scallions and Maltaise Sauce*

*Scallops are sweet to eat and taste even better if seared with almost burned edges to give a crisp, bitter-sweet finish. The 'homemade' pasta can, of course, be replaced with a dried or fresh, store bought variety.*

| | |
|---|---|
| **Serves 4** | A pat of butter |
| 16–20 large, fresh scallops, cleaned and trimmed of roe | 6 tablespoons Orange Oil (page 238, optional) or olive oil |
| 1 recipe of Homemade Pasta dough (page 234) or dried or fresh, store bought spaghetti/tagliolini | 8 tablespoons Carrot Butter Sauce (page 237, optional) |
| 1 bunch of scallions | 1 recipe of Maltaise Sauce (page 235), to serve |
| Olive oil | Salt and pepper |

If using homemade pasta dough, roll out the pasta thinly on a floured or semolina covered surface. Cut it into 4 in (10 cm) thick strips and roll it through a hand-cranked pasta machine several times, then cut it through the 'spaghetti' attachment. Place the spaghetti on a tray covered with a cloth and leave it to relax and dry for 30 minutes. If you do not have a pasta machine, simply roll the pasta with a rolling pin until you have a ⅛ in (3 mm) thickness. Roll the sheet of pasta carefully into a cylinder and cut thin strips with a sharp knife. Unroll each slice into strands as you cut, otherwise the pasta will stick together. Dry on a cloth. Cook the fresh pasta in salted, boiling water for 3–4 minutes until tender or follow the package instructions for the dried pasta. Strain in a colander and leave to cool.

Slice the scallions at an angle. Heat a frying pan and a small saucepan. Add a few drops of olive oil to the frying pan and, when hot, sear the scallops. While the scallops are browning, melt the butter and fry the scallions for 2–3 minutes, without letting them brown. Season with salt and pepper. The scallops should now have a rich, dark tinge on the edges and be golden in the center. Turn the scallops in the pan, seasoning them with salt and pepper. The total cooking time of the scallops will be 2–3 minutes, 4 minutes maximum.

Warm the pasta in 2 tablespoons of orange or olive oil and a pat of butter. Season.

To serve, place a pile of pasta at the top of each plate with a good spoonful of scallions on top of each. Spoon 2 tablespoons of the carrot butter sauce, if using, over each pile. Place the scallops in the front and drizzle a tablespoon of orange oil on each portion. Hand the maltaise sauce separately.

**Note:** If you do not have the time to make the orange oil and carrot butter sauce, simply serve with the maltaise sauce mixed into the pasta at the last moment.

The carrot butter sauce could also be the one to use on its own and, for a sharp orange flavor, add ¼-½ cup (50–85 ml) of strongly reduced juice.

# Steamed Turbot *with Potato Gnocchi Tartare and French Beans*

*Turbot is one of the best fish that you can buy and eat. The quality of the fish is amazing with a firm but succulent texture. It is quite expensive but, if you get the chance to spoil yourself, buy some and try it.*

*Other fish will also work with this recipe — halibut, salmon, cod and sea trout in particular.*

---

**Serves 4**

4 x 6–8 oz (175–225 g) portions of
  turbot fillet, with skins
2 cups (275 g) fine green beans
A pat of butter
1 recipe Gnocchi Tartare
  (page 134)

1 tablespoon grated Parmesan
1 recipe Basic Butter Sauce
  (page 236)
Salt and pepper
Coarse sea salt (optional)

The green beans should be trimmed at the stalk end only. This leaves the fine points still attached, giving a better presentation. Cook the beans in salted, boiling water without a lid for 2–4 minutes until tender. They can also be cooked while the turbot is steaming if you wish. Drain them once tender, season with salt and pepper and roll them in a small pat of the butter.

To steam the fish, place the fillets, flesh side down, on buttered and seasoned wax paper or foil. Now steam the fillets over a pan of boiling water covered with a lid for 6–8 minutes, depending on the thickness of the fish.

While the fish and beans are cooking, pan fry the gnocchi tartare in butter for a few minutes until golden brown. Once cooked, sprinkle with the Parmesan and roll the gnocchi around in it to coat them. Warm the butter sauce and the dish is ready to serve.

To serve, put a pile of the seasoned green beans onto each plate at six o'clock and the gnocchi at the top. Pour the warmed butter sauce over and around the French beans. Remove the skin from the turbot fillet, sprinkle it with a few coarse sea salt granules and place the fish on top of the beans. The dish is ready!

# Grilled Mustard Halibut *with Warm Pickled Potatoes*

*The pickled potatoes are just new potatoes, cooked, skinned, and then marinated while still warm in a fresh mixed herb pickling liquor. I like to overcook the potatoes slightly so that when steeped in the pickling liquor and then eaten the soft, creamy centers help balance the whole taste.*

*The halibut (more or less any fish can be used for this recipe) is just brushed with a mustard butter and broiled: few ingredients, lots of taste – always a good combination.*

---

### Serves 4
4 x 6–8 oz (175–225 g) halibut fillet
   portions
1–1½ lb (450–750 g) hot, very
   well-cooked new potatoes, peeled
   and halved
1 tablespoon butter
1 heaping teaspoon Dijon mustard
Salt and pepper
all-purpose flour, for dusting

### For the Pickling Liquor:
4 tablespoons white wine
4 tablespoons white wine vinegar
A few black peppercorns
1 star anise (optional)
4 shallots, sliced into rings
1 large garlic clove, finely chopped
The juice of 1 lemon
6–8 tablespoons olive oil
1 teaspoon chopped fresh chives
1 teaspoon chopped fresh tarragon
½ teaspoon chopped fresh parsley,
   basil or chervil

Heat the wine and vinegar together with the black peppercorns, star anise, if using, and shallot rings. Reduce by a third, which should take 3–4 minutes. Add the garlic while still warm. Pour this over the warm new potatoes with the lemon juice and leave to marinate for 20–30 minutes.

Mix the butter with the mustard. Season the halibut fillets with salt and pepper and then lightly dust them with flour on the presentation side. Place the fillets on a buttered baking tray and brush each one with the mustard mixture.

Don't cook the fillets until the potatoes have been marinated. Put the fish under the broiler on a medium heat and cook for 8–10 minutes until golden and only just firm. (If the fish is quite thin, 6 minutes may be enough.)

Add the olive oil and chopped herbs to the potatoes and lightly warm. Spoon the pickled potatoes onto the serving plates with the broiled mustard halibut.

**Note:** This dish goes very well with a simple green or watercress salad.

# Confit of Sea Trout *with Caramelized Shallots, Lemon, Olives, and Capers*

*The word* confit *comes from the French word meaning 'to preserve'. Most things that are cooked in the confit style are cooked in their own fat and preserved in it. Sea trout doesn't have its own fat to cook in, but it cooks beautifully when poached slowly in goose fat or a flavored oil. The oil keeps all of the natural juices in the fish and it certainly doesn't leave a greasy, oily finish.*

*Goose fat is the best to cook it in but for this recipe I am using a flavored oil. Should the confit method turn you off, just pan-fry or broil the sea trout which will still give you great results.*

---

**Serves 4**

4 x 6–8 oz (175–225g) sea trout
   fillet portions, skinned and boned
12 large shallots, cut into ½ in
   (1 cm) dice
5 tablespoons olive oil
A pat of butter
1 teaspoon light brown sugar
   (optional)
1 large lemon, peeled, segmented
   and sliced
12–16 pitted black olives, quartered
1 tablespoon of capers
1 tablespoon chopped fresh chives

Mustard Hollandaise Sauce
   (see Quick Hollandaise Sauce,
   page 235), to serve
Salt and pepper

**For the Flavored Oil :**

2½ cups (600 ml) peanut or cooking
   oil
1¼ cups (300 ml) olive oil
1 lemon, quartered
A pinch of sea salt
A few black peppercorns, crushed
½ bunch of fresh tarragon
1 bay leaf
1 star anise

To make the flavored oil, mix all the ingredients together in a pan. Bring to the simmer and then remove from the heat. Leave to infuse for a few hours. After the oil has infused, pour it through a sieve and discard the infusing ingredients. The oil is now ready to use.

You can make the mustard hollandaise 20–30 minutes in advance.

For the garnish, the shallots first need to be caramelized. This can be achieved by placing them in a saucepan with a tablespoon of the olive oil and cooking them slowly until they reach a rich, deep, golden caramel color and flavor. The natural juices and sweetness of the shallots have now caramelized. This will take 8-10 minutes. To speed up the process, simply heat a frying pan with the tablespoon of olive oil and add the shallots with a pat of butter. Fry to a quick golden brown and add a teaspoon of light brown sugar. This will instantly caramelize, giving you rich, tasty shallots. Season with salt and pepper.

Add the sliced lemon segments, black olives and capers to the remaining 4 tablespoons of olive oil. This 'dressing' should not be too oily. All of these flavors work together, giving off lots of tastes that will neither mask the other nor overpower the sea trout.

Heat the flavored oil until it is just warm. Salt the sea trout fillets and put them in the oil. They will take 10–12 minutes to cook slowly, keeping the fish pink inside. After the first 5–6 minutes, check the sea trout in case the temperature of the oil is too high. It is then best to check every 2–3 minutes. Lift out of the oil and leave to drain slightly.

To serve the dish, add the chopped chives to the shallot dressing and spoon over the plate, spreading it out evenly. Place the sea trout in the center and spoon the mustard hollandaise over the sea trout.

The dish is now ready to eat.

**Note:** For an extra flavor in the dish, I like to spoon a couple of tablespoons of the fennel *jus* (from Steamed Fillet of Cod with a Cilantro Butter Sauce and Ratatouille Cake, page 64) around the plate.

# Open Cod Hash

*Everyone's usual idea of a hash is corned beef fried with potatoes and onions. That's exactly what I'm going to do with this cod hash: it's composed of fried potatoes, scallions and chunks of cod. It could also be made in the classic way, using mashed potatoes and then frying the whole thing as a cake.*

---

**Serves 4**

1½ lb (750 g) cod fillet, skinned and
    cut into 1 in (2.5 cm) chunks
1 lb (450 g) new potatoes in skins
1 large bunch of scallions

2–3 tablespoons olive oil
A pat of butter
all-purpose flour, for dusting
Salt and pepper

Boil the new potatoes for 25–30 minutes; this will overcook them, with the outside beginning to crumble. Once cooked and while still warm, peel the potatoes and cut in half. Slice the scallions into ½ in (1 cm) thick slices. The potatoes can now be fried in 1 tablespoon of hot olive oil and a pat of butter. Fry until golden and beginning to break up. Season with salt and pepper. The scallions can also be fried quickly in a tablespoon of oil, making them tender with only tinges of golden brown and maintaining the rich green and white colors. Season the cod cubes and roll them very lightly through the all-purpose flour.

Heat the remaining oil and another pat of butter in a hot pan and fry the cod pieces for 5–6 minutes. This will give them a good color and still leave a moist, flaky interior. All of the ingredients can now be mixed together and served. The fish will break up: don't worry about this.

**Note:** The fish is best fried a handful or two at a time. This will prevent the pan from becoming too cold and stop the fish stewing and flaking.

This can be finished with a drizzle more olive oil and some lemon juice. The Basic Butter Sauce on page 236 can also be poured over.

Other flavors can be added, such as tomatoes or sweet peppers. Or try a sprinkling of cheddar across the top, which you then brown under the broiler.

The softness of the overcooked potatoes is one of the real winners in this dish – they create creaminess and help to bind simply because they have been overcooked. Fresh herbs could be added, such as tarragon or parsley. Tartare sauce also goes very well with the hash.

This recipe can also be used for a corned-beef hash. Just replace the cod with a can of corned beef.

# Grilled 'Crunchy' Salmon *with* Gravlax Sauce

*Gravlax is basically salmon that has been marinated or cured with equal quantities of salt and sugar, flavored with brandy, dill and pepper. After a few hours or days, you have gravlax (if you are thinking of making any, it is ¼ cup (25 g) salt and 2 tablespoons (25 g) sugar per 1 lb (450 g) of fish).*

*This dish isn't gravlax but what I have done is to take those flavors and turn them into a sauce. The salmon itself is mock-grilled with a skewer or trussing needle (it can be pan-fried or cooked directly under the broiler instead) and then sprinkled with coarse sea salt and finished under the broiler. The sea salt gives a crunchy finish, which balances with the sweet, brandy-flavored dressing.*

---

**Serves 4**
4 x 6–8 oz (175–225 g) fillet
   portions of salmon, skinned
all-purpose flour, for dusting
A pat of butter, melted
Salt and pepper
2 teaspoons coarse sea salt

**For the Sauce:**
1 egg yolk
4 teaspoons Dijon mustard

2 tablespoons white wine vinegar
8 tablespoons olive oil
4 tablespoons peanut or vegetable
   oil
A pat of butter
½ teaspoon light brown sugar
2 tablespoons finely chopped
   shallots or onions
¼ cup (50 ml) brandy
1 heaping teaspoon chopped fresh dill
Salt and pepper

To make the mayonnaise style sauce, mix the egg yolk, mustard and vinegar. Mix the two oils and slowly whisk them into the mustard and vinegar.

Melt the butter and the sugar, add the shallots and cook without coloring them for 2–3 minutes. Add the brandy and reduce for 2–3 minutes until almost dry. Allow to cool to room temperature. Add the shallots to the sauce with the dill. Season with salt and pepper.

To cook the salmon, heat some skewers or trussing needles on an open flame (or use a ribbed grill pan). Season the salmon and lightly dust the skinned side with all-purpose flour. Use the hot skewers to mark the flesh or sit the salmon, skinned side down, on the grill pan for 4–5 minutes by turning it round by 45° half-way through to give an attractive crisscross 'grilled' effect.

Place the finished salmon, grill-marked side up, on a buttered baking tray. Brush with butter and sprinkle over the sea salt. Cook the salmon under a preheated grill. The salmon will take 8–10 minutes to gain a good, golden, crunchy finish. If using a grill pan, turn the fish over once marked, cook for 4–5 minutes maximum and sprinkle with the sea salt. Serve with the sauce.

**Note:** A good green salad and lemon wedges will go very well with this dish or perhaps some fresh spinach or peas with new potatoes.

The gravlax sauce also goes well with smoked salmon or cold, poached fresh salmon.

# Whole Roast Mackerel *with Red Onion and Tomato Salad*

*The mackerel is best bought already cross-cut filleted with the central bones to both fillets removed. This basically means the fish is filleted before being gutted and cut along either side of the backbone and then the main 'carcass' is removed. The fish is then gutted and any remaining bones are removed and rinsed.*

*I like to make a spicy garam masala butter with which to stuff the fish. So, while it is roasting the butter is melting and giving the fish a rich, spicy taste. Garam masala is a mixture of spices used to flavor Indian curries. It can be bought already made, but I am going to give you the recipe (as featured in* Open Rhodes) *to make your own.*

**Serves 4**

4 x mackerel, filleted as above

8 tablespoons (100 g) butter

1 heaping tablespoon finely chopped shallot or onion

1 x heaping teaspoon garam masala (see below)

1 pork caul (crépine, optional)

2 tablespoons olive or cooking oil

**For the Garam Masala:**

2 tablespoons all-purpose flour seeds

2 tablespoons cumin seeds

1 teaspoon cardamom pods

2 bay leaves

1 tablespoon black peppercorns

2 teaspoons cloves

½ teaspoon grated nutmeg

¼ teaspoon ground mace

¼ teaspoon ground ginger

**For the Red Onion and Tomato Salad:**

8 plum or salad tomatoes

2 red onions, sliced

2 tablespoons olive oil

2 tablespoons peanut oil

1 teaspoon balsamic vinegar

A squeeze of lemon juice

A pinch of ground cumin (optional)

1 tablespoon water

1 tablespoon chopped fresh cilantro

Salt and pepper

For the garam masala, dry roast all of the ingredients except the nutmeg, mace, and ginger, in a dry frying pan over a medium heat until they color and become aromatic. Leave to cool. Add the remaining spices and grind to a powder in a coffee grinder or blender. This can now be kept in an air-tight jar until needed.

To make the butter, melt 1 tablespoons (15 g) and add the shallot or onion, with a heaping teaspoon of garam masala. Cook without letting the shallot or onion color for 3–4 minutes; allow to cool. Mix with the remaining 7 tablespoons (85 g) of softened butter.

To stuff the mackerel, divide the spicy butter among all four. Fold the fillets together into a whole fish (except the head). These can now be seasoned and wrapped in pig's caul to hold the fillets together or wrapped in buttered foil. The fish are best refrigerated for half an hour before roasting. This will set the butter, holding the fish together.

Preheat the oven to 400°F/200°C. To roast the mackerel, heat some olive or cooking oil in a frying pan that can be used in the oven or a flameproof roasting pan. Pan-fry the fish (in foil, if using) for 2–3 minutes on each side, allowing them to color, before roasting for 12–15 minutes in the oven.

To make the salad, blanch the tomatoes in boiling water for 8–10 seconds and then plunge them into iced water. Remove the skins and slice into rings. Make the dressing by mixing the olive and peanut oils together and flavoring with the balsamic vinegar, a squeeze of lemon juice and salt and pepper. I also sometimes add a pinch of ground cumin to the dressing. Loosen the dressing slightly with the tablespoon of water. Season the tomato and onion slices and build the salad up in layers, putting some dressing and chopped cilantro between each layer. These salad 'cakes' can be built in individual pie or tart rings on the presentation plates.

Put the roasted mackerel on the plates. Pour any cooking juices from the foil if used over the fish and serve.

**Note:**  Mackerel fillets can be used in this recipe; simply broil them and serve with the butter melting over, alongside a tossed tomato and red onion salad.

FISH

# Monkfish Fritters 'à la Scampi' *with Roast Tomato Relish*

*Monkfish, when cut into fingers and either breadcrumbed or battered and deep-fried, takes on a scampi-like texture and image. It is a very meaty fish and has a succulent flavor.*

*This recipe can also be used to cook Dublin Bay prawns, jumbo shrimp or just chunks of fish. The roast tomatoes are my chunky replacement for tomato sauce. They give a good, fresh tomato flavor, spiced to sharpen your taste buds.*

**Serves 2**

12 oz–1 lb (350–450 g)
   monkfish fillet
Salt and pepper
A squeeze of lemon juice

**For the Batter:**

1½ cup (175 g) self-rising flour
Salt
1 egg
⅔–1¼ cups (150–300 ml) lager
   or beer
Oil, for deep-frying

**For the Roast Tomatoes:**

6 plum or salad tomatoes, cut into
   six wedges and seeded
1 tablespoon olive oil
½ garlic clove, crushed
A pinch of English mustard powder
A pat of butter
1 tablespoon white-wine or
   malt vinegar
½ teaspoon light brown sugar
Salt and pepper
1 lemon, halved or cut in wedges
Fresh parsley or watercress sprigs

Trim and cut the monkfish fillet into fingers 2 x ½ in (5 x 1 cm), season with salt and pepper and a squeeze of lemon juice.

To make the batter, sift together the self-raising flour and salt into a bowl. Whisk in the egg and lager or beer. Heat a domestic fat fryer to 350–375°F/180–190°C. Lightly dust the monkfish fingers with flour and dip them into the batter. This is best achieved by lifting them with a toothpick. Carefully place the fingers in the hot fat and fry in batches if necessary until golden. Lift from the fat and sprinkle with salt.

While the fish is cooking, heat the olive oil in a frying pan. Once hot, drop the tomatoes in and fry for 30 seconds to 1 minute before adding the garlic and mustard powder. Also add the butter and continue to fry, giving a golden brown edge to the tomatoes. After 3–4 minutes, the tomatoes should have softened. Add the vinegar and sugar and quickly reduce for 2–3 minutes. Season with salt and pepper and the roast tomato relish is ready.

To serve, sit a pile of monkfish scampi on each plate with a spoonful or two of the roast tomatoes. Garnish with lemon wedges or halves and perhaps a sprig of parsley or watercress.

**Note:** The relish can be given more heat with a dash or two of Tabasco sauce.

Other dips that go very well with this dish are sour cream mixed with lemon juice and chives, or guacamole (see below).

# Guacamole

*The main ingredient for guacamole is avocado, which is spiced up with chilies and other flavors. Guacamole should be used almost immediately after a while the avocado will begin to discolor. Chopped red and green peppers can also be added and lemon juice can be used instead of lime. Here's a recipe for two generous portions:*

---

**Serves 2**

2 ripe avocados, peeled, halved and pitted

The juice of 1 lime

2 shallots or ½ onion, finely chopped

1 fresh green chili, seeded, if wished, and finely chopped

2 tomatoes, blanched, skinned and seeded

1 garlic clove, crushed

1 tablespoon chopped fresh cilantro

Salt and pepper

Chop the avocado and fork in the lime juice. Add all the remaining ingredients and season with salt and pepper.

# poultry
# and meat

*t*his is a section for meat lovers, with most dishes carrying a British influence. I've used a lot of the traditional methods and styles with twists and influences from here and there to help them along.

On the poultry side, there are chicken, duck and pigeon dishes, with chicken appearing in two roasts. One is a pot-roast, creating its own stock as it roasts in the large pot. The other is just a roast chicken leg with bacon; well, it's not quite *just* that; it's prepared, boned, stuffed, wrapped, roasted and on page 86, you'll find it!

I've also featured homemade pies, which give a great sense of achievement and pure culinary satisfaction when eaten. The Steak and 'Kidney Pie' (page 118) is, for me, an incredibly exciting dish, along with the Slow-honey-roast Duck (page 82) and Braised Pig's Feet (page 96). Steak and kidney pie is a British classic with all of the flavors working under one (pastry) roof. In my version, the kidney pie is a completely separate item, flavored with a mixture of caramelized onions and cream. Sitting next to it you have the piece of steak, slowly braised until melting. Hence the title – Steak and 'Kidney Pie'.

The slow-honey-roast duck is just as tasty, with a rich honey glaze caramelizing the whole bird. There are also recipes for Four-hour Lamb (page 109), Tournedos of Pork (page 106), Rabbit Carbonara (page 89), Boiled Brisket of Beef (page 121) and lots more.

# Pot-roast Chicken *with Mushrooms, Peas and Mint*

*Pot-roasted chicken, presented on the table still in its cooking pot, is a mouth watering sight. The semi-roasted, poached chicken will just be golden in the pot, with the finished sauce around.*

*Wild mushrooms, which will give the end result an even more 'earthy' taste, could be used instead of the button or chestnut mushrooms. Cremini mushrooms are rich brown in color and are so named because of their nutty flavor.*

---

**Serves 4**

3–4 lb (1.5–1.75 kg) chicken
2 tablespoons olive oil
A pat of butter
1 onion, roughly chopped
2 celery sticks, roughly chopped
1 garlic clove
4–5 fresh mint leaves
3¾ cups (900 ml) Chicken Stock (page 240) or alternative (page 243) or water
Salt and pepper

**For the Sauce Garnish:**

2 cups (225 g) fresh peas, cooked (frozen can be used)
3¼ cups (225 g) button or cremini mushrooms
⅔ cup (150 ml) heavy cream
4 tbs (50 g) cold butter, cubed, plus a pat of butter
6 fresh mint leaves, finely shredded
Salt and pepper

Preheat the oven to 400°F/200°C. Season the chicken with salt and pepper. Heat the oil and butter in a frying pan and cook the chicken for 4–5 minutes until golden brown.

Sit the chicken in an earthenware braising pot or casserole dish. In the same frying pan, lightly fry for 4–5 minutes the onion, celery and the stalks from the sauce garnish mushrooms, along with the whole glove of garlic and mint leaves. Add to the chicken. Heat the chicken stock or water and pour it into the pot. Cover and place in the oven. The chicken will now take an hour to cook. During this time, baste the bird now and then with the cooking liquid.

Prepare and cook the peas and mushrooms for the sauce while the chicken is pot-roasting. Cook the peas in rapidly boiling, salted water until absolutely tender. This will take 10–15 minutes for fresh and 3–5 minutes for frozen. Once they are cooked, refresh immediately in ice water. Quarter the mushroom caps, season and sauté in a pat of butter for a few minutes until golden brown and tender.

After an hour, check that the chicken is cooked by pressing the thigh/drumstick between forefinger and thumb. The flesh should give and feel tender when pressed. Remove the chicken and cover with foil to keep warm. Strain the cooking liquid through a sieve and reduce it by half; this will take 8–10 minutes. Add the cream and simmer for 3–4 minutes.

To finish the sauce, add the peas and mushrooms and warm through for a few minutes. Add the cubed butter and stir in. Check for seasoning. The sauce should still have a fairly loose consistency. At the last minute, add the shredded mint.

# Slow-honey-roast Duck

*The flavors from this dish remind me of the taste found in Chinese pancakes with scallions and cucumber. The duck is so tender and gives a very full flavor, which makes you just want to eat more and more of it. I think that's exactly the 'problem' you are going to find here: you just won't be able to stop wanting more! For this reason, it's best to allow half a duck per person!*

**Serves 2**
2½–3 lb (1.25–1.5 kg)
   oven-ready duck
5 heaping tablespoons clear honey

1 teaspoon crushed white
   peppercorns
1 tablespoon coarse sea salt

Preheat the oven to 325°F/160°C. The duck breast skin should first be scored four or five times, just cutting into the skin itself. Put the duck in a small roasting tray. Sprinkle the peppercorns over the duck with the salt, pushing the salt onto the skin. Spoon the honey over the duck, making sure it is completely covered. Place the duck in the oven.

After the first half hour, baste the duck with the honey and duck residue in the roasting tray. Leave to slow roast for a further 30 minutes. The salt sprinkled over the duck will draw the excess water and fat from the skin itself and this will obviously collect in the roasting tray. After the second half hour, remove the duck from the roasting tray and carefully, from one corner, pour off as much excess fat as possible; it will be sitting on top of the honey in the tray. Replace the duck in the tray, baste with the honey residue and return to the oven. The duck can now be left to slow roast, basting every 15 minutes for a further hour.

The duck has now been slowly cooked for 2 hours. Remove the duck once more from the tray and again pour off any excess fat. Baste the duck with the honey and return to the oven.

During the last half hour of cooking, baste the duck every 5–10 minutes. The honey will now have reduced and become very thick, glazing the duck even more. After the 2½ hours are up, remove the duck from the oven and tray. If any excess honey seems to be still a little thin, simply boil it in the tray and reduce it to a thick, coating consistency. Pour over the duck and leave to rest for 15 minutes.

Remove the legs along with the breasts, making sure they are left whole. Sit the breast and leg, for each portion on the plates, spooning over a tablespoon of honey and any residue. The slow roast duck will be well done throughout; the meat will have become very tender and moist, just crumbling nicely as you eat it.

**Note:** You may well find that after 2 hours the duck is completely roasted, tender and glazed.

I like to simply serve a good green salad, trickled with olive oil and a squeeze of lemon with this dish.

Another favorite is to serve with the Mashed Potato Sauce (page 140). The potato sauce helps balance the richness of the honey.

# Red Wine Mallard *with Buttered Greens*

*Mallard is a wild duck which is in season between September and the end of January. It is the largest of the wild duck family, feeding two people per bird. Other wild 'ducks' in the same family are wigeon and teal. You may have to order mallard in advance from your butcher.*

*This recipe can be made using an 'oven-roast' duck, but the cooking times will be longer.*

**Serves 4**

2 mallard, legs removed
1 bottle of red wine
Vegetable oil
1 carrot, roughly chopped
1 onion, roughly chopped
½ leek, roughly chopped
Fresh thyme sprig
1 bay leaf
2 juniper berries, lightly crushed
(optional)

⅔ cup (150 ml) Chicken Stock
(page 240) or alternative
(page 243)
1¼ cup (300 ml) Veal or Beef
Jus/Gravy (page 242) or
alternative (page 243)
1½ lb (750 g) scallions, stalked and
shredded ½ in (1 cm) thick
A pat of butter
2–3 tablespoons water
Salt and pepper

The mallard legs can be marinated in half a bottle of red wine for 24 hours beforehand if you wish to guarantee a good strong flavor from them.

Preheat the oven to 400°F/200°C.

Warm a drizzle of vegetable oil in a large saucepan and add the chopped vegetables, thyme, bay leaf and juniper berries. Cook for 10–15 minutes, allowing the vegetables to color. Add the red wine from the duck legs and the remaining half bottle and boil rapidly until reduced by three-quarters. To help increase the duck flavor of the sauce, the main carcass of the ducks can be removed. This will leave the duck breasts still sitting on the bone, but with no carcass beneath them. Chop the carcasses from both ducks into small pieces and fry for a few minutes in a little oil until golden. Add the fried carcass pieces to the red wine reduction. The duck legs can now also be browned in oil and added to the reduction.

Add the chicken stock and *jus*/gravy to the pan and bring to the simmer. Braise the legs in the preheated oven for 45 minutes–1 hour. The duck legs will now be totally tender. Remove the legs and strain the sauce through a fine sieve. Bring the sauce back to the simmer, skimming off any excess fat and cook until it is reduced to a coating consistency. The flavor will have a combination of strong red wine and duck. Season to taste with a little salt and pepper.

Lay the remaining double breasts, skin side down, in a heavy-bottomed, ovenproof frying pan and fry over a high heat until golden. Turn the breasts over and roast in the oven for 20–25 minutes. This will give you wonderful pink duck still sitting on the bone.

Remove from the oven cover with some foil and leave to rest somewhere warm for 10–15 minutes.

While the duck is resting, cook the greens. Melt the butter with 2–3 tablespoons of water. Bring to the boil and add the shredded greens. Season with salt and pepper and cook, stirring, on a medium heat for a few minutes until tender. Also, return the duck legs to the finished sauce and warm through.

To serve, put a spoonful of greens at the top of a plate or bowl and sit a duck leg next to it. Cut the duck breasts off the bone by following the direction of the carcass. Carve each breast into three and then lay the slices at the front of the plate. Pour the finished sauce over and around and serve.

**Note:** The cooking of the duck legs and finishing of the sauce can be done 24 hours in advance. Then just reheat the legs for 10–15 minutes in the warming sauce. If buying from a local butcher, I am sure they will remove the legs and take out the central carcass (and chop it) for you, leaving the two breasts of each duck still attached to the bone. This guarantees a tender finish and the shape of the duck is not lost.

**I** Cut either side of the thigh bone and around the knuckle at the top of the thigh. Scrape towards the drumstick and cut knuckle, leaving a single bone.

**2** Skin the legs. Mix together the ingredients for the butter. Divide between the 4 legs, filling each empty thigh.

**3** Place a bacon strip on the drumstick end and fold round the leg. Continue with more strips until all the legs are covered. Fry and then roast.

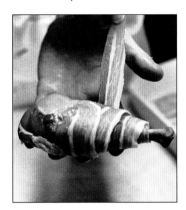

# Roast Chicken and Bacon *flavored with Tarragon, Garlic and Lemon*

*The title 'roast chicken' may be a little deceptive when in fact all it's going to be is a roast chicken leg! That's one of the features of this dish that makes it so exciting. Once you've tried it, you'll be amazed at just how good a roasted chicken leg can be. For this recipe, I'm boning out the thigh bone, which will leave me space to fill with the flavored tarragon butter. This melts as the chicken roasts and leaves a wonderful flavor in the chicken.*

**Serves 4**
4 legs of chicken
12–16 strips of bacon
Vegetable oil

**For the Butter:**
6 tbs (75 g) butter, softened
2 tablespoons chopped fresh tarragon
2 small garlic cloves, crushed
2 tablespoons finely chopped
  shallots or onions
The finely grated zest of 1 lemon
Salt and pepper
**For the Sauce:**
A pat of butter

½ onion, roughly chopped
2 garlic cloves, crushed
1 bay leaf
2 glasses white wine
The juice of 1 or 2 lemons
1¼ cup (300 ml) Chicken Stock
  (page 240) or alternative
  (page 243)
⅔ cup (150 ml) heavy cream
Salt and pepper

Preheat the oven to 400°F/200°C. To make the sauce, melt the butter and add the onion, crushed garlic and bay leaf. Cook without coloring for 3–4 minutes. Add the white wine and reduce until almost dry. Add the juice of 1 lemon and reduce by half. Add the chicken stock and reduce by two-thirds. Pour on the heavy cream and bring to the simmer. Simmer gently for 10–15 minutes. Strain through a sieve and season with salt and pepper. To make the sauce fuller and sharper, add another squeeze or two of lemon juice. The sauce is now ready.

First remove the bone from the thigh part of each leg. Cut either side of the bone and then cut around the knuckle showing at the top of the thigh. Scrape down the bone to the joint connecting the thigh with the drumstick. Now simply break or cut at the knuckle. This will leave you with a single 1½–2 in (3–5 cm) bone in the drumstick. Skin the legs.

For the butter, mix together the softened butter, tarragon, garlic, shallots or onions, lemon zest and seasoning. Divide the flavored butter between the four legs, filling the empty thigh. Now wrap the chicken legs in the bacon. Start by placing a strip of bacon on the drumstick end of the leg. Fold the strip round and round the leg, slightly overlapping as you do to keep the bacon in place. Continue covering the leg with the strips, starting where the last strip finished. You will need 3–4 strips to cover each leg. Once completely covered, pierce with a toothpick to hold the bacon in place.

Warm a roasting tray on a medium heat with a drizzle of vegetable oil. Add the legs to the pan, cooking and browning the bacon all the way around until crisp. This is best achieved by browning over a medium heat. Place the chicken legs in the oven and roast for 15–20 minutes. During this time, the bacon will become even more golden and crisp. Leave to rest for 5–6 minutes before carving.

Carve three slices through the thigh part of the cut and sit the slices, overlapping, on the plates. The drumstick can be presented standing up, revealing its bone behind the slices. To finish, just pour some of the cream sauce around.

**Note:** This dish goes very well with buttered spinach as featured in the photograph on page 87. To cook buttered spinach, pick and de-stalk and wash the spinach several times to remove any grit. Heat a pat of butter and a tablespoon or two of water to boiling point and add the washed spinach. Cook on a fast heat for a few minutes until tender. Season the spinach with salt, pepper and grated nutmeg.

# Rabbit Carbonara

*I've chosen rabbit as an alternative to the obvious chicken but the recipe can be made replacing the rabbit legs with four chicken breasts, so please don't be turned off if you don't like rabbit. The flavor of rabbit is richer and stronger, which is why I use them. I must have seen literally hundreds of different recipes for carbonara sauces. This is mine; it's simple to make and extremely tasty to eat.*

**Serves 4**
4 rabbit legs
12 oz (350 g) fresh or dried noodles
   or spaghetti

**For the Sauce:**
2½ cups (600 ml) Chicken Stock
   (page 240) or alternative
   (page 243)
1 onion, finely chopped
1 garlic clove, crushed

2 tablespoons olive oil
4 oz (100 g) bacon strips
⅔ cup (150 ml) heavy cream
1 cup (50–75 g) Parmesan, grated
2 tablespoons chopped fresh flatleaf
   or curly parsley
A squeeze of lemon juice (optional)
Salt and pepper
A drizzle of good olive oil, to serve

Poach the rabbit legs in the chicken stock for 20–25 minutes until tender. Remove the legs and reduce the stock to ⅔ cup (150 ml). Cook the onion and garlic in a tablespoon of olive oil for a few minutes without letting them brown. Fry the bacon separately in the remaining olive oil until crisp (or just cook it with the onions). Add the reduced stock and the cream and bring to a simmer. Cook for a few minutes. Add the bacon, if cooked separately. Season with salt and pepper.

Cook the noodles or spaghetti in salted, boiling water, following the package instructions, if dried. If fresh, they will take 4–5 minutes.

Meanwhile, take the meat from the rabbit legs off the bone. Shred it into strips. Add the rabbit to the sauce to warm through.

As soon as the noodles are cooked, drain in a colander. Season and mix with the rabbit sauce. Add a tablespoon or two of grated Parmesan with the parsley. A squeeze of lemon juice will lift all of the flavors. Divide between bowls, finishing each with a drizzle of olive oil.

**Note:** Mushrooms can also be added to the recipe and a good twist of pepper at the end will really fire up the dish.

# Roast Wood Pigeon *with Sautéed*
## *Red Wine Potatoes*

*Wood pigeons have a strong, almost beefy flavor so a good red wine always goes well with them. The potatoes are flavored with red onions and then caramelized in red wine – the flavor is so good. I also like to sauté the potatoes in goose fat for a very rich flavor. You can of course sauté the potatoes in butter, which is almost as good.*

*The pigeons are going to be roasted on the breast bones. The rest of the carcass and the legs are going to be removed, chopped up and turned into a 'game' sauce.*

---

**Serves 4**

4 large wood pigeons
4 potatoes, boiled in their jackets
Vegetable oil
5 red onions, sliced
1 carrot, chopped
1 bay leaf
Fresh thyme sprig
¾ bottle of red wine
2½ cups (600 ml) Chicken Stock (page 240) or 1¼ cups (300 ml) Veal *Jus*/Gravy (page 242) or alternative (page 243)

4-6 tbs (50–75 g) cold butter
2 tbs (50 g) butter or goose or duck fat, for frying the potatoes and onions
1 teaspoon light brown granulated sugar
¼ cup (50 ml) brandy or Armagnac (optional)
1 tablespoon chopped fresh flatleaf parsley
Salt and pepper

Preheat the oven to 400°F/200°C. Remove the legs from the birds and detach the breasts on the bone from the rest of the carcass. Chop the legs and the discarded parts of the carcass into small pieces and brown them in a drop of cooking oil in a large, deep frying pan or saucepan. Add one of the onions, the carrot, bay leaf and thyme and cook for 10–15 minutes or until all have taken on some color.

Add two-thirds of the wine and boil rapidly until reduced by three-quarters. If using chicken stock in place of *jus*/gravy (which is what I shall be using), add it now and simmer for 20 minutes before starting the final reduction. Now increase the heat and boil rapidly. Once the liquid is reduced to ⅔ cup (150 ml), you will have a good, rich, strong pigeon stock. Now you can whisk in the 4-6 tbs (50–75 g) of cold butter, cut in small cubes, to give a red-wine butter sauce. If using veal *jus*/gravy instead, add to the sauce and simmer very gently for 20–30 minutes. It will not need the final reduction by rapid boiling. Strain the sauce through a fine sieve into a clean pan.

Peel the cooked potatoes and cut into ¼ in (5 mm) thick slices. Classic sauté potatoes should start to break down as they are fried: this gives them a much better crumbly texture. Pan fry the potato slices in some of the goose or duck fat or butter over a medium high heat until golden and beginning to crisp. Season with salt and pepper.

Meanwhile, pan fry the remaining onions in the remaining butter or duck or goose fat, in a separate pan on a high heat until slightly softened and browned. Add the remaining third of the wine and reduce until almost dry. Add the sugar, which will caramelize quite quickly. Mix together the potatoes and onions and keep warm.

The pigeons can now be roasted. Season them with salt and pepper and cook, skin-side down, with a drop of cooking oil on top of the stove in a roasting pan or heavy ovenproof frying pan. Finish the pigeons in the oven, breast side up, for 15 minutes. This will keep the breasts nice and pink. Another 10 minutes will make them well done.

Once cooked, remove them from the oven, cover with foil and allow to rest somewhere warm for 5–6 minutes. Remove the breasts from the bone and sprinkle the pink side with the Armagnac or brandy (if using). The flavor will be absorbed by the meat, which will be wonderfully enhanced. Leave to stand for a further 5 minutes. Meanwhile, reheat the sauce and finish the sautéed onions and potatoes with the chopped parsley. Spoon some onto each plate and add the pigeon breasts (two per portion) either sitting at the front or on the top of the plate. Pour the butter sauce or gravy around and serve.

**Note:** The French Bean Purée (page 156) goes very well as a vegetable with this dish; you could put the breasts on a pool of purée, offering the sauté potatoes separately.

Other game – pheasant, teal, grouse, etc. – will all work with this recipe.

# Scallops of Pork *fried with a Sage, Garlic and Anchovy Crust, served with Apple Mashed Potatoes*

*If you are not a big fan of anchovies, you can leave them out of this recipe. I prefer to use marinated anchovies which are a totally different 'kettle of fish' from the canned variety. The canned variety can be used but you'll only need about a quarter of the quantity – they are a lot, lot stronger and saltier.*

*Next is the apple mash. Apple and potato are both favorite flavors of mine, as you probably know by now! A ready-made apple sauce can be used instead of cooking your own but it is best to choose one that isn't too sweet. The combination of the pork with the apple works very well, as indeed does the mash!*

---

**Serves 4**
4 x 6–8 oz (175–225 g) pork fillets
   or pork loin portions
4 tbs (50 g) butter
2 shallots, finely chopped or ½ onion
1¾ cup (100 g) fresh white
   breadcrumbs
8–10 fresh sage leaves, chopped
8 marinated anchovy fillets or
   4 canned ones (optional)
2 garlic cloves, crushed
all-purpose flour, for dusting
1 egg, beaten

2 tablespoons olive oil
Salt and pepper
A squeeze of lemon juice

**For the Potatoes:**
1½ lb (750 g) Mashed Potatoes
   (page 140)
4 Granny Smith or
   Golden Delicious apples
A pat of butter

To make the apple mashed potatoes, peel, quarter and core the apples. Cut the apple quarters into six or eight. Melt the butter and add the apples. Cook on medium heat until the apples are completely cooked, soft and translucent. Push the apple through a sieve or purée it in a blender and then mix it with the mashed potatoes. The ratio between the two is really up to you – it's a question of adding and tasting. I find between a quarter and a third of apple to potato works well but if you prefer more simply add more.

Trim the pork fillet or pork loin portions so they are totally fat-free. Both can be found prepared and cut in most supermarkets. Put the portions between sheets of plastic wrap and bat them out to scallops ¼ in thick (5 mm) with a heavy saucepan or rolling pin.

Melt a pat of butter with the shallots or onion and cook for 2–3 minutes until softened but without browning. Leave to cool. Once cool, mix into the breadcrumbs with the sage, anchovies (if using) and garlic. Season with salt and pepper. Season the pork, dust with all-purpose flour and pass it through the egg. The pork can now be coated in the breadcrumbs; make sure the scallops are all well covered on both sides.

Heat a frying pan with the olive oil. Add a pat of butter and put the scallops in the pan. Cook them on medium heat for 4–5 minutes on each side until they have a crisp, golden finish.

Serve the apple mashed potatoes on the plates with the scallops or in a separate bowl. To finish, heat a pat of butter in the frying pan until it bubbles to a nut brown. Add a squeeze or two of lemon juice and pour over the pork.

**Note:** Chicken breasts can also be tenderized into scallops and finished as for the pork.

# Four-hour Pork – *pressure-cooked in two!*

*Trying to cook a 4-hour dish in 2 hours would normally put you under a lot of pressure. But with this recipe, that's exactly what I am going to do!*

*I'm using a pressure cooker. I have been amazed at how good these machines are. You put all the ingredients in and, in under 2 hours, the dish is virtually done! If you don't have one, this dish really takes four-hours. Just cook the dish in the oven at 300°F/150°C for 4 hours; either way, the meat simply melts and falls off the bone.*

---

**Serves 4–6**

3–4 lb (1.5–1.75 kg) cut of shoulder or leg of pork

½ cup (100 g) prunes, stoned and quartered

4 apples, peeled, cored and cut into eighths

2–3 strips of orange zest

1 bay leaf

2 potatoes, peeled and quartered

2 onions, roughly chopped

2 cloves

2½ cups (600 ml) beer

1¼ cups (300 ml) Chicken Stock (page 240) or alternative (page 243) or water

½ teaspoon light brown granulated sugar

A pat of butter

Salt and pepper

1 tablespoon chopped fresh parsley

The pork cut can be cooked as it is with the skin left on or removed, scored, salted and roasted separately for 30–40 minutes at 400°F/200°C to make crackling. If you want to do this, retie the pork joint into shape.

Place all of the ingredients, except the butter and the chopped parsley, in the pressure cooker and bring to the simmer. Fit the lid on top, set the pressure weight and adjust the heat as required. Cook for about 1½–2 hours on a fairly low heat but still at full pressure and then turn off the heat. Leave to stand for at least 15 minutes to allow the steam to be released before removing the lid. Remove the succulent, overcooked pork and allow it to rest for 10 minutes.

The cooking liquid may need to be skimmed to remove excess fat. The apples and potatoes will have almost broken down, thickening the liquid. Add the butter and carefully stir in. Remove the orange zest. You now have a sauce that has nothing but flavor. Season with salt and pepper and add the chopped parsley.

You can now literally break the pork into portions and put them in bowls or on plates. Spoon the sauce over and serve. This dish has a very rustic look about it, but it has immense flavor and is so easy that it relieves a lot of 'pressure' in your kitchen!

**Note:** Check the pressure cooker manufacturer's instructions for detailed instructions on pot roasting cuts of this size.

# Braised Pig's Feet

*Pig's feet are an unusual but sensational dish. Filling them with a pork sausage and black pudding stuffing and serving them with mashed potatoes and gravy gives them a traditional English touch. If you try these once, I can assure you'll be excited and delighted by the results! Ask the butcher to prepare them for you. Also get him to mince the pork belly, which gives the stuffing the right fat-to-meat content.*

**Serves 4**
4 pig's back trotters, boned
Mashed Potatoes (page 140)

**For the Stuffing:**
12 oz (350 g) pork belly, ground
6 oz (175 g) black pudding, cut into
    ½ in (1 cm) dice
2 large onions, chopped
1 garlic clove, crushed
A pat of butter
A pinch of ground mace
1 egg
2 tablespoons white breadcrumbs
1 tablespoon chopped fresh sage
A dash of Worcestershire sauce
Salt and pepper

**For the Cooking Liquor:**
A pat of butter
1 onion, roughly chopped
1 carrot, roughly chopped
1 leek, roughly chopped
Fresh thyme sprig
1 bay leaf
1 glass white wine
2 glasses Madeira
2½ cups (600 ml) Chicken Stock
    (page 240) or alternative
    (page 243)
1¼ cups (300 ml) Beef or Veal
    Jus/Gravy (page 242) or
    alternative (page 243)
Salt and pepper

Preheat the oven to 325°F/160°C. For the cooking liquid in a casserole dish or saucepan, melt a pat of butter with the chopped vegetables, thyme and bay leaf. Cook without letting them brown for 1–2 minutes before adding the white wine. Boil rapidly until reduced by half. Add the Madeira and reduce by half again. The stock and *jus*/gravy can now be added with the boned trotters. Bring to the simmer, cover, place in the oven and braise for 2½–3 hours. After 2½ hours, check the trotter skin for tenderness. If pinched, it must tear very easily. If slightly firm, cook for the remaining half hour.

Once cooked, remove the trotters and sit on individual, buttered foil strips, skin side down.

Strain the cooking liquid through a fine sieve and if necessary boil rapidly until reduced to a sauce consistency.

As it is reducing, the sauce may need to be skimmed of any excess fat. It should be rich in color with a glossy finish. Season with salt and pepper. The sauce can also be lifted with an extra dash of neat Madeira. Set aside while you finish the trotters.

For the stuffing, cook the chopped onions and crushed garlic in the butter without letting them brown for 5–6 minutes or until softened. Leave to cool. Mix the onions into the ground pork belly with the black pudding. Season with salt, pepper and ground mace.

Beat in the egg and then add the breadcrumbs and chopped sage. Check the seasoning and finish with a dash of Worcestershire sauce.

Once the trotters have cooled to room temperature, roll some of the stuffing into a sausage shape. Sit this on the trotter, adding enough to make the trotter resemble its original shape. Fold over the remaining skin and roll in the foil, twisting either end to help maintain a good cylindrical shape. Refrigerate the trotters for 1–2 hours to set. They will keep very well, refrigerated, for 2–3 days.

To finish and serve the trotters, steam the trotters over a pan of boiling water for 15 minutes. Carefully unwrap them. An alternative method is to sit them in a roasting tray with ¼ in (5 mm) of hot water from the kettle and bake them at 375°F/190°C, also for 15 minutes. Spoon or pipe through a ½ in (1 cm) plain tube, some creamy mashed potatoes at the top of the plate. Sit the trotter in front. Now just pour the reduced, finished sauce over the trotter and serve.

# Pan Fried or Broiled Liver *with Young Sprouting Cabbage and Gorgonzola Rarebit*

*Rarebit was never going to escape from this book! There are so many different cheese flavors that can be used. This recipe can be made with stilton or roquefort — I just can't ignore them.*

*The liver I'm going to use is calves', which is obviously the very best but also the most expensive. Lamb's liver will also go very well. The greens and gorgonzola go very well with pork too; a good pork roast served with them is delicious.*

---

**Serves 4**

4 x 6–8 oz (175–225 g) thick slices
   of calves' or lamb's liver
all-purpose flour, seasoned
A drizzle of vegetable oil
A pat of butter
Salt and pepper

**For the Cabbage:**

1½–2 lb (750–900 g) young cabbage,
   or savoy cabbage, or spring greens
2 tbs (25 g) butter

8 oz (225 g) Gorgonzola Rarebit
   (page 233)
Salt and pepper

**For the Sauce:**

2 tablespoons sherry vinegar
1 teaspoon light brown granulated
   sugar
⅔ cup (150 ml) thick Jus/Gravy
   (page 242) or alternative
   (page 243)
Salt and pepper

Wash the young sprouting cabbage, keeping the leaves intact with their stalks which cook very tender. If using savoy cabbage or spring greens, just cut into wide strips. Cook in salted, boiling water for 2–3 minutes or until tender. Drain. If you want to cook the cabbage in advance, refresh it in plenty of cold water and re-heat it in the microwave when you are ready. Season the cabbage with salt and pepper and add the butter. Mix thoroughly. You can now serve it separately in a vegetable dish with the Gorgonzola Rarebit just golden and melting over or put individual portions on the serving plates, mold the rarebit into ¼ in (5 mm) thick discs and lay them on top, so they melt over the cabbage when broiled. If using savoy cabbage or spring greens, it is best served glazed in a separate vegetable dish.

For the sauce, quickly boil together the sherry vinegar and sugar until slightly reduced and then add to the *jus*/gravy. Bring to the simmer and season with salt and pepper.

Preheat the broiler to high. For the liver, dust the thick liver slices in the seasoned flour. Heat a frying pan or grill pan with a drizzle of cooking oil. Put the liver in the pan and add the butter. For thick liver slices, cook for 2–3 minutes, turn over and cook for a further 2 minutes. For thin slices, cook for 1–2 minutes on each side. Meanwhile, slide the cabbage under the broiler to color. Season the liver, put next to the glazed cabbage (if presenting on plates) and either serve the sauce separately or trickle over or around the liver.

# Rib Steak 'au Poivre' *with*
## *Sweet Brandy Butter*

*Steak* au poivre *has many variations: one of these is the type of steak you use (fillet, sirloin, T-bone, chateaubriand or rib). The other variation depends on your choice of pepper for the* au poivre *– crushed black peppercorns or green peppercorns in a brandy cream sauce. This one is going to be a combination of both. The steak will be smothered with the crushed black peppercorns and the brandy is used in the butter along with sweet white wine, shallots or onions, parsley and mustard.*

*One of the advantages of cooking a rib steak is that it is a cut of meat for two people. The weight of the meat is 1½–2 lb (750–900 g) and that includes the rib bone as well! Consequently, the steak will be 1½–2 in (3–5 cm) thick. If a 8 oz (225 g) sirloin steak is being cooked, the strong flavor of the crushed peppercorns may take over because of the size of the meat. With the thick rib steak, the flavor is totally different. You have the peppery outside with the rich, almost sweet, flavor of the beef to look forward to. When you are eating the rib with the tasty butter just melting over the taste is really quite sensational. Remember that the rib is for two people so, although it sounds so good, you really will have to share it!*

*I like to serve a good watercress or green salad with the steak, accompanied by either Mashed Potatoes (page 140) or French fries.*

---

**Serves 2**

1½–2 lb (750–900 g) rib steak, on
    the bone, trimmed
2 tablespoons black peppercorns
2 tablespoons olive oil
A pat of butter
Salt

**For the Sweet Brandy Butter:**
2 tablespoons finely chopped
    shallots or onions

¼ cup (50 ml) brandy
4 tablespoons sweet white wine,
    or dry white wine with a pinch
    of sugar
6 tbs (75 g) butter, softened
2 teaspoons chopped fresh parsley
1 teaspoon Dijon or English mustard
    (optional)
Salt and pepper

To make the sweet brandy butter, warm the shallots or onions with the brandy and then boil until reduced and almost dry. Add the wine and reduce until almost dry. Let cool. Once cold, mix into the butter with the parsley and mustard, if using. Season with salt and pepper.

Crush the peppercorns, not too finely, in a mortar and pestle, coffee grinder or with the back of a knife. Shake the crushed peppercorns in a sieve to release the powdered pepper, which will make the pepper flavor too strong. Press the crushed peppercorns into each side of the meat – be quite firm. Season with salt.

Heat the olive oil in a frying pan and, once hot, add the meat. It is important now not to fry too quickly, otherwise the steak will burn before it is cooked. Also, I only like to turn the meat once. This ensures a good, crusty finish and that the peppercorns are cooked.

For a medium-rare to medium steak, it is best to turn the steak after 8–10 minutes. This may seem a long time to cook it, but a rib on the bone does take quite a time to cook. Once turned, add the butter, which will turn to a good nut brown as the steak continues to cook. The steak will now take a further 8–10 minutes and during that time you should spoon over the cooking juices to baste the meat.

Once cooked, leave the meat to rest somewhere warm for 6–7 minutes before carving. This will relax the meat, giving it a more tender finish. Spoon the brandy butter on the rib, leaving it just to melt over before serving; or reheat the rib cooking pan with all the residue still in the pan. Add some of the brandy butter, stirring it into all the other flavors and then pour it over and around the steak to serve.

# One-piece Irish Stew

*I featured Irish stew in my first book* Rhodes Around Britain. *That was done in the good old-fashioned way with everything in one pot and just ladled up and ready! This method gives you the same flavors but in a totally different form.*

*Chumps of lamb are cuts of lamb that come in pairs at the rear of the saddle. They are usually cut into chump chops but I prefer to use them as individual cuts for roasting, braising or stewing. With all fat and sinew removed (ask your butcher to do this), they can be tied into cuts.*

*This recipe may appear long-winded, but I promise you it really is very simple and easy. Basically, it is just boiled meat with one potato and three veggies – I'd call that a traditional British dish, wouldn't you?*

---

**Serves 4**

**For the Lamb:**

4 cuts of lamb, or chumps, trimmed
   of all fat
A pat of butter
2 carrots, roughly chopped
1 large onion, roughly chopped
2–3 celery sticks, roughly chopped
2 garlic cloves, finely chopped
1 bay leaf
Fresh thyme sprig
3¾ cups (900 ml) Chicken Stock
   (page 240) or alternative
   (page 243) or water

A few lamb bones (optional)
**For the Garnish:**
4 small onions
8 tbs (100 g) butter
1 small savoy cabbage
4 carrots, peeled
½ teaspoon sugar
2 large potatoes, peeled
1–2 teaspoons roughly chopped
   fresh flatleaf parsley (optional)
Salt and pepper

To cook the lamb, melt a pat of butter in a large pan and add the chopped vegetables, garlic, bay leaf and thyme. Cook for 5–6 minutes until slightly softened. Add the lamb chumps and top with the chicken stock or water. Because of the slow cooking method, the chumps will create their own stock if cooked in water. A few extra lamb bones can also be added to increase the flavor. Using chicken stock rather than water will obviously leave you with a stronger broth.

Bring to a simmer and continue to simmer, covered, for 1½ hours. The stock may need skimming from time to time to remove any impurities.

Once cooked, remove the meat and keep warm. Strain the cooking liquid through a sieve and discard the vegetables. Taste the stock for strength and reduce it to increase the flavor and thicken the consistency.

All the vegetable garnishes can be prepared and cooked while the lamb is braising. I prefer to cook these separately from the stew to give a better finish to the dish.

For the onions, preheat the oven to 400°F/200°C. Melt a pat of butter in a frying pan. Put the onions in the pan and cook for 4–5 minutes until golden brown on the presentation side. Transfer the onions to a braising dish and fill to half-way up the sides with some of the braising liquid from the lamb or some extra chicken stock. Cook them in the oven for 30–35 minutes until completely tender. They can just be reheated in the liquid when needed.

For the cabbage parcels, peel the outside leaves from the cabbage, wash, and remove the stalks leading through the center of the leaf. Cook four large or eight small leaves in salted, boiling water for 2–3 minutes until completely tender. Refresh in ice water. Quarter the center of the remaining cabbage and remove all the stalks. Shred the cabbage leaves very finely. Melt another pat of butter with 2–3 tablespoons of water in a saucepan and add the shredded cabbage. Cook on a medium heat for 3–4 minutes until tender. Season with salt and pepper and allow to cool.

Once it's cool, divide the mix into four balls and wrap each one in the cooked leaves. These can now be wrapped tightly in plastic wrap to maintain a good ball or parcel shape. To reheat, steam them over boiling water for 5–6 minutes or microwave for 1–2 minutes on full power.

For the carrots, place in a small saucepan, barely covering them with cold water. Add a pat of butter, sugar and a pinch of salt. Cover and bring to the simmer, cooking them for 10–12 minutes until they are tender. Remove the lid and reduce the cooking liquid with the carrots until a buttery syrupy consistency is achieved. The carrots are now glazed with their own cooking liquid. To reheat, toss in a little water and butter over a low heat.

For the potatoes, halve the peeled potatoes lengthwise. Each piece can now be cut into barrel shapes with a sharp knife, or leave them as half-potatoes. Boil them in salted water until tender but still keeping their shape. Melt a pat of butter. Once the potatoes are cooked, brush with melted butter.

We now have the lamb and the garnishes ready.

Sit the vegetables at the top of the plate and the chump of lamb at the front. Add the remaining butter to the reduced cooking liquid and also the chopped parsley. Spoon the sauce over the lamb and serve: one piece Irish stew!

# Cornish Pasty Pudding

*This steamed version of the traditional favorite is lovely to eat; the beef cooks with potatoes, onions and rutabega in its own juices with a touch of stock to help it along.*

*All it needs then is a good spoonful of mustard to go with it and the dish is complete. Some* jus*/gravy (page 242) can also be offered separately.*

---

**Serves 4**

**For the Suet Pastry:**

1 lb (450 g) all-purpose flour
¼ cup (25 g) baking powder
10 oz (275 g) dried suet
1 tablespoon dried English mustard
 (optional)
1¼ cup (300 ml) water
A pinch of salt

**For the Filling:**

1 lb (450 g) beef chuck or skirt,
 sliced into very thin strips
1 large potato, peeled and sliced
1 small rutabega, peeled and sliced
1 large onion, sliced
A pat of butter
⅔–1 cup (150–250 ml) Beef Stock
 (page 242) or alternative
 (page 243)
Worcestershire sauce
*Jus*/Gravy (page 242, optional)
Salt and pepper

Sift the flour, baking powder and salt together. Mix the suet and mustard powder, if using (the mustard fires up the flavor of the pastry and the rest of the pasty), and add to the flour mix. Add the water and work to a good suet dough. Before rolling, allow the dough to rest for 20 minutes.

Butter a 5 cups (1.2-liter) pudding mold. Roll out three-quarters of the dough and line the mold, making it at least ¼–½ in (5 mm–1 cm) thick. Roll the remaining quarter of the dough into a circle to cover the pudding.

Season the meat, vegetables and onion separately with salt and pepper. Melt the butter and drizzle it over the vegetables. The meat can now be layered between individual layers of the rutabega, potatoes, and onions. Once the suet pudding bowl is filled, mix a few shakes of the Worcestershire sauce with the beef stock and pour over.

Brush water around the edge of the pudding and cover with the lid. Press to seal all around and then cover with buttered foil, pleating it to leave room for rising. The pudding can now be steamed for 2 hours. Once it's cooked, remove from the steamer and leave to rest for 10 minutes before turning out. If gravy is being served, pour it over or offer it separately.

**Note:** Fresh chopped thyme can be added to the mixture with a pinch of ground mace and cayenne pepper to spice up the filling.

# Tournedos of Pork *with Caramelized Apple and Mashed Potato Sauce*

*Another tournedos dish with exactly the same concept as the lamb on page 122. Of course you'll not be needing a whole leg of pork – that would give you about 40 portions! I buy 3 lb (1.5 kg) of pork meat from the leg. This can be broken down and prepared as for the lamb recipe. This recipe also illustrates exactly what I feel about British dishes: working with classic British flavors and then turning them into something even more special by enhancing their taste. Pork with apples and mashed potatoes is a classic. Here's a 'new' classic.*

**Serves 8**

3 lb (1.5 kg) leg of pork meat, boned
   and skin removed
8 oz (225 g) pig's caul (crépine) or
   15–18 strips of smoked bacon
10 fresh sage leaves, chopped
A pat of butter
Salt and pepper

**For the Sauce:**

2½ cups (600 ml) Jus/Gravy (page
   242) or alternative (page 243)
1¼ cups (300 ml) apple juice
A squeeze of lemon juice

**For the Garnishes:**

4 Granny Smith apples
A pat of butter
A sprinkling of sugar
1 quantity Mashed Potato Sauce
   (page 140)

To prepare the pork, cut and prepare it in exactly the same way as for the lamb (page 122). Remove all sinews, cut the lean meat into strips and mince the trimmings. Instead of adding cumin, just add salt, pepper and the chopped sage. Arrange the meat strips and farce as for the other recipe, roll into a cylinder and wrap in pig's caul, foil, or bacon strips. Refrigerate, cut and tie as in the lamb and the tournedos are ready.

Preheat the oven to 400°F/200°C. The sauce can be kept very simple. Just reduce the apple juice by two-thirds and then add the *jus*/gravy. Add a squeeze of lemon juice, if you like, to sharpen the apple flavor.

Peel the apples and remove the cores. Cut through the middle, trimming off the ends to give you ½–¾ in (1–1.5 cm) thick slices.

Season the pork tournedos with salt and pepper and sauté in butter on all sides until nicely browned. Finish cooking in the oven for 12–15 minutes. This will leave the pork still moist in the center. Leave to rest for 5–6 minutes.

While the pork is cooking and resting, pan fry the apples in butter until golden and

tender. This will take 5–6 minutes. Once cooked, sit them on a tray, wider side up, and sprinkle with sugar. Caramelize under a hot broiler.

To serve the dish, spoon some warmed mashed potato sauce on the top half of the plate. Place the apples towards the front with the pork tournedos sitting at the side. Drizzle the pork apple gravy around and serve. You can also serve this with pork crackling (see Note below) as shown in the picture on page 107.

**Note:** It is best to reduce the apple gravy to a good, thick consistency, so it easily coats the back of a spoon. Any pork skin can be cut into thin strips and well salted. Bake in a preheated oven (350°F/180°C) for 30–40 minutes. This will remove all excess fat, and leave you with pork crackling. These can be salted and left to cool. A few to eat with the tournedos are lovely. A glass or two of Madeira, reduced into the sauce, will make it even stronger.

A stronger pork flavor for the sauce can also be achieved by taking 1 lb (450 g) of chopped pork bones and roasting them with onions, leeks, celery, sage leaves and garlic. Once golden brown, add 2 ½ cups (600 ml) of chicken stock and cook for 1–2 hours. Reduce by three-quarters and add to the *jus*/gravy. Continue to simmer gently for 20–30 minutes and strain through a sieve. Now reduce the apple juice, add to the gravy and the sauce is ready.

# Four Hour Lamb

*I'm sure you all know by now how much I love slow cooking methods. Waiting 4 hours for this leg of lamb is worth every minute!*

*Pierre Koffman, one of the most talented and wellknown chefs in the UK and Europe, featured this recipe (or one very similar) in one of his books. I tried it, loved it and now I'm just passing it on. It's that good.*

*This recipes uses a leg of lamb, which will feed eight people generously.*

---

**Serves 8**

**For the Vegetable *Mirepoix***

2 onions, diced
2–3 carrots, diced
1 leek, diced
2–3 celery sticks, diced

**For the Lamb:**

1 leg of lamb
Fresh thyme sprig
1 bay leaf
5 tbs (65 g) butter
4 oz (100 g) garlic, tied in muslin
1 bottle of white wine
Cooking oil
3¾ cups (900 ml) Chicken Stock
(page 240) or alternative
(page 243)
Salt and pepper

Preheat the oven to 350°F/180°C. Soften the *mirepoix* vegetables, thyme and bay leaf in 1 tbs (15 g) of butter in a deep ovenproof braising pan. Once softened, add the bag of garlic cloves and the white wine. Bring to the boil and reduce the wine by three-quarters. While the vegetables and wine are cooking, season the leg of lamb and brown all over in a hot frying pan with the cooking oil. Once browned, put the lamb in the braising pan. Add the chicken stock and top with water, so the lamb is half covered. Return to a simmer and cover with a lid. Cook the lamb in the oven for 4 hours. I like to turn the lamb over after 2 hours, so it cooks evenly.

After 4 hours, remove the lamb which will now be very tender. Leave to rest. Strain and reduce the liquid by half or more. Taste the stock for strength: a really good, strong stock will give a better finish to the sauce. About *1¼ cups* (300 ml) of well reduced stock should be plenty. Take the almost puréed garlics from the bag and press them to a smooth paste. Add this paste as a thickener to the sauce and then whisk in the remaining 4 tbs (50 g) butter. The sauce is now finished. Carve the lamb or break it into chunks. Spoon over the sauce and serve.

**Note:** Vegetables that go well with this dish are Mashed Potatoes (page 140), roasted carrots, Turnip Purée (page 152) or peas.

# 'Piece' of Beef Braised *with a Rich Glaze (and more!)*

*The 'piece' is a cut of beef taken from the chuck steak, which you can get from the butcher. Chuck is normally sold diced and used for stews and pies. The texture is reasonably soft and open. This means that, while braising or stewing, the meat is absorbing all of the sauce it is being cooked in. Consequently, you end up with very tender meat, which can be carved with a spoon. Closer and firmer cuts, such as topside or sirloin, stay firm and all the pores close during cooking, so although they become tender they are also quite dry to eat.*

*This dish is served with roasted onions filled with turnip purée. To lift the flavors of the purée, I've added some diced bone marrow, purely an optional extra, but a good one. You can of course leave the onions as they are and omit the turnip purée from the recipe.*

**Serves 6**

8 oz (6 x 225 g) chuck cuts,
    trimmed of all sinews and tied
A pat of butter
Salt and pepper

**For the Vegetable *Mirepoix*:**

1 onion, roughly chopped
1 carrot, roughly chopped
½ leek, roughly chopped
2 celery sticks, roughly chopped
A pat of butter

**For the Sauce:**

4 tomatoes, roughly chopped
1 bottle of red wine
3¾ cups (900 ml) Beef Stock, not
    too strong (page 242; good-quality
    bouillon cubes can be used) or
    water
6 onions, halved through middle,
    skins left on
A pat of butter
1¼ cups (300 ml) *Jus*/Gravy
    (page 242) or alternative
    (page 243)
1–2 oz (25–50 g) bone marrow
    (optional), soaked in water for
    24–48 hours
12 oz (350 g) Turnip Purée,
    (page 152)
Salt and pepper

Preheat the oven to 375°F/190°C. Cook the vegetable *mirepoix* in a braising dish with a pat of butter for 5–6 minutes until beginning to brown and soften. Add the tomatoes and continue to cook for a further 5–6 minutes. Add the red wine and bring to the boil. The wine can now be left to boil and reduce by three-quarters. This will give a powerful red wine flavor to the finished sauce. Add the beef stock or water and bring to the simmer.

Heat a frying pan. Season the mini chuck cuts with salt and pepper. Add a pat of butter to the pan and fry the cuts, sealing them on all sides. Lift the beef from the pan and place in the braising dish. Return to the simmer and cover with a lid. Place the pot in the oven and leave to braise, turning the meat every half hour or so for 2–2½ hours.

While the meat is braising, caramelize the onions. Place the onions, flesh-side down and skins left on, in a roasting tray with a pat of butter. Cover with foil and place in the oven, with the beef. After half an hour, remove the foil. This will have created steam and lightly softened the onions, releasing their natural juices. For the next 40–45 minutes, the juices will begin to caramelize while the onions are roasting. After the cooking time, pierce with a knife to check they are tender. If not, then cook for a further 20–30 minutes. Once tender, the onions should have caramelized to a golden brown with tinges of burned color.

After 2 hours, lift one of the meat from the pan and check for tenderness. The beef must really be overcooked to be at its best. When you are testing the meat, it should start to break away with just a little pressure. If not ready, return it to the oven for a further 30 minutes. The meat can sometimes take up to 3 hours.

Once cooked, remove the joints from the stock, cover and keep warm. Strain the stock and bring to the boil, reducing by at least half to two-thirds. Once reduced, add the finished *jus*/gravy. This will thicken the cooking liquid, giving you a good sauce consistency. Season with salt and pepper. At this stage I like to take ⅔ cup (150 ml) of the sauce and reduce it further to a very thick, shiny consistency – it also becomes very sticky! This I use to brush the meat before serving, giving it the most incredible shiny finish.

The bone marrow really is an optional extra. If using, it needs to have been soaked in cold water for 24–48 hours. This cleans the marrow, giving you an almost pure white finish. Divide the marrow into ¼ in (5 mm) pieces and quickly warm in a pat of butter. Heat the turnip purée and add the bone marrow. Remove the skins of the onions. I like to remove some of the center of the onions and spoon in some of the turnip purée. Spoon the purée into the onions. Place the 'pieces' of beef on top and drizzle the heavily reduced glaze over. The remaining sauce can be offered separately.

**Note:** The 'pieces' of beef can be served with the garnish of your choice, so the stuffed onions become an extra to the basic recipe. Good Mashed Potatoes (page 140) and spinach are delicious with it!

# Homemade Individual Pies

*This is an introduction to a combination of flavors that has unlimited variations and could become a complete book on its own. Making individual pies is a lovely bonus for the eater, who breaks through the crisp pastry to find a delicious filling. But they don't have to be individual at all; one large pie (approximately 10 in/25 cm in diameter) presented at the table is also very exciting. Cooking the fillings in pie dishes with just a pastry topping will also work, so feel free to adapt these recipes to suit you.*

*This first recipe is for the quantity of pastry needed to line and top four molds. After that you have some recipes and ideas for fillings, which are all cooked and finished separately before molding.*

---

**Makes 4 Pies**

1½ lb (750 g) Short crust pastry, or
 Rich Short Crust Pepper Pastry
 (page 224)

8 oz (225 g) Quick Puff Pastry
 (page 225), rolled and cut into
 4½ in (11 cm) circles
1 egg

The metal pastry rings I use for this recipe are 4 in (10 cm) in diameter and 3 in (7.5 cm) high. The rings should first be buttered. Sit them on a waxed-paper-lined baking tray. Roll out the shortcrust pastry and cut out four 4 in (10 cm) circles. Sit one in the base of each ring. Roll the remaining pastry and cut it into strips wide enough to line the sides of the rings. If you are making one large pie, cut out one 10 in (25 cm) disc of pastry and one wide strip for the sides. Once in place, press the pastry along the bottom edge, so that it makes a good seal with the base and then all the way around the sides, so it comes a little above the ring to provide an edge to join to the puff pastry lid. Line each mold with waxed paper or foil and fill with baking beans or rice. Leave to rest in the fridge for 20 minutes. Bake blind for 15–20 minutes at 400°/200°, cooking them to a light golden color. This will guarantee a crisp finish.

Make the filling of your choice (see pages 113–117) and allow it to cool completely.

To finish the pies, preheat the oven to 400°F/200°C. Pack the filling into the baked pastry case. Save any excess sauce from the filling to serve with the pies. Brush egg around the edge of the pastry and sit the puff pastry lids on top, pressing to seal the two. Brush the lids with egg for a glazed finish. Cook the pies for 40–45 minutes. This will cook the puff pastry while heating the pie filling. Sit the pies on a plate or in large bowls, remove the pastry rings and pour any excess sauce from the filling around. The pies are ready to serve.

**Note:** One large pie will take 1–1¼ hours to cook. A filled pie dish with just a pastry lid will also take approximately 1 hour.

# Hot Pork Pie

*This idea is based on traditional cold pork pies. Cold pork pies have quite a spicy finish, so I decided to take those flavors and turn them into a hot dish.*

---

**Serves 4**
4 pastry shells (see page 112)

**For the Stew:**
4½ cups (900 g) diced shoulder of pork
2 onions, roughly chopped
4½ cups (1.2 liters) Chicken Stock (page 240) or alternative (page 243)
Fresh thyme sprig
A few fresh sage leaves
¼ teaspoon mace
¼ teaspoon mixed spice
¼ teaspoon English mustard powder
A pat of butter
Salt and pepper

**For the Sauce:**
Pork cooking liquid (once pork has been stewed)
1¼ cup (300 ml) heavy cream
A squeeze of lemon juice
Salt and pepper

**For the Onion Mix:**
4 onions, sliced
A pat of butter
½ teaspoon chopped fresh thyme
½ teaspoon chopped fresh sage
¼ teaspoon mace
¼ teaspoon allspice
¼ teaspoon English mustard powder
Salt and pepper

Place all the stew ingredients in a saucepan and bring to the simmer. Stew gently for 50–60 minutes until the pork is tender. Lift the pork from the stock and keep it covered. Strain the stock and reduce it by half to two-thirds, giving you a good, strong flavored pork reduction. Add the heavy cream and bring to the simmer. Cook for 5–10 minutes until it coats the base of the spoon, before adding a squeeze of lemon juice and seasoning with salt and pepper. The sauce is ready.

For the onion mix, cook the onions in the butter, without letting them brown, for 5–6 minutes, with the herbs and spices. Once softened, season with salt and pepper and leave to cool.

Mix together the cooked pork, onions and a few spoonfuls of the sauce to moisten. Check for seasoning. Spoon the mixture into the cooked pastry shells and cover with the lids as instructed on page 112. These can now be baked and served with the remaining sauce poured around.

**Note:** When filling the pie molds, the pork and onions could be layered alternately, just spooning a little sauce between each layer. The spices used give you a flavor very similar to the traditional pork pie, but with a completely different, hot texture.

# Chicken and Leek Pie

*This recipe can be made with just chicken breasts or boned chicken legs. A combination of both can also be used.*

**Serves 4**

6 chicken breasts, skinned and cut into 1 in (2.5 cm) dice

2 medium leeks, cut into 1 in (2.5 cm) pieces

4 pastry shells (see page 112)

A pat of butter

2 onions, diced

1 garlic clove, crushed

2½ cups (600 ml) Chicken Stock (page 240) or alternative (page 243)

1¼ cups (300 ml) heavy cream

Salt and pepper

A squeeze of lemon juice

In a saucepan, melt the butter and fry the chicken for 2–3 minutes. Add the onions and continue to cook for another 3–4 minutes. Add the garlic, chicken stock and seasoning. Bring to the simmer and cook for 15–20 minutes until the chicken is tender. While the chicken is cooking, plunge the leeks into salted, boiling water and cook for 2–3 minutes until tender. Drain and leave to cool.

Lift the chicken and onions from the stock and strain the stock through a sieve. Reduce the stock by two-thirds and then add the cream. Bring to the simmer and reduce to a coating sauce consistency. Season and flavor with a squeeze of lemon juice.

Once all has cooked, mix the chicken with the leeks and moisten with half of the sauce. Divide between the pastry shells and finish and cook as instructed on page 112. The remaining chicken sauce can be warmed and poured around the pies before serving.

**Note:** Mushrooms can also be added to give the pie another flavor.

# Bacon and Spinach Pie *with Mustard and Fava Bean Sauce*

*This recipe has two options – the bacon confit used in the salad on page 38, just sliced and layered with the spinach (that's the best version); or buy some streaky or green (unsmoked) back bacon pieces and shallow-fry or boil them and then layer them. The sauce is the same for either version.*

**Serves 4**

4 pastry cases (see page 112)

**For the Pie Filling:**

2 lb (900 g) Confit of Bacon
(page 38)
2 lb (900 g) spinach, picked
and washed
2 onions, sliced
A pat of butter
Salt and pepper

**For the Sauce:**

2 shallots or ½ onion, finely chopped
1 garlic clove, sliced
2–3 strips of bacon, chopped
A pat of butter
1 cup (250 ml) white wine
2½ cups (600 ml) Chicken Stock
(page 240) or alternative (page
243)
⅔ cup (150 ml) heavy cream
English mustard, to taste (optional)
1¼ cups (175 g) fresh or frozen
fava beans
Salt and pepper

To make the sauce, cook the shallots or onion, garlic and bacon in butter for 5–6 minutes, until softened. Add the wine and reduce until almost dry. Add the chicken stock and reduce by two-thirds; this should take 8–10 minutes. Add the heavy cream and cook for 10–15 minutes. Season the sauce and strain it through a sieve. Add ½ teaspoon of English mustard and taste for quantity and strength. If you prefer more, simply add it to taste.

With the sauce I like to drop in cooked fresh fava beans a minute or two before serving. To cook the fava beans, drop into salted, boiling water and boil for 6–7 minutes until tender. Refresh in ice water before removing their outer skins and adding to the sauce. If using frozen fava beans, simply defrost, shell and add a minute or two before serving.

For the confit of bacon and spinach pie: cook the sliced onions in the butter for 3–4 minutes until soft and slightly golden. Add the washed spinach leaves. Season with salt and pepper and cook for 3–4 minutes, stirring to ensure even cooking. The spinach can now be left to cool.

Carve the confit into thin, 3–4 in (7–10 cm) slices. Lay 2–3 slices in the base of the pie dish and then top with some spinach and onion mix. Repeat the bacon slices and spinach until all the mixture is used between the molds. Spoon 2 tablespoons of the sauce into each pie and cover.

Bake as instructed on page 112. Heat the remaining sauce with the cooked broad beans and pour around each pie.

**Note:** The cooking time can be between 3 and 10 minutes for fava beans, depending on their size.

**Variation:** If you don't have the bacon confit, buy 2 lb (900 g) thickly sliced bacon and cut into ½ in (1 cm) dice. When cooking the shallots or onion for the sauce, add the bacon pieces. Continue to the point of adding the stock – you will need an extra 1¼ cups (300 ml) of stock to cover the bacon. Water can also be used. Bring to a simmer and cook for 30 minutes until the bacon is tender. Remove the bacon pieces and reduce the stock by two-thirds. Finish the method as for the main recipe opposite. The spinach and bacon can now be layered in the pastry shells with a spoonful or two of the sauce added to moisten. Cover and bake as instructed on page 112. Serve the finished sauce (with or without fava beans!) poured around the pies.

# Homemade Pie Extras

*You now have three solid recipes for pies which are all excellent. I do prefer to use cooked ingredients rather than cooking pies or puddings raw. This means you have time to get the consistency and the amount of sauce just right before baking. The other bonus is being able to make the filling and sauce a day or two in advance, refrigerating them and then using them for pies when needed. Here are a few extra ideas for more pies:*

- Any game, such as venison, pigeon or pheasant, can make good pies.

- For a vegetarian pie: stack and layer lightly cooked ratatouille and serve with a tomato salad or sauce.

- Don't forget the classic British steak and kidney pie.

*The choice is yours!*

# Steak and 'Kidney Pie'

*This most classic of British dishes can be found just about anywhere in the UK. But not like this! That's quite a statement because I've eaten many excellent steak and kidney pies. The reason is that this dish is a piece of steak (as in the recipe on page 110) served with a separate kidney and onion pie, so the two separate dishes are presented together to create one classic.*

*The cut of steak and the method of cooking the steak is exactly the same as for the 'piece of beef' recipe (though I am using slightly smaller cuts because they are pies). The kidney pies are very easy to make with the creamed, bittersweet onions coming from the recipe on page 132.*

(as in the recipe on page 110) · page 132

**Serves 6**

6 oz (6 x 175 g) chuck cuts
(individually trimmed and tied
pieces of chuck steak)
A pat of butter
Salt and pepper

**For the Pies:**

8 oz (225 g) Short Crust Pastry
(page 224)
8 lamb's kidneys or 8–10 oz
(225–275 g) veal kidneys cut into
½ in (1 cm) dice
A pat of butter or drizzle of
vegetable oil
½ quantity Bittersweet Onion Tart
mix (page 132)
1 egg yolk, beaten
8 oz (225 g) Quick Puff Pastry
(page 225), rolled and cut into
3½–4½ in (8–11 cm) circles
Salt and pepper

**For the Sauce:**

A pat of butter
Fresh thyme sprig
3 tomatoes, roughly chopped
1 bottle of red wine
3¾ cups (900 ml) Beef Stock
(not too strong) (page 242;
good-quality bouillon cubes can
be used) or water
3–4 lamb's kidneys, roughly diced
1¼ cups (300 ml) *Jus/Gravy*
(page 242) or alternative
(page 243)
Salt and pepper

**For the Vegetable *Mirepoix*:**

1 onion, roughly chopped
1 carrot, roughly chopped
2 celery sticks, roughly chopped
(optional)

To make the sauce, melt a pat of butter with the *mirepoix* of vegetables and the sprig of thyme. Cook for 3–4 minutes until softened and then add the chopped tomatoes. Continue to cook for another 3–4 minutes.

Add the red wine, bring to the boil and reduce by three-quarters. This should take 5–6 minutes. Now just add the beef stock and bring to the simmer.

POULTRY AND MEAT

While the sauce is being made, season the chuck with salt and pepper. Heat a frying pan with a pat of butter and brown the beef on all sides. Add them to the simmering stock. The beef will take approximately 2½ hours to become completely tender: it needs to be slightly 'overcooked'. After 2 hours, check the texture of the meat. When you press the meat, the meat should start to break away very easily; if not, continue to cook for a further 30 minutes (or more).

Once completely cooked, remove the joints and cover with plastic wrap.

To finish the sauce, sauté the roughly diced lamb's kidney in some butter for 3–4 minutes. Add to the beef cooking liquid. Reduce the liquid by half, skimming off any impurities. This will increase the strength and flavor of the sauce with the kidney giving an extra taste. Once reduced, add the *jus/*gravy. Bring to the simmer and then strain through a sieve. You should have a well flavored liquid with a sauce consistency. I now like to pour off ⅔ cup (150 ml) and reduce it by at least half again to a very thick, shiny consistency – it also becomes very sticky. This will be used to brush or roll the finished beef before serving. It leaves the meat just glistening.

Season the remaining sauce, if needed (if the sauce is too thin but strong in taste, it can be lightly thickened with cornstarch or arrowroot).

The pies can be made while the steaks are cooking. Butter six 2½–3 in (6–7.5 cm) tartlet pans. Preheat the oven to 400°F/200°C. Roll out the shortcrust pastry, cut into large discs and use to line the tartlet pans, leaving any excess pastry hanging over the edges of the pans. Line with waxed paper or foil, fill with baking beans and bake for 15–20 minutes. Once cool, remove the waxed paper or foil and beans. Slice away any excess pastry to leave a neat finish.

The ½ in (1 cm) diced kidneys can now be pan-fried very quickly in a hot pan with butter or cooking oil. This takes about 3–4 minutes and is just to seal the kidneys. Season with salt and pepper and leave to cool. Once cool, mix some of the bittersweet onion mix with the lamb's or veal kidneys to bind. Spoon some more onion mix into the base of the tartlet mounds and then top with the sautéed kidney mixture.

Now top with more onion mix to leave a good dome shape. Brush around the edge of the pastry with egg yolk and top with the puff pastry, pressing and sealing all around. Leave the pies to rest in the refrigerator for at least 20 minutes. Once set, trim off any excess pastry around the sides. Brush the tops with egg yolk.

To finish the dish, bake the pies for 15–20 minutes until golden. Put the steaks back into the finished sauce to warm through. Remove them and roll or brush with the reduced sticky sauce.

To serve, sit the steaks and pies side by side in bowls or on plates and pour some sauce around.

**Note:** This dish can be made well in advance – the steaks will then take up to 20–30 minutes to reheat in the sauce. The pies will keep, refrigerated, for 24 hours before being baked.

# Boiled Brisket of Beef *and Vegetable Stew*

*Brisket is a cut of beef taken from the forequarter. It is normally pickled in brine, which is a combination of salt, saltpeter and water. The beef can be kept in brine for up to 10 days. This will help tenderize the cut. If buying brisket already salted, I suggest it is soaked in fresh water for 24–48 hours to release some of the salt flavor. This goes very well with mashed potatoes.*

**Serves 4**

2 lb (900 g) brisket, soaked
  in fresh water
1 carrot
1 onion
1 bay leaf
2 celery sticks
1 leek
Fresh thyme sprig

**For the Vegetable Garnish:**

2 onions, cut into ½ in (1 cm) dice
3–4 celery sticks, cut into
  ½ in (1 cm) dice
1 small rutabega cut into
  ½ in (1 cm) dice
2 large carrots, cut into
  ½ in (1 cm) dice
2 leeks, cut into ½ in (1 cm) dice
A pat of butter
2–3 tablespoons heavy cream
Salt and pepper
Chopped fresh parsley and thyme

Cover the brisket with fresh cold water in a large saucepan and bring to the boil. Once boiling, pour the water off and refresh the beef in cold water. Once refreshed, top off with more cold water, adding the whole vegetables and thyme. Cover and bring to a simmer, skimming away any impurities. The beef will take 2½–3 hours to become totally tender.

While the beef is cooking, prepare the garnish vegetables and cook them separately. Cook the onions and celery in a pat of butter without browning. Blanch the rutabega, carrots and leeks in water or some of the brisket cooking liquid until tender.

When the beef is cooked, drain off two-thirds of the cooking liquid and reduce to 1¼ cups (300 ml). Add the cream and all of the garnishing vegetables. Warm through and season with salt and pepper. Add a pat of butter and stir in. Add the chopped herbs.

Carve the brisket and place the slices in bowls or on plates. I prefer to serve this dish in large bowls and treat the sauce as a beef and vegetable soup. If the 'soup' is too thick, loosen it with more of the stock. Spoon the vegetables and sauce over and serve.

This dish works very well with a bowl of Mashed Potatoes (page 140).

**Note:** You could use whole, fairly small vegetables for the garnish (you will need to cut rutabega in chunks and celery sticks in half). Simply boil the beef in water and add the vegetables towards the end of cooking, serving them as the garnish.

# Tournedos of Lamb *with Snails, Onions and Bacon*

*Tournedos is a description usually used for beef fillet steak. Lamb doesn't carry fillets of that size but with this recipe and method the fillet is created from a leg of lamb. The technique breaks down the meat's textures, making it very tender. In addition, lamb prepared in this way will give you at least eight portions and, if it's a large leg, up to twelve. Snails are not to everyone's liking, but the snails I am using are French and canned, not fresh. This makes the job a lot easier and the quality and tenderness is superb. They have a mushroom-like texture and are not chewy at all. They are well worth trying, if not in this recipe then perhaps as the traditional snails with garlic and parsley. The tournedos really are worth having a go at and I know you'll agree when you see the results. If you tell your friends they are going to be eating leg of lamb and these turn up, it will be a more than nice surprise.*

### Serves 8–12

1 leg of lamb, boned and all fat
    removed, weighing approximately
    3½-4 lb (1.5-1.75 kg)
8 oz (225 g) pig's caul (crépine) or
    15–18 strips of smoked bacon
    (optional)
Salt and pepper
A pinch of ground cumin

### For the Garnish
### (for 8 portions):

1 bottle of red wine

2¼ cups (600 ml) Veal or Beef
    Jus/Gravy (page 242) or
    alternative (page 243)
30–35 canned snails (optional)
1 lb (450 g) small pearl onions,
    peeled
8–10 oz (225–275 g) bacon, the
    strips cut into ½ in (1 cm) dice
2–3 oz (50–75 g) spinach, cooked,
    per portion (optional)
A pat of butter
Salt and pepper

Separate the boned leg of lamb into individual muscles by breaking apart the membranes which hold them together. The next job is to remove all the sinew, which doesn't take long but is quicker done by your butcher! This will break down the meat even more, leaving you with absolutely sinew free, lean pieces of meat. It is important that all sinews are totally removed. This will guarantee the tenderness of the meat.

    Once all is cleaned, you will have a few meat scraps. These need to be ground or processed (make sure you have about 4 oz/100 g). Season with salt and pepper and a pinch of ground cumin. This 'farce' will be used to help hold the other cuts together when you start to assemble the tournedos. All of the remaining meat can now be cut into strips, approximately 4 in (10 cm) long and ½ in (1 cm) wide (lamb fingers). Next rinse the pig's caul (crépine), if using, in cold water, to loosen and clean it. Caul is not easy to get hold of so, if you can't find it, simply just use tin foil or lay thin strips of bacon, vertically, side by side, in a line on the foil first.

The lamb finger fillets can now be laid on the caul, foil or bacon and foil. Lay them lengthwise (in the opposite direction to the bacon), side by side, which will give you a line of meat approximately 3–4 in (7.5–10 cm) wide and 12 in (30 cm) long. Spread the minced lamb thinly over it until all is used and then roll or hand-shape into a cylinder. Wrap tightly in the caul, buttered foil or bacon and foil and then re-wrap in more foil, twisting at either end to firm the wrap. Leave to set in the refrigerator for 1–2 hours.

Preheat the oven to 400°F/200°C. Cut across the cylinder, still in the foil, into tournedos (fillet-steak shapes) 1½–2 in (3–5 cm) deep. This should give you at least eight portions. The portions are not huge but, remember, they do have quite a considerable quantity of garnish to give the flavors a lift. If caul or bacon have been used to wrap the meat, remove the outer foil. These portions must now be tied with two pieces of string. This will guarantee they keep their shape. If only foil has been used, tie string around the outside of the foil. The tournedos are now ready to be cooked.

The next step is to make the garnish. I have kept the sauce simple. All you need to do is to rapidly boil the wine until reduced by three-quarters and then add the *jus*/gravy. Cook for 5–10 minutes and it is made. It will take on the flavor of the garnishes that will be warmed through in it to increase the flavor.

The garnishes can be prepared and cooked well in advance. The snails just need to be halved. Panfry the pearl onions in some of the butter over medium heat. This will brown them slowly while they are becoming tender. Once golden and almost dark (this is the natural caramelizing of their juices and sugars), remove from the pan. Fry the bacon in its own fat and on a medium heat to give the bacon plenty of time to crisp.

Add some melted butter to the spinach and season. Pan-fry or microwave when needed.

To cook the lamb, season with salt and pepper and pan-fry carefully in butter on all sides. Transfer to a roasting tin if you've not used an ovenproof frying pan and finish in the oven for 8–10 minutes. The lamb will still be pink in the center (medium). Remove from the oven and leave to relax and tenderize for 4-5 minutes. While the lamb is relaxing, add the garnishes (snails, button onions and bacon) to the sauce and simmer to warm them through and infuse the sauce with their flavor.

To serve, spoon some spinach in the center of the plates and pour sauce and garnish around. Remove any string and foil from the lamb and place the tournedos on top of the spinach.

**Note:** You can add a few black peppercorns, a bay leaf and some chopped shallots or onions to the red wine reduction to strengthen the flavor. Or, instead of a wine reduction, a good lamb stock can be made by roasting the chopped leg of lamb bones with some carrots, onions, leeks and celery, garlic, thyme and peppercorns, cooking them in about 1–2 pints (600 ml–1.2 liters) chicken stock for a couple of hours and then reducing it by three-quarters. This will give you a good, strong, lamb flavor, which, when added to the *jus*/gravy, will need no wine at all. Just simmer and strain and an excellent lamb sauce is made.

You do not have to stick with this garnish and sauce. A good redcurrant gravy, with sautéed potatoes and Spring greens, is another option.

# vegetarian and vegetables

*V*arious flavors and tastes have been added to some of the vegetables featured in this section to give them a whole new dimension. This always helps make a feature of them and will also help to lift the flavor of a simple roast or other basic main course.

The Lemon Buttered Broccoli (page 149), Spicy Fried Cauliflower (page 155) and French Bean Purée (page 156) are good with many a dish.

As for vegetarian main courses, how does Pasta with 'Pork Stuffing' Sauce (page 136) sound? Not exactly vegetarian, but it is. The sauce simply uses some of the stuffing ingredients; it tastes delicious and is obviously also a great accompaniment to virtually any pork recipe.

The Green Tomato *Tarte Tatin* (page 130) will give you a whole new feeling and taste for green tomatoes, which are normally just made into a chutney. The Potato and Onion Torte (page 126) is absolutely packed with flavor and the Hot-Pot (page 141) is a dream. It's been put together by taking all of the classic ingredients from Lancashire hot-pot (featured in *Rhodes Around Britain*), except the lamb, and building them into a potato and vegetable hot-pot cake. Cutting into and through all of these vegetable layers gives you a lot of texture and taste in one bite.

The vegetables can be found in their own seasons throughout the year, so when the kale has finished, move on to broccoli, and then leeks, and so on. Swap ideas and techniques from different recipes and apply them to a variety of vegetables, or just keep to a recipe and technique that suits every vegetable: simple and tasty.

# Roast Mushroom and Leek Shepherd's Pie

*This is an easy vegetarian recipe which becomes almost 'meaty,' using portabello mushrooms. The dish is layered like a lasagna with the mashed potato piped or spread across the top.*

---

**Serves 4–6**

2 lb (900 g) portabello, wiped and
    stalks removed
4–5 leeks, finely shredded
Olive or cooking oil
A tablespoon of butter
1 onion, sliced
1½–2 lb (750–900 g) Mashed
    Potatoes (page 140)
Juice of ½–1 lemon

Salt and pepper
1 teaspoon chopped fresh parsley
    (optional)
1 teaspoon chopped fresh tarragon
    (optional)
1 teaspoon chopped fresh basil
    (optional)

Preheat the oven to 450°F/230°C.

Heat a frying pan with a tablespoon or two of olive or cooking oil. Season the mushrooms with salt and pepper and place in the pan. Fry the mushrooms on a high heat, browning them well. After a minute, turn them in the pan and repeat the browning (another tablespoon of oil may be needed). Now roast the mushrooms in the hot oven for 5–6 minutes. Once cooked, remove and keep to one side. Because of the fast, hot frying and roasting, the mushrooms will have kept all of their juices, giving a richer flavor.

To cook the leeks, heat a tablespoon of olive oil with the butter and add the sliced onion. Cook on a moderate heat for a few minutes until softened with very little color. Increase the heat, add the shredded leeks and season with salt and pepper. Stir for 3–4 minutes and the leeks should now be tender.

Using a buttered ovenproof casserole or pie pan, cut the mushrooms into slices and place them in the pan. Spoon some leeks on top and then repeat with the mushrooms; continue to layer the ingredients until all are used up.

The mashed potatoes can now be finished with the lemon juice and chopped herbs, if using. Spread them on top. Brush with butter and finish under the broiler until golden brown.

**Note:** If using all-purpose mashed potato to top the 'pie', why not finish it with grated cheddar or with little pieces of Gorgonzola Rarebit (page 233) sprinkled on top and broiled.

# Potato and Onion Torte *with Mushroom Sauce*

*Here's another pastry-based dish that can be made into individual tortes or one large one.*

*If making individuals, I line the 34 in (7.5–9 cm) pans with Shortcrust Pastry (page 224) (or the Rich Shortcrust Pepper Pastry on page 224) and blind-bake them before filling and topping with Quick Puff Pastry (page 225). This gives you a combination of two pastries with completely different textures working together. If I'm making one large torte, I go for a complete puff pastry finish, although the short crust base will also work, giving you a delicious texture combination.*

*With this dish, I serve a mushroom and thyme sauce, not essential but delicious. Its basis is a very tasty mushroom stock, which will give the sauce a powerful mushroom flavor.*

---

**Serves 4**

8 oz (225 g) puff pastry, rolled into 7
  in and 9 disks and baked, plus 6 oz
  (175 g) puff pastry, rolled into
  4 x 5 in (12 cm) disks
1 egg yolk
A sprinkling of coarse sea salt
  (optional)

**For the Filling:**

4–5 large potatoes, boiled
  in their skins
3 large onions, sliced
A tablespoon of butter
1 teaspoon light brown sugar
Salt and pepper

**For the Mushroom Stock:**

8 oz (225 g) button mushrooms,
  chopped

1 garlic clove, crushed
Fresh thyme sprig
1 tablespoon olive oil
1¼ cups (300 ml) water

**For the Sauce:**

1 cup (150 ml) of reduced
  Mushroom Stock (see above)
3 tablespoons heavy cream
8 oz (225 g) button mushrooms
  (chestnut), quartered
2–3 oz (50–75 g) unsalted butter
Salt and pepper
½ teaspoon fresh thyme leaves

Preheat the oven to 400°F/200°C. If making 4 individual tortes, place the baked tartlet cases onto a baking sheet. If making the large torte, place the 7 in (18 cm) puff-pastry disk on a waxed-paper-lined baking pan.

Peel and slice the cooked potatoes while still warm and season with salt and pepper.

Melt a little butter and spoon over. This will be absorbed by the warm potatoes.

Shallow-fry the sliced onions in a tablespoon of butter, allowing them to soften and take on a rich golden color. Add the teaspoon of sugar and continue to fry. This will give a mild, sweet, caramelized flavor. Season and leave to cool.

Once the potatoes and onions have cooled, place a layer of the potatoes onto the pastry disk, leaving a ½ in (1 cm) border. Spread on some caramelized onions and then another layer of potato. Repeat this process, forming a dome shape with the larger torte until all the ingredients or almost all are used up.

Brush around the border of the torte(s) with egg yolk and cover with puff pastry disks. The egg yolk will help seal the pastries together. On individual tarts, just trim any excess pastry away. On the large tart, the border can be pinched and shaped. Refrigerate for at least 20 minutes before baking.

Meanwhile, make the stock. Fry the mushrooms, garlic, and thyme in the olive oil for a few minutes. Add the water and bring to a simmer. Cook for 15–20 minutes and then strain through a sieve, squeezing all of the juices from the mushrooms. Reduce to 1/2 cup (150 ml), doubling the flavor of the stock.

Brush the tortes with more egg yolk to obtain an even richer golden color, and if you like a slightly crunchy finish, sprinkle lightly with a little coarse sea salt. Individual tortes will take 15–20 minutes to cook and a large one will need 25–30 minutes.

To finish the sauce and give it a creamier taste, add the heavy cream to the stock and bring to a simmer.

Pan fry the mushrooms with al tablespoon of the butter until tender and season with salt and pepper. Add the remaining butter to the sauce, gently shaking the pan so the butter and sauce emulsify. Add the fried mushrooms and thyme, season with salt and pepper, and the sauce is ready.

Serve the smaller tortes whole; cut the large one into four portions, passing the mushroom sauce separately.

**Note:** Lots more fillings can be used as variations: ratatouille, spinach, and mushrooms are just a few ideas.

# Stilton and Spinach Tart

*Stilton is not the only cheese I use in this recipe. To help the flavors along, I add a little grated Parmesan.*

*The difference between a tart and this pie is the pastry. The pie variation in this recipe doesn't use any pastry at all: all I have done is layer the ingredients into a lasagna or vegetable dish. It works very well and you don't have to make any pastry!*

---

**Serves 4 as a pie or
6 as a tart**

6–8 oz (175–225 g) Quick Puff Pastry (page 225), or frozen puff pastry, thawed

2 lb (900 g) picked and washed spinach

8 oz (225 g) crumbled stilton

A tablespoon of butter

½ cup (150 ml) heavy cream

1 egg

2 tablespoons finely grated Parmesan

Salt and pepper

**For the Cream Dressing:**

4 tablespoons light cream

A squeeze of lemon juice

2 tablespoons walnut oil

Salt and pepper

1 heaped teaspoon chopped fresh chives

Preheat the oven to 400°F/200°C. If making tart(s), butter a 9 in (23 cm) removable bottomed flan ring or four 4 in (10 cm) tartlet pans. Roll out the pastry and line the pan(s), leaving some excess pastry attached. This will prevent the pastry from sinking into the pans(s). Line with waxed paper or foil and weight it with some dried beans or rice. Bake blind for 15-20 minutes. Remove the paper and beans or rice, and after it cools, trim off any excess pastry to leave a neat finish.

If making a pie, immediately melt the butter in a large saucepan with 2–3 tablespoons of water. Add the washed spinach and cook on a high heat, stirring for 2–3 minutes. The spinach will become soft and tender. Pour it into a sieve or colander and let it cool. Squeeze out the excess liquid. Season with salt and pepper.

Mix the heavy cream with the egg and one tablespoon of the Parmesan. The spinach and stilton can now be alternately layered, spooning some of the cream mix between each layer into either the large flan, the individual tartlets, or an ovenproof vegetable or lasagna dish. Sprinkle the remaining Parmesan on top and transfer to the oven. The individual tartlets will take just 15–20 minutes with the larger tart needing 20–25 minutes.

If it is a tart, whether individual or large, it will go very well with a green salad with the light cream dressing made as follows: warm the light cream. Add the lemon juice and whisk in the walnut oil. Season with salt and pepper. Add the chopped chives and spoon around the tarts. The dish is ready to serve.

**Note:** The Parmesan can be left out of the cream mixture, if desired.

# Green Tomato *Tarte Tatin*

*Tarte tatin is a French classic made with apples. The apples are caramelized in butter and sugar and topped with pastry while still in the frying pan. This is baked and then turned over onto a plate to serve. It looks stunning and the flavor is immense. Yes, you've guessed it, that's more or less what I'm going to do, but on a savory note with green tomatoes. You will need an ovenproof 8 in (20 cm) frying pan. Serve with a simple, tossed salad.*

| Serves 2 (or 1 if you're very hungry) | For the Dressing or Garnish (optional) |
|---|---|
| 6 green tomatoes | 4 tablespoons olive oil |
| Olive oil | 1 tablespoon balsamic vinegar |
| A tablespoon of butter | Salt and pepper |
| 1 teaspoon of light brown sugar | 4 teaspoons sour cream |
| 4–6 oz (100–175 g) Quick Puff Pastry (page 225) or frozen puff pastry, thawed | A squeeze of lemon or lime juice |
| Salt and pepper | A few fresh basil leaves, torn |
| | ½ small red onion, finely sliced |
| | A few fresh Parmesan shavings |
| | A little coarse sea salt and coarsely ground black pepper (optional) |

Preheat the oven to 450°F/230°C. Heat the ovenproof frying pan with a trickle of olive oil. Halve the tomatoes through the middle. Season the tomatoes with salt and pepper and place them flesh side down, in a circular pattern, totally filling the pan. Increase the heat so the tomatoes are frying and not stewing. After 1 minute, add the tablespoon of butter and sprinkle with the sugar. Continue to fry for another minute or two, shaking the pan occasionally so that they are evenly coated with butter. The tomatoes will have started to caramelize. Remove the pan from the stove and leave to cool.

Roll out the pastry into a 8 in (20 cm) circle. Put the pastry on top of the tomatoes, pressing lightly to help it take on the shape of the tomato border. Bake the tart for 15–20 minutes until the pastry is crisp and golden. Turn the tart out onto a plate (remember, the handle will be hot!). You will have rich, golden caramelized tomatoes looking right at you. For an even richer, caramelized look, brush with more butter and sprinkle with a touch more sugar. Pop under the broiler until it begins to bubble. Cut into two portions.

For the dressing, mix the oil with the vinegar and season. Season the soured cream separately and add the lemon or lime juice. Spoon threads of the sour cream across the plates and repeat with the balsamic dressing.

Sit the tart portions on top or by the side of the dressings and sprinkle with the torn basil leaves, red onion slices and Parmesan shavings. The tart can be finished with a small sprinkling of coarse sea salt and black pepper.

# Bittersweet Onion Tart *with Leek, Tomato and Lemon Dressing*

*The bittersweet onion tart stands completely on its own as an idea and dish. The pastry is of a short crust variety, enriched with the flavor of black pepper to just give it a tasty bite.*

*The leek, tomato and lemon dressing is a combination of flavors that go very well with the tart. I also like to add mushrooms to the dressing for even more texture.*

*The tart can be served with a simple tossed salad or, as I suggest in the Note, it goes beautifully with Pan Fried or Broiled Liver (page 98).*

---

**Serves 6**

1 recipe Rich Short crust Pepper
   Pastry (page 225)
6 onions, sliced
A tablespoon of butter
1 teaspoon light brown sugar
Salt and pepper
1 ¼ cups (300 ml) heavy cream
2 eggs
A few salad greens, to garnish

**For the Dressing:**

3–4 baby leeks, washed and sliced
3 tomatoes, blanched, skinned and
   seeded, cut into 6–8 wedges
12 button mushrooms, cleaned and
   trimmed (optional)
4 tablespoons olive oil
Salt and pepper
Juice of 1 lemon

Preheat the oven to 450°F/200°C. Butter six 4 in (10 cm) tartlet pans or a 10 in (25 cm), loose-bottomed flan ring. Roll out the pastry and use it to line the pan(s), leaving some excess pastry attached. This will prevent the pastry from sinking into the pan(s). Line with waxed paper or foil and dried beans or rice. Bake blind for 20–25 minutes. Remove the paper and beans and when it has cooled, trim off any excess pastry, leaving a neat finish.

Fry the onions in the butter over a high heat. This may have to be done in two or three stages, taking into account the quantity of onions being used. Fry until well softened and on the point of being burned or caramelized, which will take 5–6 minutes. The burned tinges (and we do want some of the onions burnt) will give us the bitter side to this dish. Once softened and colored in the pan, add a sprinkling of light brown sugar to caramelize the onions and add the note of sweetness against the bitter, 'burned' flavor.

Once all the onions have been cooked, mix together and season with salt and pepper. Reduce the heat to low. Whisk the cream and eggs together and pour onto the onions while still on the stove. Stir for a few minutes until thickened but not scrambled. Remove from the stove and check for seasoning. Taste the mix (it will now be coffee-colored) for the depth and balance of the bitterness and sweetness. If you feel it is too bitter, add a small sprinkling of sugar to the mixture.

The mixture can now be cooled and refrigerated (it will keep for a few days). If you want to cook it immediately, while still warm, fill the pastry case(s) and bake in the oven until set. For the individual pies this will take only 8–10 minutes; for a larger flan allow 15–20 minutes. If the mixture has been left to cool and then refrigerated, the individuals will take 15 minutes and the larger one 25–30.

Once the tarts have set, they are ready to serve.

The dressing is quite simple and quick and holds flavors that go very well with the bittersweet onion taste. If using mushrooms, quarter them and pan fry in 2 tablespoons of olive oil for a few minutes until tender and golden. Remove them from the pan and add a tablespoon more olive oil. Fry the leeks until tender; add the cooked mushrooms and tomatoes. Season with salt and pepper, adding the last tablespoon of olive oil and finishing with the lemon juice.

This chunky dressing can now be spooned over and around the tarts. A few lettuce leaves or watercress can be used to finish the dish, placing them on top of the tartlets.

**Note:** The pastry case(s) can be removed from the pan(s) before cooking with the filling; however, the rings are a good security and can simply be removed once finished.

Fresh herbs such as basil, tarragon, parsley, chervil and so on also go very well in the dressing. A little finely chopped fresh red chili will add extra fire to the flavor!

More or less all the flavors used in the dressing, the mushrooms, tomatoes and leeks, can be added to the bittersweet onion mixture to give the tarts even more texture.

The tart also goes well with the Panfried or Broiled Liver (page 98). You can serve it with the sherry vinegar based sauce from the Panfried Liver recipe and for the ultimate combination, pan fry a slice of *foie gras* and place it on top of the tart!

# Potato Gnocchi and Gnocchi Tartare

*The word gnocchi means 'small dumpling.' There are several varieties of gnocchi: gnocchi parisienne, which is choux-paste-based; gnocchi romaine, which is semolina-based; gnocchi piedmontaise, which is potato-based.*

*This recipe is for piedmontaise gnocchi. Gnocchi are very easy to make and lend themselves to any course and any meal, whether accompanying a main course or as a complete vegetarian dish on its own. The potato variety goes very well with a good tomato sauce and lots of Parmesan; or simply roll the gnocchi in pesto sauce or good olive oil with chopped herbs, tomatoes and fresh olives. This is a basic recipe for potato based gnocchi. I also give the ingredients for turning them into Gnocchi Tartare, using flavors from the classic mayonnaise-based tartare sauce: shallots, capers, and tarragon.*

---

### Serves 6

2½ lb (1.2 kg) large potatoes
4–6 oz (100–175 g ) all-purpose
   flour
1 tablespoon (25 g) butter or 2
   teaspoons olive oil
1 egg
1 egg yolk
Salt and pepper
Grated nutmeg

### For Gnocchi Tartare:

2 heaped tablespoons finely
   chopped shallots or onions
2 tablespoons olive oil
2 tablespoons chopped capers
1 tablespoon chopped fresh
   tarragon
1 tablespoon chopped fresh parsley
A tablespoon of butter
Grated Parmesan

Cook the potatoes whole in salted, boiling water until tender. Peel the warm cooked potatoes and mash to a smooth texture (the potato can simply be pushed through a sieve). Add and mix in the flour, butter or olive oil, egg and egg yolk. Season with salt and pepper and a touch of nutmeg. Roll the mix on a floured surface into ½–¾ in (1–2 cm) balls.

The gnocchi are now ready to poach in simmering salted water for 3–4 minutes; 5 minutes is the maximum they will need. If using immediately, lift from the water and serve with a sauce of your choice and grated Parmesan. If cooking ahead, either refresh in cold water or leave to stand and cool on a cloth. They can be reheated, perhaps by pan frying, when needed.

To make gnocchi tartare, first cook the shallots or onions without letting them brown in the olive oil until softened. Allow to cool.

When adding the flour and eggs to the mashed potatoes to make the gnocchi, also add the tartare sauce ingredients. Prepare and cook as for the standard gnocchi. They are best then pan fried to golden brown in butter to give a slightly crisp edge, and then rolled or sprinkled with Parmesan.

# Pasta with 'Pork Stuffing' Sauce

*I was going to call this a British pasta dish, but I'm not quite sure that pasta can really be called British! This is a vegetarian 'pork stuffing.' I've taken the traditional onion and sage combination and a couple of additions and turned them into a sauce topped with crisp, crunchy white breadcrumbs.*

**Serves 4**

1 lb (450 g) fresh or dried noodles

A tablespoon of butter

2 onions, finely chopped

1 garlic clove, crushed

½ cup (150 ml) apple juice or white wine

½ cup (150 ml) Vegetable Stock (page 240; good-quality stock cubes can be used)

½ cup (150 ml) heavy cream

A squeeze of lemon juice

12 fresh sage leaves, chopped

2 oz (50 g) pinenuts, toasted and chopped

2–3 oz (50–75 g) fresh white breadcrumbs, toasted to golden brown

Olive oil

Salt and pepper

Grated Parmesan (optional)

Melt the butter with the onions and garlic. Cook for 6–7 minutes until softened. Add the apple juice or white wine and reduce by three-quarters. Add the vegetable stock and reduce by half. Now it is time to add the heavy cream and simmer for a few minutes. Season with salt and pepper and add a squeeze of lemon juice to lift all the flavors. Keep warm while you cook the pasta.

Now it's time to cook the pasta. Fresh noodles take approximately 3–5 minutes, dried ones 10–12 minutes.

Mix the noodles with the sauce, adding the chopped sage, and check for seasoning. Spoon the noodles into bowls and sprinkle with the toasted pinenuts and breadcrumbs. Drizzle with some olive oil and serve. The grated Parmesan can also be sprinkled on top or offered separately.

**Note:** If you prefer non-vegetarian pasta dishes, add strips of ham or bacon to the sauce.

# Barbecued Vegetables

*Most summer barbecues are filled with steaks, burgers, chicken wings, and hot dogs, all of which we enjoy, but how about a nice change? The variations of colors, textures, and flavors with vegetables are almost unlimited! So here are some which I've chosen that will make a delicious change for everybody, including vegetarians who come to your barbecue.*

---

**Serves 4**

8 asparagus spears
6 baby leeks
4 baby fennel, or 1 large, quartered
2 small red onions, sliced in
    ½ in (1 cm) rings
½ red pepper, seeded and cut in
    thick strips
½ yellow pepper, seeded and cut in
    thick strips

2 plum tomatoes, halved lengthwise
1 zucchini, sliced diagonally
8 tablespoons olive oil
1 lemon
Mustard Dressing
    (page 244, optional)
Salt and pepper
A few fresh basil and tarragon leaves

The asparagus, leeks and large fennel will all need to be blanched in salted, boiling water and refreshed before grilling.

The asparagus should be lightly peeled before blanching for 1–2 minutes. Trim the leeks, removing the tougher green ends, and blanch them for 2 minutes. Small fennel bulbs can be grilled raw, but the large should first be quartered and then blanched for 2–3 minutes. To grill the vegetables, make sure the barbecue is very hot. Toss the vegetables in 2 tablespoons of oil.

Next, place the vegetables on the barbecue and then cook and turn them until they become slightly soft to touch and golden brown tinges. This will only take a few minutes for each vegetable. If you do not have room to cook all the vegetables at the same time, it's best to cook the fennel, onions, peppers and tomatoes first, keeping them warm while the rest are cooking.

Once all the vegetables have been barbecued, season with salt and pepper and arrange on plates. Mix together the remaining olive oil and lemon juice and season with salt and pepper. This dressing can now be drizzled over the vegetables. I also like to repeat the same process with the mustard dressing. Simply sprinkle over the basil and tarragon leaves before serving. You now have a colorful selection of textures and flavors to enjoy.

**Note:** The vegetables go very well with a lemon mayonnaise dip or a classic tartare sauce. Good quality crusty bread or barbecued garlic bread also go very well with this dish. Olive bread brushed with olive oil and cooked on the open broil is also sensational to eat with this dish.

# Roast Potatoes

*This is one of Britain's favorite potato dishes, along with good creamy mashed potatoes. Roast potatoes are a weekly institution in every family. It is our standard procedure: Sunday lunch means roast potatoes! And quite right too. Good roasts are just irresistible, hot or cold.*

*The first question normally asked is which potato to use? Almost any potato will taste good roasted, but for the perfect, crispy finish, I use red, new, or Yukon Gold – all are easily available.*

*If you want a good, crisp, roast finish, potatoes will take longer than you think in the oven – up to 1½ hours. If you are serving them with your roast of the day, pour off some of the fat from the roast and cook the potatoes in that to get tastier and crispier potatoes.*

---

**Serves 4–6**                                  Olive oil, cooking oil or lard
2 lb (900 g) potatoes, left in skins            Salt

Preheat the oven to 400°F/200°C. The potatoes can be first boiled for about 10 minutes in their skins before being drained, peeled, and shaken in the dry pan to help them to become crisp. Heat enough cooking oil or fat to cover the bottom of a good roasting pan. Add the potatoes and turn them in the fat until coated all over. Season, place in the oven, and roast for 30 minutes before turning and continuing to roast for a further 30 minutes. The potatoes should now be crisp and golden.

To give burnt tinges, turn the oven up to 475°F/240°C. Leave the potatoes in the oven on their own for another 10–15 minutes.

The potatoes can also be peeled before parboiling. Boil for 8–10 minutes, drain well, and then roll lightly in seasoned all-purpose flour to give them a brown edge after roasting. Add a little extra oil for the roasting time. If not parboiled, the potatoes will need up to 1½ hours in the oven.

## 'Banana' Roasts

---

To make these, you need large potatoes. Peel them and cut lengthwise with a sharp knife. Shape them, cutting away the edges from top to tail, leaving sharp points. Create a curved edge in the 'center' with the sharp knife or peeler to give a banana shape. Four 'bananas' make one portion.

To roast the 'bananas,' parboil for 3–4 minutes then drain and allow them to cool for 10 minutes. Heat olive or cooking oil in a roasting pan or frying pan and cook the potatoes to a golden brown. Before placing in the oven, add a tablespoon or two of butter. The potatoes will take 20–30 minutes to become rich in color and texture with the points almost burned. Season with coarse salt and serve.

**Note:** Any roast potatoes will taste better if you add a tablespoon of butter during cooking.

# Mashed Potatoes

*Yukon Gold is a variety of potato that works particularly well for mashing. You will find that these potatoes have a good, crumbly texture that 'creams' well without becoming too starchy.*

*The mashed potato sauce is made with light cream and milk, just enough to give the potatoes a spreading consistency.*

**Serves 4–6**

2 lb (900 g) potatoes, peeled and
    quartered
8 tablespoons (100 g) unsalted
    butter

½ cup (120 ml) heavy cream or milk
Salt and freshly ground white
    pepper
Grated nutmeg

Boil the potatoes in salted water until tender, about 20–25 minutes, depending on size. Drain all the water and replace the lid. Shake the pan vigorously, which will start to break up the potatoes. Add the butter and cream or milk, a little at a time, while mashing the potatoes. Season with salt, pepper and nutmeg. The potatoes will be light, fluffy and creamy.

# Mashed Potato Sauce

*For this potato dish, you will only need 1 lb (450 g) of cooked, mashed potato with nothing added. The 'sauce' literally just melts in the mouth and will go with so many dishes. I recommend serving it with Slow-honey-roast Duck (see page 82).*

**Serves 4–6**

1 lb (450 g) Mashed Potatoes
    (above)
1 ¼ cups (150 ml) light cream

4 tablespoons (50 g) butter
Salt, pepper, and grated nutmeg
Milk or extra light cream, if needed

Warm the cream.

Season the potato with salt, pepper, and nutmeg. Work the butter into the potato to give it a richer consistency.

Pour the warmed light cream a little at a time and work until you have a good, soft, dropping and spreading consistency. Check the seasoning and the 'sauce' is ready. If the 'sauce' is made in advance, when reheating it, you may find it will have thickened and will need more warm milk or cream to loosen it.

# Potato and Vegetable Hot-pot Cake

*This dish can be served as a complete vegetarian main course or as a vegetable accompaniment to a meat main course. I am making a Lancashire hot-pot without the lamb: lots of vegetables layered in the pot with vegetable stock and baked in the oven. The result is succulent flavors, topped with crisp potatoes. The dish can be made in a deep baking pan, but I prefer to use an ovenproof baking pan.*

**Serves 4–6**

1½ lb (750 g) potatoes, thinly sliced
3 onions, sliced ¼ in (5 mm) thick
6 tablespoons (75 g) butter
4 carrots, sliced ¼ in (5 mm) thick
4 parsnips, peeled and quartered
   lengthwise
1 small rutabega, peeled, halved and
   sliced ¼ in (5 mm) thick
4 cups (350 g) turnips, peeled and
   sliced ¼ in (5 mm) thick
3 ¾ cups (900 ml) Vegetable Stock
   (page 240; good-quality bullion
   cubes can be used)
Salt and pepper

Preheat the oven to 425°F/220°C.

Fry the onions for a few minutes in a tablespoon of the butter until softened. Leave to cool. Butter the baking pan, place half of the potatoes in the bottom and season with salt and pepper. Spoon a third of the onions on top and then place the carrots on top. Season and dot with butter and then cover with the parsnip quarters. Season again and spoon another third of the onions on top. Lay the rutabega on top, season and brush with butter. Lay the turnips over, season and lay the remaining onions on top. Overlap the potatoes neatly to make the top layer, brush with the remaining butter and season with a sprinkle of salt. Add 2 ½ cups (600 ml) of the vegetable stock and bring to a simmer.

Place in the hot oven for 30 minutes. During this time, the potatoes will start to brown. Cover with a lid or foil and continue to cook for a further 50 minutes. During this time, press the potatoes down into the vegetables to help form a cake. If the vegetables are absorbing the stock too quickly and turning dry, add the remaining 1¼ cups (300 ml) of vegetable stock. For the last 10 minutes of cooking, remove the lid or foil to crispen the potatoes.

**Note:** The potato finish can be crisped even more under the broiler. To give a Lancashire feel to the dish, serve the hot-pot with roast lamb.

**1** Break the stalk from the the artichokes. Cut ⅛ in (2–3 mm) from the base, revealing the artichoke bottoms.

**2** Cut around the artichokes, removing the outside leaves. Cut the tops away, leaving 1 in (2.5 cm) deep chokes.

**3** Trim off any excess green on the bottoms. Scoop out the furry 'chokes' from the center.

# Cooking Globe Artichokes

*Globe artichokes can have so many uses. The outside leaves can be cooked and used as garnishes or in salads. There is a small bite of flesh to be eaten at the base of them. The small, younger leaves attached to the artichoke bottoms in the center can be cooked still attached and then used in salads, or as complete vegetarian dishes. I'm really after the artichoke bottom itself, which for me is the best and most succulent part.*

*To cook them, I like to make a tomato and lemon stock. The acidity from the lemon and sweetness of the tomato give the artichoke even more flavor without masking its own.*

**Serves 6**

**For the Stock:**
6 over-ripe tomatoes, roughly
  chopped
Juice of 1 lemon
1 ¼ cups (300 ml) water
Salt

1 teaspoon coriander seeds
  (optional)
1 bay leaf (optional)

**For the Artichokes:**
6 globe artichokes
Juice of 1 lemon

To make the stock, place all of the ingredients together in a pan and bring to a simmer. The stock is now ready to use.

Break the stalk from the base of the artichokes. Cut ⅛ in (2–3 mm) from the base with a sharp knife, revealing the artichoke bottom. Cut around the artichoke, removing the outside leaves; this will leave you with a cylinder shape. Cut the top of the cylinder away, leaving you with about a 1 in (2.5 cm) deep choke. Trim off any excess green left on the bottoms and scoop out the furry 'choke' from the center.

Once each artichoke is prepared, roll in the lemon juice to prevent any discoloring. The artichokes can now be placed in a simmering cooking liquid. Cover with waxed paper.

The artichokes will take 20–25 minutes to become completely tender. Remove from the heat and leave to cool. Once cooled, lift the artichokes from the stock and strain the stock through a sieve. Pour the stock over the chokes and keep refrigerated until needed.

# Garlic Mushrooms and Spinach *with* *Melted Gruyère*

*Garlic mushrooms are a very popular favorite as appetizers or side dishes. This dish can be either of these. You can leave out the spinach and cheese and just make the garlic mushrooms. But having the spinach to balance the strong garlic flavor, along with the grated melting cheese, is quite special.*

**Serves 4**

1 lb (450 g) button, cup or chestnut mushrooms
12 oz (350 g) spinach, picked and washed
3 tablespoons olive oil
4 tablespoons (50 g) butter
3 garlic cloves, crushed
1 shallot, finely chopped (optional)
A squeeze of lemon juice (optional)
1 cup (100 g) gruyère, grated
Salt and pepper

Wipe the mushrooms clean, and if they are large, cut into quarters. Heat the olive oil in a large frying pan until very hot. Add the mushrooms and fry quickly to brown immediately. Add the butter and continue to fry for a further minute. Add the garlic and season with salt and pepper. The mushrooms will have been cooking now for 3–4 minutes. Add the chopped shallot, if using, and the spinach. Continue to fry for 2–3 minutes more and check for seasoning. Add a squeeze of lemon, if using, and divide among four serving dishes or plates. Sprinkle the cheese on top and finish by melting under the broiler.

**Note:** Cheddar can also be used.

# Glazed Lemon Fava Beans *on Spinach Toast with Tomato Sauce*

*The cheese is being used to make cheese on toast as a base for the dish. Parmesan is my first choice, or a slice of gruyère; cheddar can also be used.*

**Serves 2**

6 oz (175 g) shelled fresh
   fava beans

8 oz (225 g) picked and
   washed spinach

2 large slices of crusty bread,
   1 cm (½ in) thick

3 tablespoons olive oil

6 tomatoes, blanched in boiling
   water for 10 seconds and skinned

1 small garlic clove, crushed

A tablespoon of butter

2 tablespoons grated Parmesan,
   cheddar or gruyère

2 egg yolks

Juice of ½ lemon

Salt and pepper

Brush the bread with olive oil and toast until golden brown; keep warm.

Cook the fava beans in salted, boiling water for 6–8 minutes. If they are particularly big, they may need an extra few minutes. Once cooked, drain, keeping two tablespoons of the cooking liquid. Slip the beans out of their skins and season.

Seed the tomatoes and chop the tomato flesh into a ¼ in (5 mm) dice. Heat a tablespoon of olive oil with the clove of garlic and add the tomatoes. Cook them until tender and almost reduced to a pulp, allowing the natural waters to reduce. Once reduced, season with salt and pepper and add the remaining olive oil.

In another pan, melt the butter and add the spinach. Cook for a few minutes until tender and season with salt and pepper.

Melt the cheese on the toast under the broiler.

Quickly whisk the egg yolks with the reserved fava bean cooking liquid and lemon juice in a bowl over simmering water to a thick *sabayon* consistency (like soft-peak whipped cream). Season with salt and pepper and use 1 tablespoon to bind the warm fava beans. Squeeze any excess liquid from the spinach and sit it on top of the cheese toasts. Spoon the fava beans onto the spinach. Coat the fava beans with the remaining lemon *sabayon* and glaze to a golden brown under the broiler. Spoon the tomato sauce around and serve.

**Note:** Chopped fresh basil, tarragon or parsley can be added to the tomato sauce.

# Parsleyed Crispy Carrots

*For this dish, I like the carrots to be slightly overcooked. This makes them softer and more succulent to eat, once you've crunched through the crispy crumbs!*

**Serves 6**

1 lb (450 g) baby carrots with tops
Finely grated zest of ½ orange
8 oz (225 g) fresh white
    breadcrumbs

1 heaping teaspoon chopped fresh
    parsley
6 tablespoons all-purpose flour,
    seasoned
1–2 eggs, beaten
Oil, for deep-frying
Salt and pepper

Peel the carrots and trim the stalk tops to a ½–¾ in (1–2 cm) stem. Cook them in salted, boiling water until completely tender. This will take 15–20 minutes, depending on the thickness of the carrots.

Once cooked, drain the excess water and leave the carrots to cool. Rub the orange zest into the breadcrumbs, season with salt and pepper and add the parsley. The carrots can now be rolled in the seasoned all-purpose flour, dipped in the beaten egg and then rolled in the breadcrumbs. Roll the crumbs reasonably firmly around the carrots, leaving the green tops uncoated. The carrots are now ready to be carefully fried in the hot oil. They will take just a few minutes to become golden and crisp. Lift them from the oil and put them to drain on paper towels. Season with a pinch of salt.

The parsleyed crispy carrots are now ready to serve.

**Note:** For an even crispier finish, put the carrots through the egg and crumbs again for a second coating.

The parsley can be left out and the orange zest added to give you crisp, crunchy, orange carrots.

# Cooking Kale

*Kale is a member of the cabbage family of vegetables, grown in the winter or early spring. It is similar to spring greens in flavor but with a thicker and firmer texture. When raw, it has a 'curly' parsley look about it.*

*Although similar to spring greens, kale holds its own texture and flavor and keeps an amazing deep green color when cooked. I like to eat it just boiled and then tossed in butter and seasoned. It can also be used in stir-fries (once blanched) and mixed with spices, pasta or potatoes.*

*In this book, I have recommended serving curly kale with the Parsleyed Cod on page 62, where it is just lightly bound with a mustard butter sauce. Or how about glazing kale with the soft Gorgonzola Rarebit (page 233)?*

---

**Serves 4**
1½–2 lb (750–900 g) curly kale

Salt and pepper
A tablespoon of butter

Remove the stalks from the kale and wash the leaves. The kale can now be cooked in salted, boiling water for 3–4 minutes. Drain in a colander, removing excess water. Season with salt and pepper and stir through the butter.

The kale can also be cooked ahead and refreshed in iced water. Then season and butter it while cold and refrigerate until needed. Now all you need to do is microwave and serve.

# Lemon-buttered Broccoli *with* Crisp Anchovies

*This is a vegetable dish that is packed with flavor. It goes best with fish, chicken or pork. A simple broiled sole with a portion of the broccoli creates a totally different dish. As with most of my recipes using anchovies, I am using the marinated rather than the panned ones.*

**Serves 4**

2 lb (900 g) broccoli
10–12 marinated anchovy fillets
2–3 tablespoons milk
1 tablespoon self-raising flour, mixed
  with ¼ teaspoon cayenne pepper
Oil, for deep-frying
Salt

**For the Lemon Butter:**

4-6 tablespoons (50–75 g) butter,
  softened
Juice of 1 lemon
3 tablespoons Vegetable Stock (page
  240; good-quality bullion cubes
  can be used), water or light cream
Salt and pepper

Split the anchovies down the center, separating the two fillets and then cut at an angle into ½ in (1 cm) pieces. Drop the anchovies into the milk and then into the cayenne flour, shaking off any excess. Deep-fry the anchovies until golden and crisp. A deep-fat fryer is not necessary; 1 in (2.5 cm) of hot oil in a saucepan will also do the trick.

Bring the lemon juice and stock, water or light cream to a simmer. Whisk in the butter to emulsify. Once all is whisked in, it is important that it doesn't boil or the butter will separate. Season with salt and pepper. If you have an electric blender, a quick processing will totally emulsify the sauce and lighten the flavor.

Trim excess stalk and leaves from the broccoli, leaving nice, small florets. Cook them in salted, boiling water until just tender. The cooking time will range between 2 and 6 minutes, depending on the size of the florets.

To serve the broccoli, season the florets and place them in a vegetable dish. Spoon the lemon sauce over and finish with a good sprinkling of crisp anchovies.

**Note:** This dish can be turned into a vegetarian one by replacing the anchovies with roasted or toasted pinenuts. The pinenuts can also be added to the anchovy version for an extra nutty finish.

# Roast Pumpkin

*Pumpkin has quite a large family – English, American, squash and butternut squash all being part of it. Yellow summer squash, zucchini, and cucumber are also relatives.*

*Pumpkin and butternut squash make good purées and soups and roast very well too. It is best to buy small pumpkins, which can easily be cut into wedges and roasted.*

---

**Serves 6**
A 2 lb (900 g) pumpkin
3 tablespoons cooking oil

2 tablespoons (25 g) butter
Salt and pepper
Grated nutmeg

Preheat the oven to 400°F/200°C. Cut the pumpkin into 12–16 wedges and remove the seeds. The skin can be left or cut off. It will not become tender and edible; however, it does guarantee that the pumpkin wedges don't break up, so they keep the nice half-moon shape. The cooking time will be the same.

Heat a frying pan with a drop of the oil. Season the pumpkin with salt and pepper and fry to a golden brown on both sides (5–6 minutes). When ready, transfer to a roasting pan. Repeat this process until all the wedges are browned. Add the butter and roast in the oven for 20 minutes, turning them half way through. If the pumpkin still feels a little too firm, return it to the oven for another 5–10 minutes.

Once cooked, transfer to a serving plate or bowl, pouring any buttery juices over it, and finish with a little grated nutmeg.

**Note:** Chopped pinenuts, lightly roasted and sprinkled over, go very well with the pumpkin.

# Turnip Purée

*A classic British vegetable, which can be used with almost as much variety as potatoes, turnips seem to have an overcooked, boiled, and bitter image, so that none of us really wants to know or try them.*

*This recipe does away with all that. Cooking the turnips in milk gives them a totally different flavor and they retain a brilliant white finish. So now there's no excuse – this dish has got to be tried.*

---

**Serves 4–6**
2 lb (900 g) turnips
2 cups (450 ml) milk
½ cup (150 ml) water

1 small garlic clove (optional)
¼ cup (50–85 ml) heavy cream
   (optional)
Salt and pepper

Peel the turnips and cut them into a rough dice. Cover with the milk and water in a saucepan and add a pinch of salt and the garlic clove, if using. Bring to a simmer and cook for 5–10 minutes until tender. When the turnips and garlic are soft, push them through a sieve or purée in a food processor. If the purée is too liquid, return it to a saucepan and cook over a low heat. This will slowly evaporate the liquid content, giving a firmer consistency.

Add the cream, if using, to enrich the flavor and create a creamy texture. Season with salt and pepper and serve.

**Note:** In place of the heavy cream, some of the cooking milk can be used.

# Sautéed New Potatoes *with Onions, Garlic and Orange*

*The flavor of orange is an old fashioned favorite with duck. This potato dish goes perfectly with duck or game dishes.*

---

**Serves 4**

1½ lb (750 g) new potatoes, slightly overcooked in their skins

4 tbs (50 g) butter, with a few drops of cooking oil

1 large onion, sliced (or 2 small onions)

1 garlic clove, crushed

Zest of 1 large orange, finely grated

Salt and pepper

1 teaspoon chopped fresh parsley or tarragon (optional)

Peel the cooked new potatoes and halve. Because they have been lightly overcooked, they will break up a bit. This is exactly the texture we are looking for, to give an almost creamy, sautéed flavor. Heat a frying-pan with a small amount of oil. Add half the butter and, once bubbling, add the potatoes. Season with salt and pepper and sauté on a high heat to give a golden color and texture (4–5 minutes).

While the potatoes are sautéing, heat another pan with the remaining butter and fry the onion with the garlic and orange until softened and golden brown. Season with salt and pepper. When the potatoes are sautéed, add the onions, and toss together. Finish by sprinkling with the chopped parsley or tarragon, if using.

# Sautéed, Vinegared Peppers

*This sounds like quite an acidic dish with the sharp flavor of vinegar finishing it off. In fact, the vinegar just lifts and adds lots of flavor to the peppers. I serve these with barbecued dishes (fish or meat) and also with roast chicken or lamb.*

**Serves 3–4**

1 large red pepper
1 large green pepper
1 large yellow pepper
2 tablespoons olive or peanut oil

A tablespoon of butter
1–2 tablespoons white wine or
  other vinegar e.g. red wine,
  tarragon or sherry vinegar
Salt and pepper

You can leave the skin of the peppers on or blanch them and remove their skins. Blanching and skinning will leave the peppers with a more tender finish. To blanch, place in salted, boiling water for 3–4 minutes. Remove from the water and peel off the skins. Split the peppers lengthwize and remove all seeds and core. If you're not blanching and peeling the peppers, just seed them.

Cut the peppers into strips or 1 in (2.5 cm) dice. Heat the oil in a frying pan and add the peppers. Cook for a few minutes, adding a tablespoon of butter to give a nutty taste. Once the peppers have started to brown and soften, season with salt and pepper, and add the vinegar. This will evaporate very quickly as the peppers absorb the flavor.

**Note:** Fresh herbs can be added at the end of cooking – parsley, tarragon or basil all work well and garlic can also be used.

A sprinkling of sugar will give the peppers a sweet and sour finish.

The peppers can also be skinned by broiling until almost burned and then placing in a plastic bag. This creates steam and helps loosen the skin.

# Spicy Fried Cauliflower

*This recipe is a vegetarian version of the spicy fried chicken in* Open Rhodes. *I was cooking for some friends and had decided to keep it simple with spicy fried chicken, rice, salad and naan bread. One friend was a vegetarian, so I made this with florets of cauliflower and finely chopped sweet peppers to finish. It turned out to be a winner, so here's the recipe.*

**Serves 2**

I small cooked cauliflower,
  cut into small florets
2 tablespoons natural yogurt
Juice of I lime
½ teaspoon ground turmeric
½ teaspoon paprika
2 cardamom pods, finely crushed
¼ teaspoon salt
I garlic clove, crushed
I tablespoon vegetable oil

A tablespoon of butter
I tablespoon sesame oil
  (or more vegetable oil)
⅓ red pepper, seeded and cut in
  small dice
⅓ green pepper, seeded and cut in
  small dice
Salt and pepper
I teaspoon chopped fresh coriander
  (optional)

Mix together the yogurt, lime juice, turmeric, paprika, cardamom, salt and garlic. Heat a tablespoon of vegetable oil and butter in a wok or frying pan to a medium heat. Add the cauliflower and fry to a light golden color. Add the yogurt marinade and increase the heat. Continue to fry for 1–2 minutes until the marinade has thickened and coated the cauliflower.

While the cauliflower is frying, heat another small pan and heat the sesame or vegetable oil. Quickly fry the peppers for a few minutes, season with salt and pepper. Spoon the cauliflower into a bowl and sprinkle with the peppers and chopped coriander, if using.

**Note:** This recipe will work with other vegetables; perhaps you could make a spicy fried ratatouille.

# French Bean Purée

*I have always said that good-quality green vegetables should never be puréed but now I'm changing my mind. Spinach purée has always been good, along with broccoli and asparagus, so why not French beans? This purée is very good, with the flavor of bubbling butter giving the beans a lovely nutty finish.*

**Serves 4**

1 lb (450 g) French beans, topped and tailed

1 tablespoon butter
2 tablespoons heavy cream
Salt and pepper

Cook the beans in salted, boiling water until completely tender but still with their brilliant green color. Drain off the water and place the beans in a food processor. Season with salt and pepper and blend to a smooth purée. While blending, heat a small frying-pan and add the butter. Once bubbling and at a nutty brown stage, add to the purée. Finish by adding the heavy cream. The green bean purée is now ready to serve.

**Note:** This recipe will work very well using almost any green vegetable.

# Curried Fried Potatoes

*These potatoes are 'parmentier', as featured in* Open Rhodes: *a shallow-fried, diced potato cooked until golden and crisp and soft in the center. The difference with these is that I'm rolling the potatoes in Madras curry powder before frying. As the potato cooks, so does the curry flavor. The potatoes are very, very tasty!*

*A sour cream dip can easily be made to go with them by mixing ½ cup (150 ml) of soured cream with the juice of 1–2 limes or lemons, seasoned with salt and pepper. (Natural yogurt can also be used.) Another finishing touch is garam masala. This is often sprinkled on top of finished curry dishes to spice them up even more. It is simply a mix of roasted spices (see my recipe on page 76 or it can be bought in small jars and keeps almost indefinitely in an air-tight container).*

---

**Serves 4**

1½ lb (750 g) potatoes, cut in
   ½ in (1 cm) dice
1 teaspoon Madras curry powder
4 tablespoons cooking oil
   (preferably peanut)

A tablespoon of butter
Salt
A pinch of garam masala (optional)
1 teaspoon chopped cilantro
   (optional)

Heat the oil in a large frying-pan. Make sure the diced potatoes are dry and then roll them in the curry powder, making sure they are all well coated. Season with salt. Once the oil is up to a medium high temperature, add the potatoes. Allow the potatoes to fry and turn a light golden color, which takes 3–4 minutes, before turning the heat down. This will prevent them from overcoloring before being cooked. Continue to fry, adding the butter and turning the potatoes from time to time, for 8–10 minutes. Towards the end of the cooking, increase the heat to give a richer golden color. To finish, sprinkle with garam masala and chopped cilantro, if you like.

**Note:** Any remaining cooking oil will have taken on the curry flavor, so you can use this as a dressing to drizzle over the finished crispy potatoes.

   These potatoes go very well with chicken and fish dishes.

DESSERTS

# desserts

*t*he dessert chapter always seems to be the busiest. I start off with just a few ideas and then tend to get totally carried away, tasting and testing as many as possible. The desserts have taken one or two new directions – one of which is a sort of 'afternoon snack' theme. Homemade Eccles Cakes (page 218), which are lovely to serve as a complete dessert with custard and extra-thick cream, Homemade Crumpets (page 221), Golden Ginger 'Flapjack' Cake (page 220), Molasses Loaf (page 217) and Mini Madeira Prune Cakes (page 205) are all well suited for desserts or just to accompany a good pot of English tea.

There are also some interesting combinations; Potato and Mascarpone Cheesecake Tart (page 180) is certainly one, with the everyday vegetable becoming a dessert, enlivened with a squeeze of lemon.

Pumpernickel Bread and Butter Dessert (page 193), I promise you, is not just an excuse to feature 'B & B' again, although I have to admit I just can't leave the whole concept of that dish alone! The pumpernickel dessert is a proper loaf, but with custard and molasses in place of sugar to give you a toffee-like dream.

The sorbets have moved on to sherbets, which are a slightly different concept. The basic syrup mixture is made with milk and has egg white added near the end. The finished result gives you a very lively 'sorbet' that sparkles on the palate. There are also parfaits, fritters, tarts, pies, different flavored pastry recipes, creams, brûlées and two desserts that I promised from *Open Rhodes* – Bourbon Cookies (page 210) and Wagon Wheel® Dessert (page 190)! The cookie-as-dessert revival lives on in these with two very tasty results: a chocolate cookie, which cuts through to a slice of brownie and then some chocolate ganache, or shortbread cookies sandwiched with jam, through to marshmallow in the center, all totally covered in chocolate. These varied desserts have one thing in common – taste!

# Soft Fruit Ice Creams

*This has to be one of the easiest ice cream recipes you will ever find. It is made simply with soft fruit, stock syrup, a squeeze of lemon and crème fraîche.*

*This recipe is for fresh fruits but canned ones can be used – just purée almost any fruit in its own syrup, sweeten further, if necessary, with powdered sugar and add a few tablespoons of crème fraîche, and the ice cream is finished.*

*Here's the fresh fruit version.*

---

**Serves 4**

2 cups (225 g) soft fruit, raspberries, blackberries, strawberries, etc.

¼ cup (50 g) sugar

½ cup (120 ml) water

A squeeze of lemon juice

3 heaping tablespoons crème fraîche

Powdered sugar, to taste (if needed)

To make the fruit purée, boil together the sugar and water. Let it cool. Add the soft fruit and lemon juice and purée in a food processor. Push through a sieve. Add the crème fraîche and taste for sweetness. If it's too tart, add powdered sugar to taste. The ice cream mix is now ready to churn for 15–20 minutes. If you don't have an ice cream machine, freeze the mixture in a bowl and stir every 5–10 minutes. When almost set, whisk to a smooth, creamy finish and then leave to freeze completely.

**Note:** An extra ½ cup (50 g) of soft fruits can be chopped and added just before the setting point for a different texture.

You can also serve a drizzle of fruit syrup (page 229) with this soft fruit ice cream.

# Iced Pear Parfait *with Caramelized Pears in a Hazelnut Tart*

*This recipe has many steps, with tarts, parfaits, sauces, and caramelizing all to be made. But most parts, if not all, can be made well in advance. Also, as with all of my recipes, all the parts don't have to stay together. The pear parfait can become a dessert on its own.*

*For this particular recipe, I use quite an unusual mold. To freeze the parfait in a cylinder shape, which can then be sliced and put in the tart case, I use drain pipes! I buy 3 in (7.5 cm) diameter plastic drain pipes, about 6–8 in (15–20 cm) long, from a local hardware store. Wash them well, and you have cylindrical parfait molds!*

---

**Serves 4**

**For the Pear Purée:**
4 fresh or canned pears, peeled, cored and cut in rough dice
A pat of butter
2 tablespoons (25 g) sugar

**For the Parfait:**
4 egg yolks
¼ cup (50 g) sugar

A splash of Poire William liqueur (optional)
1¼ cup (300 ml) heavy cream, lightly whipped to soft peaks
4 Hazelnut 'Marzipan' Tart shells (page 164)
4 Caramelized Pears (page 164)
1 quantity of Red Wine Caramel Sauce with Hazelnuts (page 165)
8–12 tablespoons Anglaise Sauce (page 223)

For the purée, cook the fresh pears in the butter and sugar until completely tender; blend to a smooth purée in a food processor or blender. If using canned pears, just blend with some of their own syrup. For the parfait, whisk the egg yolks and caster sugar together over a pan of simmering water until it holds a thick ribbon trail (*sabayon* stage). Remove from the heat and continue to whisk until cold. Fold in the pear purée and the Poire William liqueur, if using. Now fold in the whipped cream. Cover one end of the 'pipe' with plastic wrap and stand it upright on a tray or plate. Pour the parfait in and place it in the freezer. It will take 3–4 hours to freeze totally.

Prepare the Hazelnut 'Marzipan' Tart shells, the Caramelized Pears, the Red Wine Caramel Sauce with Hazelnuts and the Anglaise Sauce.

To assemble the dessert: spoon a line of the red wine and hazelnut caramel sauce around the plate. Spoon 2–3 tablespoons of the anglaise sauce in the center. Remove the parfait 'pipe' from the freezer and run the pipe very briefly under warm water. The parfait will now push out quite easily. Cut a ½–¾ in (1–2 cm) slice per portion and place one in each hazelnut tart. Put two or four halves of caramelized pear (depending on the size) on top of the parfait, spooning or brushing some of the excess caramel syrup over to glaze. Put the tarts on top of the anglaise sauce. The complete dessert is ready to serve.

# For the Hazelnut 'Marzipan' Tart Shells

*These tart shells are very similar to a marzipan, using hazelnuts instead of almonds. They become very crisp, with a cookie-like texture. I use pans that are 3½ x ½ in deep.*

**Makes 4**

1 cup (100 g) ground hazelnuts
¼ cup (50 g) sugar
½ cup (50 g ) powdered sugar, plus
    extra for rolling out paste

1 egg yolk
1 teaspoon lemon juice

Sift together the hazelnuts and sugars. Add the egg yolk and lemon juice and combine to a marzipan paste. Roll the pastry out very thinly on a surface covered with more powdered sugar and use to line the loose-bottomed tartlet pans, trimming off any excess paste. These can now be left out to dry at room temperature for 24 hours. This will allow the marzipan to set and leave very crisp tart shells.

# For the Caramelized Pears

*The recipe I am giving you here actually cooks the pears in a caramel syrup. The pears can also be cooked in a basic stock syrup and, once cool, caramelized with powdered or regular sugar under the broiler or with a gas gun.*

**Serves 4**

4 large, firm or 8 small, firm pears,
    peeled, halved and cored

2 cups (225 g) sugar
1¼ cups (300 ml) water

Bring the sugar and water to the boil and continue to boil rapidly until it turns into a light golden caramel. Add the pears along with another 6 tablespoons of water and continue to cook for 15 minutes until the syrup turns into a darker, richer colored caramel. Remove from the stove and leave to cool. Once cooled, remove the pears. They will have a good full caramel flavor and color. The remaining caramel can be kept to glaze them just before serving.

**Note:** Instead of caramel poached pears, you can use canned halves, glazed under the broiler with powdered or regular sugar.

# For the Red Wine Caramel Sauce with Hazelnuts

*Another caramel sauce made with wine and hazelnuts gives the dish a totally different taste and finish. The finished consistency is very thick.*

**Serves 4**

1 cup (200 ml) red wine, preferably
  burgundy
1 tablespoon red wine vinegar
¾ cup (200 g) sugar

4 tablespoons (50 g) butter
1 vanilla pod, split and scraped or
  1 teaspoon vanilla extract
⅔ cup (50 g) chopped hazelnuts

Bring the wine and vinegar together to the boil and then boil rapidly until it has reduced by half. Set aside. Gently melt the sugar in a separate pan over a medium heat until it has turned into a golden caramel. Add the butter and the scraped vanilla pod or essence and cook for a further 2 minutes. Add the reduced wine mixture, remove from the heat and add the chopped hazelnuts. Leave the sauce to cool to room temperature. It is best served at this temperature.

# *sherbets*

These are essentially recipes for sorbets with a sharp, zingy finish. Sorbets are made from a fruit purée, mixed with stock syrup and usually a twist of lemon. Sherbets have milk and whipped egg whites added to them. If you want to make sorbets instead, simply omit the egg whites and milk.

# Lemon Sherbet

*This recipe can be made into lime, orange or grapefruit sherbet by replacing the lemon with the citrus fruit of your choice.*

---

**Serves 6–8**
Finely grated zest and juice of
   5 lemons

1½ cups (375 ml) Basic Stock Syrup
   (page 227)
½ cup (120 ml) milk
2 egg whites

Boil the lemon juice, zest and stock syrup. Remove from the heat, add the milk and leave to infuse and cool. Once cooled, churn the mixture in an ice cream or sorbet machine. It will take 20–25 minutes to churn to a creamy texture.

Five minutes before the sherbet is ready, beat the egg whites to the soft peak stage and add to the sherbet while mixing. Continue to churn until ready. The sherbet is now ready and can be left in the freezer to firm.

**Note:** If preferred, the zest can be strained from the mixture before churning. This sherbet is featured with the Charbroiled Glazed Pumpkin Slices on page 200.

# Bellini Champagne Sherbet

*Bellini is a famous cocktail made from puréed white peach juice and Prosecco, which is an Italian alternative to champagne. These aren't white peaches I am using but the flavor is fantastic and tastes like an iced cocktail!*

---

**Serves 6–8**

1 lb 2 oz (500 g) fresh peaches, chopped

1½ cups (350 ml) Basic Stock Syrup (page 227)

1½ cups (350 ml) champagne or sparkling wine

A squeeze of lemon juice

½ cup (120 ml) milk

2 egg whites, beaten to soft peaks

Bring the chopped peaches and stock syrup to a simmer. Cook for a few minutes or until the peaches have softened. Add the champagne or sparkling wine and lemon juice and return to a simmer. Remove from the stove and purée in a food processor or liquidizer. Push the purée through a sieve and leave to cool. Add the milk and churn in an ice cream machine for 20–25 minutes. When almost ready, add the whisked egg whites and continue to churn. When the sherbet is thick and creamy, remove from the machine and finish setting in the freezer.

**Note:** Apricots, plums, and other soft fruits will also work with the champagne. Justify the Bellini name by presenting it in a cocktail glass with a trickle of champagne poured over and fresh peach slices to garnish.

Canned peaches can also be used. Purée the peaches in their own syrup and omit the basic stock syrup from the recipe.

# Raspberry Sherbet

*This is a favorite with everyone. The fresh, fruity flavor whisked to a creamy ice is so good. Adding the red-wine vinegar lifts it even more. The raspberry flavor just tastes stronger. This sherbet would go very well with the Roast Peaches or Nectarines on page 198 or with 'Burned' Peach and Mascarpone Cheesecake Tart (page 181) with thick cream (almost a peach melba tart!).*

---

**Serves 6–8**

1¾ cups (400 ml) Raspberry Purée (page 161) (canned or frozen raspberries can also be puréed)

4 tablespoons sugar

2 tablespoons strong red-wine vinegar, preferably Cabernet Sauvignon

1 cup (200 ml) milk

2 egg whites, beaten to soft peaks

Warm the purée with the sugar. Add the vinegar and milk and leave to cool. Churn for 20–25 minutes to the sorbet stage. A few minutes before it is ready, add the beaten egg whites. Once ready, remove from the machine and finish in the freezer.

**Note:** Sherbets can be turned into sorbets by omitting the egg whites and milk.

Add a bit more vinegar if you like a sharper taste.

# Madeira Sherbet

*This Madeira sherbet has a totally different flavor. I like to serve this with Mini Madeira Prune Cakes (page 205) and Madeira Syrup (page 228) to give a complete Madeira experience. Other fortified wines can also be used, such as sherry or port.*

---

**Serves 4–6**

2 cups (450 ml) Madeira

1 cup (200 ml) water

¾ cup (150 g) sugar

½ cup (120 ml) milk

2 egg whites, beaten to soft peaks

Boil the Madeira to reduce the quantity by half. Add the water and sugar and return to a boil. Remove from the heat, add the milk, and leave to cool. Once cool, churn in the machine for 20 minutes. After 20 minutes, add the beaten soft peak egg whites and continue to churn for another 5–10 minutes. Remove from the machine and leave to set in the freezer.

# Cinnamon Ice Cream

*Baked apples, apple pies, apple crumbles and tarts would all benefit from being served with this ice cream. In this book, I recommend serving it with the Date and Orange Mascarpone Fritters (page 208). Hot fritters and cold ice cream always sounds tasty to me!*

---

**Serves 4–6**

1 cup (250 ml) heavy cream

1 cup (250 ml) milk

2 cinnamon sticks, broken

½ cup (100 g) sugar

6 egg yolks

¼ cup (50 ml) rum

Bring the cream, milk and broken cinnamon sticks to a boil. Cream together the sugar and egg yolks. Pour the boiling cream mixture onto the creamed yolks, stirring from time to time until cooled. Pour through a sieve and then churn in the ice cream machine for 15–20 minutes until very thick. Freeze. The ice cream will be nice and rich and packed with cinnamon flavor.

# Blood Orange Sorbet

*Rich, zesty and tasty!*

---

**Serves 4–6**

The juice and finely grated zest of
10 blood oranges

⅔ cup (150 g) sugar
⅔ cup (150 ml) water
The juice from 2 lemons

Place the sugar, water and orange zest in a saucepan and bring to a simmer. Cook for 10–15 minutes. Strain the juice of the oranges and lemons together. Add to the syrup and leave to cool. The sorbet syrup is now ready to be finished in the ice cream maker and churned for 20–25 minutes to a smooth consistency. Freeze until firm. If you do not have an ice cream machine, freeze the mix, whisking occasionally to help create the same consistency.

**Note:** Diced blood orange segments can be stirred into the finished mix for a more pulpy, coarser texture.

Blood oranges are not essential for this recipe. Any fresh, ripe orange will also work to give you a rich orange sorbet.

# Chocolate Banana Bread Dessert *with Chocolate Sorbet*

*This dessert will fulfill all chocolate lovers' fantasies! Imagine a rich chocolate and banana cake filled with melting chocolate ganache. And then imagine a chocolate sauce and chocolate sorbet to go with it. Just thinking about eating this dessert makes me melt! The beauty of this recipe is that it can be made well in advance and then just microwaved. This process obviously warms the cake and starts the chocolate melting inside.*

*I'm giving you the recipe for banana loaf, but a bought variety will also work. In fact, you don't have to stick to banana bread – a golden syrup or Jamaican gingerbread loaf will also work very well and, if you're the ultimate chocolate freak, use a chocolate cake!*

---

**Serves 6**

**For the Banana Bread:**

9 tablespoons (120 g) butter
⅔ cup (100 g) soft light brown sugar
½ cup (100 g) granulated sugar
2 medium eggs
4 large (250 g) very ripe bananas, mashed
3 cups (325 g) all-purpose flour
1 teaspoon baking powder
A good pinch of salt

**For the Chocolate Custard:**

¾ cup (175 ml) heavy cream
2½ cups (575 ml) milk
5 tablespoons (65 g) butter, diced
9 oz (250 g) bittersweet chocolate, broken in small pieces
3 eggs
2 egg yolks
¾ cup (150 g) soft brown sugar

**For the Chocolate Ganache:**

¾ cup (190 ml) heavy cream
2 tablespoons granulated sugar
4½ oz (120 g) semisweet chocolate, broken in small pieces
1 tablespoon butter, diced

**For the Chocolate Tuile Cookies (Makes about 10–12):**

2 tablespoons (15 g) cocoa powder
½ cup (50 g) powdered sugar
½ cup (50 g) all-purpose flour
1 egg white
4 tablespoons (50 g) butter, melted

Preheat the oven to 350°F/180°C. Butter a 2 lb (900 g) loaf pan and line it with waxed paper. Cream the butter with the soft light brown and granulated sugars. Beat the eggs together and add slowly to the butter mix. Mix the mashed ripe banana into the butter mixture. Sift together the flour and baking powder with the salt and fold into the banana-butter mix. Spoon the mixture into the lined pan and bake for 50–60 minutes. Let it cool for 10–15 minutes before turning out of the pan. Once cold, remove all the crust from the loaf. The banana bread can now be cut into ½ in (1 cm) dice. This is now ready to be soaked with the chocolate custard.

To make the chocolate custard, bring the cream and milk to a boil in a saucepan. Put the butter and chocolate in a bowl, pour on the cream mixture and stir, melting the two together. Whisk together the eggs, egg yolks and sugar. Pour on the chocolate cream and strain through a sieve. Pour the chocolate custard onto the diced banana bread; mix in well to help the banana bread soak up the chocolate flavor. Leave to soak for 30 minutes.

For the chocolate ganache, bring the heavy cream to a boil with the sugar, and pour over the chocolate and butter in a bowl and mix well. Leave to chill and set.

Once set and firm, roll the ganache into balls approximately 1 in (2.5 cm) in diameter and refrigerate until needed. These ganache balls will be placed in the center of the cakes, creating the melted chocolate filling.

Now make the chocolate tuiles. You will need a large sheet of baking parchment to spread the cookies on and a stencil to shape them, which could be a triangle, leaf shape, circle, etc. I prefer to cut a circle 3–4 in (7.5–10 cm) in diameter from a plastic carton or lid. This gives you a permanent stencil to wash and use time and time again. Preheat the oven to 325°F/160°C.

Sift together the cocoa powder, powdered sugar and flour. Slowly mix in the egg white, then the melted butter. Place the stencil on the baking parchment. Spread over enough of the mixture to give a thin shape. Lift and repeat the stencil shapes. Bake for 5–6 minutes. Once they are cooked and while still warm, lift the cookies off the paper with a palette knife and drape them over upturned cups or small bowls to give you a cookie-cup shape to place the sorbet in. You could also cut a cardboard cylinder from the center of a roll of foil or plastic wrap in half lengthwise. Push a tuile into it, which will give you a curved cookie once it has cooled. The cooked tuile cookies will keep for 48 hours if kept in an air-tight container.

Prepare the Chocolate Sorbet and the Ultimate Chocolate Sauce.

To finish the dish, preheat the oven to 325°F/160°C, or a little higher. Butter six 3 in (7.5 cm) diameter, 2 in (5 cm) deep pastry rings. Put them on greased baking parchment or waxed paper on a baking sheet. Spoon a layer of the soaked cake into the molds and put a ball of ganache in the center. Continue to fill the moulds with care until the ganache ball is covered. Bake the desserts for 10–15 minutes.

During the baking, the chocolate custard and banana cake mixture will set and give a baked cake finish with melting ganache inside. Let the desserts cool or serve immediately. The advantage of this dessert is that these desserts can be left to cool and then refrigerated. To serve, they then simply need to be microwaved.

To finish the presentation, thread some of the chocolate sauce across each plate and place the warm dessert on top. Next to the dessert, put a tuile cookie and using a tablespoon or ice cream scoop, fill with the chocolate sorbet.

The dessert is now complete and ready to eat!

**Note:** Whipped cream, placed on top of the cake, goes very well with this dish.

# For the Chocolate Sorbet

**Serves 6**

5 oz (150 g) semisweet chocolate,
  broken in pieces

2 cups (500 ml) water
⅔ cup (150 g) sugar
2 tablespoons (25 g) corn syrup

Put the chocolate pieces in a bowl. Bring the water, sugar and corn syrup to a boil and pour onto the chocolate pieces. Stir until the chocolate has melted, and allow to cool and then chill in the fridge. The sorbet mix is now ready to churn in an ice cream maker, which should take approximately 20-25 minutes. Transfer the sorbet to a box, cover and slide into the freezer. If you do not have an ice cream machine, simply freeze this mix, whisking it occasionally as it hardens to help create a smooth consistency.

# For the Ultimate Chocolate Sauce:

**Makes about 1¼ cup**
  **(300 ml)**

8 oz (225 g) semisweet chocolate
1 cup (250 ml) heavy cream

2 tablespoons (25 g) unsalted butter

To make the ultimate chocolate sauce, melt the chocolate with the cream in a bowl over a pan of hot water and, when it is warm, add the butter. You now have a thick, rich chocolate sauce. This is best eaten cold or just warm. Trying to serve this as a hot sauce will simply cause the butter to separate.

# Lemon Yogurt Ice Cream

*This ice cream is packed with lemony flavor and the consistency is helped along by the yogurt and cream. It is totally different from the Lemon Sherbet on page 166 and, if you can't choose between them, make both! If you want to test this recipe for maximum flavor, the best way is to eat lots of it!*

---

**Makes enough for the whole family!**

The juice and finely grated zest of 2 lemons

½ cup (100 g) sugar
2 cups (425 g) natural yogurt
⅔ cup (150 ml) heavy cream

Blend the lemon juice and sugar together until fine.

Mix the yogurt with the heavy cream. Stir the sugared lemon juice into the yogurt and churn in the ice cream machine.

As with most ice creams, this will take 15–20 minutes to churn, which still keeps it creamy before finishing in the freezer.

If you do not have an ice cream machine, freeze until almost set and then whisk and refreeze until completely frozen.

# fruit tarts

Fruit tarts can be made to suit almost any fruit. The simplest are often the best: a crisp pastry shell filled with pastry cream and with lots of baked fruit on top. Raw fruits will also make very good tarts. To appreciate all the wonderful fresh flavors from the fruit, cream and crisp, crumbly pastry, never serve tarts straight from the fridge. Eating them at room temperature or slightly warm will keep every taste alive. A selection of fruit tarts – such as rhubarb, gooseberry and raspberry meringue – is featured here with suggestions and recipes for different flavors of pastry bases to go with them. Here's a list of pastries you can find in this book with suggestions of the fruits to go with them:

**Sweet Short Crust Pastry (page 224):** raspberries, strawberries, gooseberries, plums, damsons, cherries and greengages

**Sweet Lemon and Raisin Short Crust Pastry (page 224):** raspberries, strawberries, gooseberries, plums, damsons, cherries and greengages

**Sweet Black Pepper and Crunchy Sugar Pastry (page 225):** strawberries, raspberries and most other summer fruits

**Shortbread Pastry (page 226):** rhubarb, strawberries and raspberries

**Hazelnut Pastry (page 226):** Summer fruits, plums, damsons, peaches, nectarines and apricots

**Quick Puff Pastry (page 225):** apples, figs, peaches and nectarines

# Rhubarb Tart

*This rhubarb tart can take on two or three different cooking and serving combinations. The pastry base is a basic sweet short crust pastry. This can either be pre-baked or the pastry and filling can be baked together raw. There is a choice of two bases to place in the pastry case: the first is Pastry Cream (page 231) and the second is a slice of Lemon Genoise Sponge (page 222). The pastry cream will give a creamy base, while the sponge absorbs all of the fruit juices.*

**Serves 6**

8 oz (225 g) Sweet Short Crust
   Pastry or Short Crust Pastry shell
   (page 224)
1½–2 lb (750–900 g) fresh rhubarb
½ in (1 cm) thick, round slice
   (8–10 in/20–25 cm diameter) of
   plain or Lemon Genoise Sponge

(page 222) or 12 tablespoons of
   Pastry Cream (page 231)
2 tablespoons (25 g) butter
4–6 tablespoons water
4–6 oz (100–175 g) sugar
2–3 tablespoons apricot jam glaze
   (optional) plus 2 tablespoons water,
   or powdered sugar, sifted (optional)

Preheat the oven to 425°F/220°C. Put the sponge or spoon the pastry cream in the base of a 8–10 in (20–25 cm) unbaked pastry shell. Peel the rhubarb (if stringy) and cut into ¾ in (2 cm) slices. Melt the butter in a large saucepan and add the rhubarb, water, and sugar. Carefully turn the rhubarb in the syrup for 1–2 minutes. Remove from the stove and allow to cool. Drain off any liquid and keep separate. Spoon all the rhubarb into the tart shells and bake for 35–40 minutes.

The rhubarb will have cooked and broken down slightly in texture. Remove the tart from the oven and place on a wire rack to cool for 10–15 minutes. Remove the tart from the ring and let it cool at room temperature. If using apricot jam as a glaze, mix any rhubarb liquid and the 2 tablespoons of water with the jam and warm. Strain through a sieve and brush the rhubarb for a glazed finish. If you're not using the jam, drizzle any excess liquid over and dust with powdered sugar.

Here is an alternative method: line the pastry case with foil or waxed paper, fill with baking beans or rice and bake for 20–30 minutes until golden and crisp. Leave to cool. Remove the foil or waxed paper and beans or rice. Trim off any excess pastry to give you a neat edge. Spread with pastry cream or line with the genoise sponge. Melt the butter and add the sliced rhubarb with the sugar. Cook and stir carefully until completely tender. This will only take 5–6 minutes. If the pastry shell is sponge-based, spoon the hot rhubarb on top; the sponge will then soak up any juices. If using pastry cream, allow the rhubarb to cool before spooning it on top. Make apricot glaze, warming the jam with just the water, straining and then brushing or spooning it over. An alternative to the jam for both versions of the tart is to dust liberally with powdered sugar.

**Note:** This recipe can be used to make fresh raspberry tarts. The fruit to sugar quantities are the same but very sharp gooseberries may well need ¼ cup (50 g) of extra sugar.

The gooseberry tart will also go well with either a pastry cream or a sponge base and will become even tastier if the Sweet Lemon and Raisin Short Crust Pastry (page 224) is used. For a neater finish with the gooseberry tart, arrange the fruits standing up in the tart case. With this method, it is best to cook them almost from raw in the pastry. For an absolutely fool-proof method of cooking fruit (e.g. raspberries, plums, cherries, or blackberries) for tarts, use ½ cup (100 g) of sugar for every 1 lb (450 g) of fruit with 4 tablespoons of water. Bring to a boil and then remove from the stove and leave to cool in the liquid. The liquid can be used to loosen the apricot jam for the glaze.

# Baked Fig Tart or Tartlets

*This recipe can be used to make four individual tartlets or one large one. If making just one large tart, you will need a 8–10 in (20–25 cm) ovenproof frying pan and for individual tartlets, four 4 in (10 cm) diameter tartlet pans. The advantage of making these into individual tartlets is that their size is perfect for the shape of the fruit. For each tart, three figs are needed to cover the base. The quantities and method are identical for either size, and only the cooking time varies slightly.*

---

**Makes a 8–10 in (20–25 cm) Tart or four 4 in (10 cm) Tartlets**

12 fresh figs, halved lengthways
4–6 oz (100–175 g) Quick Puff Pastry (page 225)
⅔ cup (100 g) soft light brown sugar
6 tablespoons (75 g) butter

Preheat the oven to 400°F/200°C. Butter the ovenproof frying pan or the individual tartlet pans very well. It is very important that the mold(s) are very well buttered. This will prevent the figs from sticking and also help the sugar to caramelize. Sprinkle 2 tablespoon (15 g) of the sugar in each pan or ¼ cup (50 g) in the frying pan. Heat the frying pan and melt a tablespoon (15 g) of butter. Fry half the figs, cut-side down, very quickly on a high heat to a golden brown. Remove from the pan and set aside or arrange in two of the tartlet pans, facing the points towards the center. Melt another tablespoon (15 g) of butter and fry the remaining figs. Fill the remaining tartlet pans. If making one large tart, return the first batch of cooked figs to the pan.

Roll out the puff pastry thinly and cut it into four 4 in (10 cm) circles or a 8 in (20 cm) circle. Place a circle of puff pastry on top of the fruit and bake for 20 minutes (small) or 25–30 minutes (large).

Once baked, remove from the oven and leave to rest for 5–6 minutes. This relaxes the figs and when turned out they will have a neater finish. Warm the base of the frying pan or pans and turn the tarts out. They will place caramelized on a crisp puff pastry base and look very appetizing.

For extra butter caramel to spoon over, melt the remaining 4 tablespoons (50 g) of butter with the ⅓ cup (50 g) of soft, light brown sugar to a silky, golden syrup and drizzle over and around. The tarts are ready to serve and will go very well with vanilla or Cinnamon Ice Cream (page 169) or just thick cream.

**Note:** A shallow cake pan can be used in place of the frying pan for the large tart.

# Potato and Mascarpone Cheesecake Tart

*Potato cheesecake is a great British dessert that always eats well, but I have decided to give it an Italian touch with the addition of mascarpone. I find this gives the dessert a richer and creamier finish, almost like a baked custard tart. I am using lemon zest in this recipe to lift all the other flavors, but orange zest can also be used.*

---

### Makes a 9 in (23 cm) Tart

8 oz (225 g) Sweet Short Crust
   Pastry (page 224)
1⅓ cup (100 g) plain mashed
   potatoes
½ cup (100 g) mascarpone

The finely grated zest of 3 lemons
1 cup (100 g) powdered sugar
4 tablespoon (50 g) butter, softened
4 egg yolks and 2 egg whites,
   beaten together

Preheat the oven to 400°F/200°C. Butter a 9 in (23 cm) spring form tart pan. Roll the pastry out thinly. Line the flan ring with pastry, leaving any excess pastry hanging over the edge of the ring. Line with foil or waxed paper and fill with baking beans or rice. Bake for 20–25 minutes. Once cooked, leave to cool. Remove the waxed paper or foil, beans or rice and trim off any excess pastry. Turn the oven down to 350°F/180°C.

Place the finely grated lemon zest in a small saucepan of cold water, bring to a simmer and simmer for a few minutes. Drain through a fine sieve, refresh under cold water and squeeze out any excess liquid. Mix with the powdered sugar.

Whisk the mashed potato and then whisk in the mascarpone and butter. Add the beaten 4 egg yolks and 2 egg whites and pour into the pre-baked pastry shell.

The tart will take 35–40 minutes to become baked, golden and set. Once cooked, remove from the oven and leave to rest. This dessert is best eaten just warm with lots of cream!

**Note:** Before placing the tart in the oven, it can be topped with finely grated nutmeg. This dessert also goes very well with raspberries and most other Summer fruits. Put the raspberries on top, completely covering the warm tart, and leave them natural or brush with a raspberry-jam glaze.

# 'Burned' Peach and Mascarpone Cheesecake Tart

*The base for this recipe is a sweet shortcrust pastry tartlet. Puff pastry can also be used. If using a biscuit base, the homemade ginger shortcake (see Rhubarb and Ginger Shortcake Dessert, page 189) can be rolled out and cooked in the cake ring. Or just make a mixture of half crushed ginger snaps and half graham crackers for a quick and easy base (see Note below).*

---

**Makes a 8 in (20 cm) deep Tart**

6 small–medium fresh peaches (canned can be used)
The juice of ½ lemon
1¼ cup (250 g) sugar
2½ cups (600 ml) water
8 oz (225 g) Sweet Short Crust Pastry (page 224) or Quick Puff Pastry (page 225)
The juice of 1 lemon or lime
½ cup (100 g) mascarpone
⅔ cup (150 ml) heavy cream
powdered sugar, sifted, for dusting

Preheat the oven to 400°F/200°C. Butter a 8 in (20 cm) diameter, 1 in (2.5 cm) deep, spring form tart pan. Roll out the pastry thinly and use it to line the tart pan. Bake for 20–30 minutes until golden and crisp. Once cooked, leave to cool. Remove the waxed paper or foil, beans, or rice and trim off any excess pastry.

Put the peaches in a saucepan with the lemon juice, 1⅓ cup (225 g) sugar and water. Add more water, if needed, just to cover. Cover with waxed paper to allow the tops of the peaches also to cook, and bring to a boil. Simmer the peaches for 5 minutes and then leave to cool in the sweet liquid. Do not poach the peaches if using canned.

To make the cheesecake, beat the remaining 2 tablespoons (25 g) sugar and lemon or lime juice into the mascarpone cheese. Whisk the heavy cream to soft peaks and fold into the mascarpone. Spread or pipe the mixture into the pastry shell. Refrigerate for 30 minutes to set. Take the peaches from the syrup and peel them. Carefully cut into halves and remove the pits. The peaches can now be packed on top of the tart.

To finish, dust the peaches heavily with powdered sugar and glaze under the broiler or with a gas gun. Dust and broil again; this will give an almost crème-brûlée-like crunchy topping and also a 'burned' edge to the sweet peaches. Before glazing, the pastry edge can be covered with foil to prevent it from burning.

**Note:** For a basic cookie crust base, take 2 cups (100 g) of ginger snaps and 2 cups (100 g) graham crackers and crush with a rolling pin or in a plastic bag. Melt 2 tablespoons (25 g) of butter and mix into the crumbs. Press the mixture into a 8–10 in (20–25 cm) greased, spring form tart ring and refrigerate to set before spreading the cream on top. To spice the pastry case, take ¼ in (50 g) of ginger, chop it and add it to the pastry recipe; or add a teaspoon of ground ginger.

# Raspberry Meringue Pie

*I call this dish 'upside-down meringue dessert.' This is because the fresh raspberries place on top of the meringue, which is directly on the pastry shell, rather than the meringue being the topping, as is usual. I have used Italian meringue as the filling. This is a meringue that is made with boiled sugar and then continuously whipped until cold, which gives it a fuller flavor and texture. In this recipe, I add some grated zest of lemon, a citrus fruit that goes very well with raspberries, although the basic meringue recipe is the same with or without the lemon. The hazelnut pastry goes very well with the meringue; the crumbly, nutty flavor with the meringue and raspberry topping is delicious.*

*You will need a sugar thermometer for this recipe.*

---

### Makes a 10 in (25 cm) Pie
3 cups (350 g) fresh raspberries, washed
8 oz (225 g) Hazelnut Pastry (page 226)
Powdered sugar, sifted, for dusting (optional)

### For the Meringue:
¾ cup (175 g) sugar
⅓ cup (85 ml) water
The finely grated zest of 2 lemons
4 egg whites

Preheat the oven to 350°F/180°C. Butter a 8 in (20 cm) loose-bottomed tart pan. Roll the pastry out thinly and line the pan. Line with foil or waxed paper, fill with baking beans or rice and bake for 25–30 minutes until set and golden. Remove the foil or waxed paper and beans or rice. Trim off any excess pastry to give you a neat finish.

For the meringue, boil the sugar and water with the lemon juice to 230°F/121°C. While the sugar is boiling, beat the egg whites to soft peaks. When the sugar has reached the right temperature, pour it slowly onto the egg whites, whisking all the time. Once it all has been added, continue to whisk until cooled. Spread the meringue in the baked pastry shell almost to the top and bake for 10 minutes. During the cooking time, the meringue will rise. Once baked, it will cool and relax back into the case.

Once the pie has cooled to room temperature, spoon the raspberries all over or arrange them upright side by side, covering the whole tart. Dust with powdered sugar, if using, just before serving.

**Note:** The raspberries can be tossed in a pat of butter, water, and sugar to give them a glaze before you spoon them over the tart.

# Pumpkin and Raisin Crumble Tart

*Pumpkin is a vegetable that is reported to have been used for at least 400 years. The members of the pumpkin family run into literally hundreds – summer squash, including yellow squash and zucchini – and winter squash, butternut and acorn, for example. It is best to select smaller pumpkins for this tart for a richer color and flavor. Serve with custard, cream or whipped cream.*

---

### Makes a 10 in (25 cm) deep Tart

8 oz (225 g) Sweet Short Crust Pastry (page 224)

1½ lb (750 g) fresh pumpkin flesh, cut in ½ in (1 cm) dice

½ cup (75 g) raisins

1 tablespoon (25 g) candied mixed peel

½ cup (75 g) soft light brown sugar

2 tablespoons (25 g) butter, melted

1 teaspoon ground mixed spice

### For the Crumble Topping:

3 cups (350 g) all-purpose flour

1 cup (225 g) butter, diced

1 cup (100 g) sugar

100 g (4 oz) chopped mixed nuts e.g. pecan, walnut, almond and hazelnut

Preheat the oven to 400°F/200°C. Butter a 10 in (25 cm), loose-bottomed tart pan that is at least 1–1½ in (2.5–3 cm) deep. Roll and line the pan with the pastry, leaving any excess pastry hanging over the edge. Line with waxed paper or foil and fill with baking beans or rice. Bake for 20–25 minutes until golden.

Once cooked, remove the paper and beans or rice and trim the excess pastry, leaving a neat finish to the tart.

Mix the pumpkin with the raisins, mixed peel, sugar, butter, and allspice. Pack the mixture into the pastry shell.

For the crumble topping, put all the ingredients into an electric mixer, using the beater attachment, or a food processor. It should be slightly over-mixed if anything to give a lumpy, textured crumble mixture. Spoon on top of the pumpkin and bake for 40–45 minutes. The 'lumpy' crumble topping will cook to a crunchy finish with the pumpkin underneath very tender. It is now ready to serve.

# Glazed Lemon and Apple Rice Pies

*I'm basically making a lemon-flavored baked rice dessert, which is going to be served cold in a pastry shell, finished with a crème brûlée style crisp topping. The apples are the dominant feature, adding a coarser texture to the finished dish.*

---

**Makes a 8 in (20 cm) shallow Pie**

8 oz (225 g) Sweet Short Crust Pastry (page 224)
1¼ cup (300 ml) milk
The finely grated zest of 2 lemons
¼ cup (25 g) long-grain rice
3 tablespoons heavy cream
1 lb (450 g) green apples, peeled, cored and diced
1 tablespoon (25 g) candied mixed peel
A pinch of ground cinnamon and nutmeg
¼ cup (50 ml) white wine
A pat of butter
1 tablespoon (15 g) sugar
2 eggs, separated
Powdered sugar, sifted, to glaze

Preheat the oven to 400°F/200°C. Butter a shallow 8 in (20 cm), loose-bottomed tart pan. Roll out the pastry thinly and line the pan with it, leaving any excess pastry hanging over the edge. Line with waxed paper or foil and fill with rice or baking beans. Bake for 20 minutes. Remove the waxed paper or foil and beans or rice. Trim the excess pastry and you will have a neat finish.

Reduce the temperature of the oven to 350°F/180°C. Boil the milk in a pan with the lemon zest, add the rice and slowly simmer for 30–35 minutes.

Remove from the heat. Add the heavy cream, apples, candied peel, cinnamon, nutmeg, white wine, butter, sugar, and egg yolks. Beat the egg whites to soft peaks and gently fold them in.

Spoon the mixture into the pastry shell and bake for 30–35 minutes. Once cooked, remove from the oven and let cool. Dust with powdered sugar and glaze under the broiler or with a gas gun. Repeat the same process with extra powdered sugar to give a thicker, caramelized topping.

**Note:** When glazing, it is best to cover the pastry edge with the foil to prevent it from burning.

# Apricot Pies

*All apricots used in this recipe can be replaced with canned, so there's no excuse for not trying this dessert when fresh apricots are not in season.*

### Makes 6–8 Individual Pies or one 9 in (23 cm) Pie
12 oz (350 g) Sweet Short Crust Pastry (page 224)

### For the Frangipane (Almond Paste):
2 cups (250 g) butter, softened
1¼ cup (250 g) sugar
4 eggs
1½ cup (175 g) ground almonds
½ cup (50 g) flour
4 oz (100 g) dried, ready-to-eat apricots, chopped

### For the Chunky Apricots:
1 lb (450 g) apricots, cut in rough ½ in (1 cm) dice or a 1 can (420 g) of apricot halves

About ¼ cup (50 g) sugar, if using fresh apricots

### For the Topping:
1 apricot half (canned or fresh) per individual tart or 8 for 1 large tart
⅔ cup (150 ml) water
¼ cup (50 g) sugar

### For the Apricot Syrup Glaze:
4 tablespoons apricot jam

### To Serve:
1¼ cup (300 ml) Anglaise Sauce (page 223)

Preheat the oven to 275°F/140°C if you're making one large pie and 325°F/160°C if you're making individual ones. Butter six or eight 3 in (7.5 cm) diameter, 2 in (5 cm) deep tartlet pans or a 9 in (23 cm) loose-bottomed tart pan. Roll out the pastry and use to line the pan(s).

The frangipane (almond paste) can be made in an electric mixer. Cream together the butter and sugar. Add the eggs one at a time until all are incorporated. Mix together the ground almonds and flour and fold into the creamed butter mixture. Add the chopped, dried apricots. Spread a little of this mixture over the base of each pastry-lined pan.

Now make the 'chunky' apricots. If using canned, simply take 8–10 halves and cut into ½ in (1 cm) dice. Divide between the pan(s). If using fresh, mix the chopped apricots with the sugar and cook on a low heat to a chunky purée. Taste, and add more sugar if too sharp. Place a heaping tablespoon of the mixture into the pan(s), leaving at least ¼ in (5 mm) space from the top. Any remaining chunky apricot mixture can be used to serve separately or added to the apricot glaze.

Bake the individual pies for 25–30 minutes and the large one for 1–1¼ hours. During cooking, the frangipane mixture will rise, leaving a domed finish. Remove from the oven and leave to rest for 10 minutes. Lift the pie(s) out of the pan(s).

Prepare the apricots for the topping. If using canned, just drain and cut carefully into thin slices and overlap around the top of the pies. If using fresh fruit, bring the water to a boil with the sugar and simmer for 3–4 minutes. Reserve the syrup. Halve the apricots and remove the pits. Slice very thinly and drop straight into the hot syrup. Remove the pan from the heat and let the syrup cool. Lift the slices out of the syrup (reserve the syrup) and arrange, overlapping, around the top of the pie(s). Dust with powdered sugar and glaze under the grill or with a gas gun to give a 'burned' edge to each slice.

For the apricot syrup glaze, bring the jam to a simmer with 4–6 tablespoons of the reserved syrup from the can or that used for cooking the fresh apricot slices. Simmer for 2–3 minutes to a coating consistency. The glaze is now ready. If you're using canned apricots, simply add water to the jam.

To present the dish, spoon some anglaise sauce in the middle of the plates, place an individual pie or a wedge from the larger pie on top and pour some apricot syrup over. The flavors are just immense.

**Note:** For a richer and thicker glaze, add any remaining chunky apricot mixture to the jam and syrup. Once tender, simply push through a sieve for a deeper glaze.

You can also use pears or peaches for this recipe.

A ¼–½ in (5 mm–1 cm) thick slice of Lemon Genoise Sponge (page 222) can be placed in the base of each pie for an even richer texture and taste.

# Rhubarb and Ginger Shortcake Dessert

*This classic dessert is built up like* mille-feuilles: *extra-thin ginger shortcakes are layered with rhubarb pieces and pastry cream. The pastry cream works very well with this dish, but simple whipped cream will also do the trick.*

---

### Serves 4

1½ lb (750 g) rhubarb

2 tablespoons (25 g) butter

¾ cup (150 g) sugar

4 tablespoons ginger ale

Powdered sugar (optional)

⅔ cup (150 ml) Pastry Cream
   (page 231), or whipped cream

### For the Cookies

1¼ cup (150 g) flour

1 teaspoon ground ginger

8 tablespoons (100 g) butter

½ cup (50 g) powdered sugar

¼ in (50 g) ginger, finely chopped

2 egg yolks

Preheat the oven to 400°F/200°C.

To make the cookies, sift the flour with the ground ginger. Rub the butter into the flour. Add the sugar and the ginger. Mix in the egg yolks and work to a smooth dough. Leave to rest for 20 minutes. Roll the dough very thinly. Using a pastry cutter of 3 in (7.5 cm) diameter, cut into about 12 discs, allowing three per portion. Place the discs on a waxed paper lined baking sheet and allow to rest for 10 minutes. Bake for 15–18 minutes. They will be golden brown and crisp. Remove from the oven and leave to cool.

Take 1¼ lb (650 g) of the rhubarb and, if it's young and tender, just wash and cut into ¾ in (2 cm) thick rounds. If it feels stringy, lightly peel it and then cut into rounds. Melt the butter in a large saucepan and add the rhubarb rounds. Stir for 2–3 minutes before adding the sugar and ginger ale. The rhubarb will cook and become tender within 3–5 minutes. Once cooked, remove four-fifths from the pan and set aside to cool. This is the rhubarb filling. Continue to cook the remaining one-fifth rhubarb to a purée and then push through a sieve to give you a rhubarb syrup. Finely dice the remaining 4 oz (100 g) raw rhubarb, add to the syrup to give it some texture and bring to a simmer for 2–3 minutes. Remove from the stove and leave to cool. If the syrup now tastes too sharp, add a sprinkling of powdered sugar.

To serve per portion: put the rhubarb filling around the edge of two of the cookies, leaving a narrow border. Spoon some pastry cream or cream in the center of the rhubarb. Stack the rhubarb covered biscuits one on top of the other (so you have two layers of rhubarb and cream) and finish by topping with one last cookie. Dust the top biscuit with powdered sugar. Spoon around the rhubarb syrup and serve.

**Note:** The cookies can be made without ginger. Fresh raspberries or strawberrries can also be used.

# Wagon Wheel® Dessert

*This recipe came from memories of canteen days at school. The Wagon Wheel® had just come out in Britain and it was a revelation: a chocolate topping encasing two cookies, filled with marshmallow. They are still available and seeing them again gave me the inspiration to turn them into a dessert. This might remind you of its American counterpart, S'mores.*

*If you want a perfect finishing touch to your dessert, I suggest you double the topping quantities and apply the chocolate in stages. The chocolate keeps the cookies fresh for days, so this dessert can be made in advance.*

---

**Serves 6**

Raspberry or strawberry jam,
   for spreading

**For the Marshmallow:**

2 cups (225 g) powdered sugar
⅓ cup (85 ml) water
2 tablespoons (25 g) corn syrup
½ oz (15 g ) leaf gelatin, soaked in
   water, or 1½ x 11.7 g sachets of
   powdered gelatine, dissolved in
   4 tablespoons of water and then
   gently heated until clear
1 egg white
Cornstarch, for dusting

**For the Cookies
  (Makes 12–15):**

1 cup (225 g) butter
⅓ cup (75 g) sugar
1 egg yolk
1 tablespoon maple or golden syrup
1¼ cup (250 g) flour

**For the Chocolate Topping:**

4 oz (100 g) good quality milk
   chocolate
⅔ cup (150 ml) heavy cream
4 tablespoons (50 g ) butter

Preheat the oven to 350°F/180°C. First make the marshmallow. Mix the powdered sugar, water and glucose together and bring to a boil. Simmer for 2–3 minutes. Add the gelatin and as soon as it has fully dissolved pour onto the egg white in a mixing bowl. Beat immediately (preferably with an electric mixer) to a thick, creamy consistency.

Dust well a large, shallow baking tray or dish (it must be at least ½ in/1 cm deep and big enough to allow you to cut six 3½ in discs/8 cm) with the cornstarch and pour in the marshmallow mix. Refrigerate and leave to set for 1–1½ hours. Once set, cut out six 3½ in (8 cm) discs with a plain cookie cutter and keep ready for the finished dessert.

Next, make the cookies. Cream together the butter and sugar and then add the egg yolk and corn syrup. Fold in the flour and mix to a smooth dough. Refrigerate for 15–20 minutes.

Roll out to ⅛ in (2–3 mm) thick. Cut out twelve 3½ in (8 cm) discs, allowing two per

portion, and bake for 10–15 minutes until golden. Remove from the oven and allow to cool.

To make the chocolate topping, melt the chocolate with the cream in a bowl over simmering water. Once melted, add the butter and stir in. Remove from the heat to prevent the butter from becoming too liquid. The butter should have melted and emulsified into the chocolate mixture. If the mixture is a little too thin, leave to cool to thicken slightly.

Spread some of the jam fairly generously onto four cookies. Place a marshmallow disc on each and then spread some more jam on top. Finish with another cookie on top to create a 'sandwich.'

For a perfect chocolate finish, spoon on the chocolate mixture in stages. First, place the cookies on a wire rack and set over a baking tray or plate and spoon some of the chocolate topping over to cover completely. Refrigerate for 15–20 minutes until set. Remove and turn the cookies upside down on the rack. Spoon some more of the chocolate over the cookies to cover. Refrigerate again until set. Remove and spoon over any remaining chocolate again (you might need to reuse some of the topping from the tray) for a smoother, thicker finish. Refrigerate and leave to set.

For an even more luscious ending, serve with a drizzle of pouring cream.

**Note:** This dessert can be made more fruity and even richer by placing fresh raspberries or strawberries on top of the marshmallow and finishing as above.

# Pumpernickel Bread and Butter Dessert

*Pumpernickel is a dark rye bread that tastes of sweet molasses flavor. It is best to find a pumpernickel bread that has a light texture and one that's not too dense and heavy. As for the dessert, I couldn't resist adding yet another bread and butter dessert recipe! This one is very rich, fudgy, and sweet.*

---

**Serves 6**

10 slices of soft pumpernickel bread
   (crusts can be left on)
4 tablespoons (50 g) unsalted butter
¼ cup (50 g) chopped prunes
8 egg yolks

2 tablespoons soft light brown sugar
2 tablespoons dark molasses
1¼ cup (300 ml) heavy cream
1¼ cup (300 ml) milk
4 tablespoons sugar

Preheat the oven to 350°F/180°C. Butter the bread and lay five slices, overlapping, in a baking dish. Sprinkle with the prunes and top with the remaining overlapping slices. Whisk the egg yolks with the brown sugar and molasses for 1–2 minutes until paler in colour. Bring the heavy cream and milk to a boil and pour onto the egg yolk mixture. Pour the custard over the bread and leave to stand for 20 minutes. During this time, the bread will soak up and absorb some of the custard.

Put the baking dish in a baking tray, half filled with warm water. Bake for 20–30 minutes. The custard will have thickened and almost have reached setting point but will still be liquid in the center. Remove from the oven and baking tray. Dust with sugar and glaze under the broiler or with a gas gun.

**Note:** The chopped prunes can be substituted with raisins.

# Steamed Lemon Dumpling Desserts

*These are more than just simple steamed desserts. The rich moistness and flavor of the lemon and suet dough bites into your taste buds. These go very well when just calmed with a spoonful of cream. If you're a real lemon lover, then serve with a rich lemon custard (Lemon Anglaise Sauce, page 223), or simply with a trickle of maple syrup.*

**Serves 6**

2½ cups (175 g) white breadcrumbs
1 cup (175 g) suet
¾ cup (175 g) sugar

1½ cups (175 g) self rising flour
The finely grated zest of 4 lemons
The juice of 2 lemons
2 eggs, beaten

Butter and lightly flour six ⅔ cup (150 ml) individual ramekins. Mix together the breadcrumbs, suet, sugar, flour, and grated lemon zest. Bind the dough together with the lemon juice and beaten eggs. Fill each ramekin three-quarters full and top with buttered foil, leaving enough space for the dumplings to rise.

Steam on a trivet in a large pan of boiling water (keeping a check on the water level) covered with a lid for 40-45 minutes. The desserts can now be turned out and served.

**Note:** You can of course use the juice and zest of oranges or limes to give you a different flavored dessert.

# Lemon and Golden Raisin Savarin
## *served with Lemon Yogurt Ice Cream*

*You can't find a more moist cake to eat than a savarin dipped in a syrup. The lemony flavor can be changed to orange or lime or left plain (without the fruit juices) and garnished with fruit.*

**Serves 6**

Lemon Yogurt Ice Cream
  (page 175), to serve

**For the Savarin:**
2 teaspoons (10 g) sugar
¾ oz (20 g) fresh yeast or ¼ oz (7 g)
  dried easy-blend yeast
¼ cup (50 ml) tepid milk
3 eggs
2¼ cups (250 g) all-purpose flour
⅔ cup (100 g) golden raisins

¼ lb (135 g) butter, diced and
  softened

**For the Syrup:**
⅔ cup (150 ml) lemon juice
Very thinly sliced julienne strips of
  lemon zest (optional)
1¼ cups (300 ml) water
½ cup (100 g) sugar
2 cinnamon sticks (optional)
1 vanilla pod or 1 teaspoon of
  vanilla extract

Preheat the oven to 375°F/190°C. Butter six 3 in (7.5 cm) savarin rings or one 9 in (23 cm) ring. Work the sugar and fresh yeast together until liquid and then add to the instant milk. Beat the eggs and add to the milk mix. Sift the flour and mix with the raisins. If using yeast, just add it to the flour and golden raisins. Pour the yeast or egg mix into the flour and work to a dough. Spoon the diced butter onto the dough and cover. Keep in a warm place, allowing to proof for 20–30 minutes. Once proofed, punch down, incorporating the butter. Scrape the mixture into a large nylon piping bag, pipe into the prepared ring(s) and bake for 20–25 minutes. Once cooked, remove from the oven and let cool.

The next stage is to make a syrup for soaking. It is from this syrup that the savarin will pick up the rich lemon flavor. The lemon julienne strips, if using, must first be blanched in fresh boiling water three times. This will take out any bitterness. Mix all of the other ingredients together and bring to a boil with the addition of the lemon zest. Simmer for 5 minutes. Remove the cinnamon and vanilla pod. The lemon zest can also be removed and kept separate in some syrup. Spoon some of the warm syrup over the savarins and leave to soak in for a few minutes before turning out onto serving plates. Any remaining lemon syrup can be reduced by half. This will result in a thick, very rich, lemony syrup to decorate the savarin(s).

To present the dish, spoon some lemon yogurt ice cream in the center of the savarins, drizzle the reduced lemon syrup over and place the lemon zest julienne on top.

**Note:** For an even better finish you can serve with Golden Raisin Syrup Sauce (page 228) or add chopped fresh mint to the lemon syrup.

# Baked Apple and Lime Syrup Dessert

*This is a classic Sunday lunch dessert. It is nice and easy to make and will suit the whole family. The lime flavor can be swapped with lemon or orange (add a spoonful or two of marmalade to the sponge mixture, if using orange) and other fruits can be added to the apples – raspberries, blackberries, red currants and so on. I like to serve this dessert with custard, cream or crème fraîche.*

---

**Serves 6**

6 green dessert apples, peeled and quartered

8 tablespoons (100 g) butter, melted

A generous pinch of ground cinnamon

2 tablespoons (25 g) sugar

2 eggs

¼ cup (50 g) soft light brown sugar packed

2 tablespoons corn syrup

6 tablespoons milk

2 cups (225 g) self rising flour

The finely grated zest and juice of 2 limes

Preheat the oven to 350°F/180°C. Butter a 8–10 in (20–25 cm) ovenproof baking dish. Remove all cores from the apple quarters and halve each quarter, giving you eight pieces per apple. Using a tablespoon or two of the melted butter, fry the apples with the cinnamon and sugar for 2–3 minutes. Remove from the heat and allow to cool. This will soften the apples. Place the apples in the dish.

Beat the eggs with the light brown sugar and corn syrup. Stir in the remaining melted butter and the milk. Sift the flour into the egg mixture and whisk it in with the lime juice and zest.

Pour the batter over the apples and bake for 25–30 minutes. Once golden brown and baked, glaze the dessert with a mixture of powdered sugar and lemon or lime juice. Simply mix the sugar with the juice until a thin icing consistency is achieved. Spread over the dessert and serve. Apricot jam or a dusting of powdered sugar can also be used.

# Roast Peaches or Nectarines *with*
## *Blackberry Ice Cream*

*Apples or bananas are probably the most common fruits that are 'roasted' yielding baked apples and barbecued bananas. Both are excellent, but I thought I would introduce another two. Roasting whole peaches or nectarines keeps all of the fruit texture and the flavor gets even better. The blackberry ice cream finishes the dish off beautifully.*

---

**Serves 4**

4 whole peaches or nectarines,
   skin left on
4 tablespoons (50 g) butter
2 tablespoons (25 g) soft light
   brown sugar packed
4 tablespoons of water
Blackberry Ice cream (page 161) or
   store bought vanilla ice cream, to
   serve

Preheat the oven to 400°F/200°C.

Heat an ovenproof frying pan with 2 tablespoons (25 g) of the butter. Add the fruits and fry for 4–5 minutes until they start to become golden brown. Turn occasionally. Arrange the fruits stalk-side down and bake for 15–20 minutes (20–25 if underripe). Remove from the oven and lift the fruits from the pan. Pour off any excess butter and wipe the pan clean. Add the remaining butter with the sugar and water. Bring to a simmer and return the fruit to the pan. Simmer and reduce the syrup while rolling the fruit to coat them with the glaze. Once the syrup has reached a coating consistency, put the peaches or nectarines on serving plates and drizzle any remaining syrup over. Serve a large scoop of blackberry ice cream next to the fruit.

**Note:** Extra syrup can be made by doubling the sugar, water and remaining butter quantities.

You don't have to serve homemade ice cream: a good quality, store bought variety will also go very well.

The fruits can be glazed with warm honey or golden syrup.

The peaches or nectarines will also go very well with custard and/or cream.

A scoop of vanilla ice cream with Raspberry Syrup (page 229) will give you 'roast peach Melba'!

DESSERTS

# Char-broiled Glazed Pumpkin Slices
## with Lemon Sherbet and Cream

*This dish works wonders on a barbecue grill. The real charred flavor is good and strong and is nicely balanced with the sweetness from the glaze, giving a bittersweet finish. All of these tastes are sharpened with a spoonful of the lemon sherbet, balanced by the fresh cream. I think I've said enough!*

*This recipe doesn't have to rely on a barbecue. A small ridged, cast-iron grill pan can also be used. If you don't have either, simply pan fry and glaze and you'll still be very happy with the results.*

---

**Serves 4**
1–1½ lb (450–750 g) small pumpkin
2 tablespoons (25 g) butter, melted
Powdered sugar, sifted

**To Serve:**
4 portions of Lemon Sherbet
  (page 166)
⅔–1¼ cups (150–300 ml) extra thick
  heavy cream

Cut the pumpkin into 8–12 wedges. Remove the seeds and with a sharp knife cut away the skin. Brush each slice with butter and place them on the hot barbecue or grill pan. The pumpkin will only need 7–8 minutes before being turned; repeat with the same cooking time for the other side. The pumpkin will now be tender without being overcooked.

Lay the slices on a buttered baking tray and dust heavily with powdered sugar. Put the tray under a very hot broiler and the sugar will begin to caramelize. Once the sugar has totally melted and begins to bubble, remove the tray, dust heavily again with powdered sugar and slide back under the broiler. This time, the powdered sugar will brown and begin to form a sweet crust. Once totally golden and crisp, the pumpkin wedges are ready. Arrange them on plates with a large scoop of the lemon sherbet and a good spoonful of extra thick heavy cream.

**Note:** A third dusting of powdered sugar and glazing will give an even crispier topping. Another form of glaze is to omit the sugar and simply drizzle golden syrup or honey over the broiled pumpkin.

Lime sherbet also goes very well with the pumpkin slices.

# Clotted Cream Brûlée

*Crème brûlée – thick vanilla custard topped with a caramel glaze – is a dessert I cannot resist. Imagine eating a crème brûlée that has clotted cream in the middle: you can taste it mingling with the custard in every bite. There's no need to imagine any more – the recipe is here!*

---

**Serves 6**

10 egg yolks

½ cup (100 g)  sugar

2 cups (450 ml) heavy cream

⅔ cup (150 ml) milk

2 vanilla pods, split lengthways, or
    2–3 drops of vanilla essence

6 heaping tablespoons clotted
    cream

powdered sugar, sifted

Cream together the egg yolks and sugar. Boil the cream, milk and vanilla pods or essence. Pour the vanilla cream onto the egg yolks and sugar and then pour this mixture into a bowl. Cook over a pan of simmering water, stirring occasionally, until thickened. This will take 20–25 minutes.

Once thickened, remove from the stove and use to half-fill all six ⅔ cup (150 ml) ramekins. Refrigerate until set. The remaining crème brûlée mix can be left to cool. Once the first half of the brûlée has set, spoon the clotted cream on top into the center. Pour over the remaining brûlée mix. Return the ramekins to the fridge to set completely.

Dust heavily with powdered sugar and glaze under the grill or with a gas gun. Dust with more powdered sugar and finish glazing. The clotted cream brûlées are now crispy on top and ready to eat.

# Crème Chiboust *with Fresh Fruit Salad*

*Crème chiboust is the cream used to finish a Gâteau St Honoré. Chiboust was the name of the chef who first put together the St Honoré and the cream to go with it. It is a pastry cream, finished with Italian meringue. In this dessert, it is flavored with lemon, frozen, cut into shapes and caramelized very quickly under a hot broiler and then served with a delicious fresh fruit salad.*

---

**Serves 6–8**

⅔ cup (150 ml) lemon juice, plus the grated zest of 2 lemons

⅔ cup (150 ml) heavy cream

4 tablespoons  sugar

2 tablespoons (25 g) cornstarch

6 egg yolks

1 x 11.7 g packet powdered gelatin, dissolved in 3 tablespoons of cold water for 5 minutes

**For the Italian Meringue:**

1 cup (200 g) sugar

¼ cup (50 ml) water

6 egg whites

**For the Fruit Salad:**

Selection of soft fruit e.g. raspberries, strawberries, peaches, bananas, kiwi fruit, oranges, melon, blackberries and/or blackcurrants, prepared as necessary

⅔ cup (150 ml) Raspberry or Strawberry Syrup (page 229)

Boil together the lemon juice, zest and cream. Mix the sugar, cornstarch and egg yolks together in a bowl and pour in the hot juice and cream mixture, whisking constantly. Return the mixture to the pan and cook on a low heat for 8–10 minutes until thickened (do not allow to boil). Dissolve the gelatin over a gentle heat until clear and add to the thickened lemon custard.

For the meringue, boil together the sugar and water to around 240°F/121–130°C, which takes 2–3 minutes. While the sugar is boiling, whisk the egg whites to firm peaks. Gradually pour a boiled sugar onto the egg whites, whisking all the time; slowly continue to whisk the egg whites until just warm. Fold the meringue into the custard. Line a large baking tray with plastic wrap and spoon in the chiboust cream (you need it to be about 1–1½ in/2.5–3 cm deep). Freeze until firm.

Once frozen, remove and cut into shapes as required. I like to serve these cut in rectangles 3½–4 × 2 in (8–10 × 5 cm). Re-freeze for 2–3 hours.

Prepare the fruit for the salad. Arrange on serving plates and pour 2–3 tablespoons of syrup over each portion.

Glaze the tops of crème chiboust shapes with a gas gun or under the broiler. Put the shapes on top of the fruit. After a few moments, the chiboust will soften. It's now ready to serve.

# Warm Cherry Chocolate Cakes

*You can use fresh or canned cherries in this recipe. If using fresh, cook them in a small pat of butter with a sprinkling of sugar, just enough to soften them lightly. You can leave out the cherries and just add extra grated chocolate to create a melting consistency.*

---

**Serves 4**

⅔ cup (100 g) fresh pitted or canned cherries, quartered

8 tablespoons (100 g) butter, plus a small pat

⅔ cup (120 g) sugar

A drop of kirsch (optional)

4 oz (100 g) bittersweet chocolate, chopped, plus 1–2 oz (25–50 g) bittersweet chocolate, grated (optional)

½ cup (50 g) all-purpose flour

3 eggs, separated

**To Serve:**

Extra thick heavy cream (optional)

Powdered sugar, sifted (optional)

Finely grated bittersweet chocolate (optional)

---

Preheat the oven to 350°F/180°C. Butter four 3 in (7.5 cm) diameter individual tartlet pans or one 6–7 in (15–18 cm) diameter tart pan. Line the base(s) with waxed paper.

Melt the small pat of butter, add the cherries, 1 tablespoon (15 g) sugar and kirsch, if using. Cook on a high heat for 1–2 minutes and then leave to cool. Melt the chocolate in a bowl over simmering water or in the microwave. Once melted, add the butter and stir until emulsified. Stir in the flour, the remaining sugar and cherries. Beat the egg yolks until pale and slightly thickened and add to the chocolate mixture.

Beat the egg whites to soft peaks and carefully fold them in. If using extra grated chocolate, add it now. Spoon into the prepared cake pans so they are just over half full. Individual cakes will now take 15–20 minutes to cook; a large cake will take 30–35 minutes.

Once cooked, remove from the oven and leave to cool to just warm. Remove from the pans and peel off the paper. Carefully cut off the crusty tops. Spoon extra thick heavy cream on top of the cake while still warm and place the crusty tops back on. The cake has a fudgy texture and is sensational to eat when served warm with the cream melting in. I like to decorate the plates with a dusting of powdered sugar and a sprinkling of finely grated chocolate.

**Note:** The cherries can be also left in halves; double the quantity to 1⅓ cups (225 g) and sauté with the butter and sugar. Flambé with brandy or kirsch and spoon over the cakes with the cream on top.

The Fruit Jam Sauce on page 230 can also be used: warm blackcurrant jam sauce works wonderfully.

# Mini Madeira Prune Cakes *with Madeira Sherbet and Syrup*

*This is a basic Madeira cake recipe, but with the addition of chopped prunes. The prunes give another flavor and a moist texture. This recipe doesn't have to be for individual cakes; an 8 in (20 cm) cake pan can be used and the prunes can be left in or out.*

---

**Serves 6**

1½ cups (175 g) butter
¾ cup (175 g) sugar
3 eggs, beaten
1½ cups (175 g) all-purpose flour
The finely grated zest of 2 lemons
¾ cup (175 g) chopped prunes

**To Serve:**

6 portions of Madeira Sherbet
(page 169)
12 tablespoons Madeira Syrup
(page 228)

Preheat the oven to 350°F/180°C. Butter six pastry rings, 3 in (7.5 cm) in diameter and 2 in (5 cm) deep. Alternatively, use six shallower 4 in (10 cm) diameter, ½ in (1 cm) deep tartlet pans or an 8 in (20 cm) round cake pan. Put the pastry rings on a waxed paper-lined baking sheet or line the bottoms of the individual pans or larger pan with waxed paper.

Beat the butter and sugar together until very light and creamy. Beat the eggs in a bowl over a pan of simmering water until thick and pale in color to a thick cream-like consistency. Fold the eggs into the butter mix and then sift in the flour. Stir in the lemon zest and chopped prunes. Divide between the rings or pans and bake for 20–25 minutes. Leave the cake(s) to cool for 10 minutes. Lift them from their mold(s) and peel off the paper if necessary.

Place the warm Madeira cakes on plates and garnish with a scoop of Madeira sherbet and drizzles of Madeira syrup.

**Note:** Cinnamon Ice Cream (page 169) also goes very well with the Madeira cake.
The cakes are very nice to offer with afternoon tea.

# Creamy Fried Slice *with Blackberry-jam Sauce and Extra Thick Cream*

*The fried slice is a ¾ in (2 cm) piece of brioche, soaked in a cream, egg and sugar mixture and then fried in butter. It's served with a loose, fresh blackberry-jam sauce spooned on top with melting extra thick heavy cream. Yum!*

**Serves 4**

¾ in (4 x 2 cm) slices of homemade or store bought brioche ( a good plain, soft loaf will also work)
4 eggs
4 tablespoons sugar
4 tablespoons heavy cream
4 tablespoons (50 g) butter
8 heaping tablespoons warm blackberry (or other fruit) Fruit Jam Sauce (page 230), warmed
Lightly whipped heavy cream, to serve

Whisk together the eggs, sugar and cream. Soak both sides of the brioche in the cream for a few minutes. Melt the butter in a large frying pan on a medium heat. Fry the slices for 2–3 minutes on both sides. This will give a golden brown, slightly crisp texture, leaving an almost warm 'doughnut' consistency inside. Put the slices on plates and spoon the warm jam sauce on top. Finish with lightly whipped cream and serve.

**Note:** Add grated nutmeg to the cream for a spicier finish.

# Date and Orange Mascarpone Fritters

*These are best made by using the sweet, thick, fleshy medjool dates which grow in Egypt and California. Although they are on the expensive side, they are worth it. The fritters are made by pitting the medjool dates and filling them with orange zest flavored mascarpone. Once battered and deep-fried, the mascarpone just melts in the mouth as you bite through the batter. I normally serve these with Cinnamon Ice Cream (page 169), along with either Orange and Rum or Golden Raisin Syrup (pages 227 and 228).*

**Serves 4**

20 medjool dates

The finely grated zest of 2 oranges

8 tablespoons mascarpone

all-purpose flour, for dusting

Oil, for deep-frying

Vanilla or Cinnamon Ice Cream
   (page 169), or cream, to serve

**For the Batter:**

1¼ cups (300 ml) sweet cider

1 cup (100 g) all-purpose flour

2 tablespoons (25 g) sugar

Heat the oil for deep-frying to 375°F/190°C or until a cube of day-old bread browns in 30 seconds.

Split the dates along one side and remove the pits. Mix the orange zest with the mascarpone. Make the batter by whisking all the ingredients together. Stuff the dates with the mascarpone mixture and push back into shape. Dust the dates with all-purpose flour and then coat with the batter. Carefully place the dates in the hot oil. Cook for 5–6 minutes until completely crisp and golden. Lift from the fat onto paper towel to absorb any excess oil.

Serve the fritters with the cinnamon ice cream and syrup, or just with vanilla ice cream.

# Chocolate Brownies

*This is the recipe I use for the Bourbon Cookie dessert (page 210) to add another texture to the cookies. But to eat them as actual brownies, I've added toasted, chopped nuts, and I've offered a recipe for a chocolate icing to finish them off. The ingredients are many, but that's what gives you the extra flavors.*

---

**Makes 12 Slices**

½ lb (225 g) butter

1¼ cups (150 g) cocoa powder

4 eggs

2¼ cups (450 g) sugar

1¼ cups (150 g) all-purpose flour

2 teaspoons vanilla extract

2 tablespoons strong coffee

1 cup (100 g) mixed chopped nuts
  e.g. hazelnuts, pecans, walnuts
  and/or almonds, toasted

**For the Chocolate Icing:**

4 oz (100 g) semisweet chocolate,
  chopped

2 tablespoons strong coffee

8 tablespoons (100 g) unsalted
  butter, softened

Preheat the oven to 350°F/180°C. Butter a 10 in (25 cm) square or round cake pan and line the base with waxed paper.

Melt the butter and mix with the cocoa powder. Whisk together the eggs and caster sugar and add to the cocoa mixture. Add all the remaining ingredients and pour into the cake pan. Bake for 15–20 minutes. Let cool before turning out of the pan and peeling off the paper. Dust with cocoa powder, leave as it is or top with the chocolate spread.

For the icing, melt the chocolate with the coffee in a bowl over warm simmering water. Once it has a smooth, creamy consistency, remove from the heat and beat in the butter, a tablespoon at a time. Leave to cool. Once at a spreading consistency, cover the brownies. These can now be cut into wedges or squares.

# Bourbon Cookies

*Another cookie idea turned into a dessert recipe, Bourbon cookies are definitely a dessert for chocoholics. The brownie between the chocolate ganache and cookie gives you more texture, more flavor and lots more chocolate. The cookie goes very well with Coffee Anglaise Sauce (page 223) and/or a drizzling of Coffee Syrup (page 230).*

**Serves 8**

1 quantity Chocolate Brownies (page 209), omitting the nuts and chocolate spread

**For the Cookies (Makes 16):**

10 tablespoons (150 g) butter
¾ cup (150g) sugar, plus extra for sprinkling
3 cups (300 g) self rising flour
A pinch of salt

8 tablespoons cocoa powder
1 egg, beaten
8–10 teaspoons milk

**For the Ganache:**

8 oz (225 g) semisweet chocolate, chopped
1 cup (250 ml) heavy cream
2 egg yolks
2 tablespoons (25 g) sugar

Preheat the oven to 350°F/180°C. Make the brownies and spread into a large, shallow baking tray to give a layer ¼–½ in (5 mm–1 cm) thick. Bake for 7 minutes to leave the brownies very moist.

**1** Make the cookie mix, roll out, cut into 16 cookies and make 15–18 holes in the top. Bake for 10 minutes.

**2** For the ganache, melt the chocolate with half the cream. Whisk the egg yolks and sugar together and add to the chocolate mix. Lightly whisk and add the remaining cream.

**3** Cut the brownies into rectangles slightly smaller than the cookies.

**4** Layer the cookie with ganache, brownie, ganache, another brownie, more ganache and top with a cookie.

For the cookies, cream together the butter and sugar. Sift together the flour, salt and cocoa powder. Add the egg to the creamed butter and then beat in the flour and cocoa mixture. Soften with the milk. Wrap the dough in plastic wrap and refrigerate for 20-30 minutes.

Roll out the cookie dough on a lightly floured surface to ⅛ in (2–3 mm) thick. Cut into 16 cookies, 4 in (10 cm) long by 2 in (5 cm) wide. Transfer to a waxed paper lined baking sheet. Make 15–18 small holes in the top (a toothpick will do the job) and bake for 10 minutes. Once baked and while still warm, sprinkle with sugar. Let cool.

For the ganache, melt the chocolate with half the cream. Whisk the egg yolks and sugar together until they hold a thick ribbon trail. Lightly whip the remaining cream. Mix the egg yolk and sugar mix with the melted chocolate cream. Fold in the whipped cream and leave to cool to a piping consistency.

Turn half the baked cookies over and spread very thinly with some ganache (to hold it to the brownie cake). Cut the brownies into rectangles just ⅛ in (2 mm) smaller than the cookies and put them on the ganache covered cookies. Pipe a ¼–½ in (5 mm–1 cm) layer of ganache on top. Put another rectangle of brownie on the ganache. Lightly spread with ganache and finish with the top cookie. Now put them on plates and dust with sugar.

**Note:** Finely grated orange zest can be added to the ganache and brownie cake recipes (1 orange for each), plus a splash of Grand Marnier, to give you a chocolate-orange Bourbon Cookie.

# Banana Fool *with Warm Chocolate Sauce*

*This is a quick dessert to make and can be made with the fruit of your choice – peaches, mangoes, summer berries, etc. The fool can be served in glasses or ramekins. If ramekins, the chocolate sauce can be replaced with grated semisweet or milk chocolate on top.*

**Serves 6**

**For the Fool:**
8 over ripe bananas
1 tablespoon lemon juice
1 egg white (optional)
¼ cup (50 g) sugar
1¼ cups (300 ml) heavy cream

**For the Chocolate Sauce:**
4 oz (100 g) semisweet chocolate,
  chopped
⅔ cup (150 ml) heavy cream
1 tablespoon (15 g) butter

To make the fool, purée the bananas in a food processor with the lemon juice. Beat the egg white, if using, to soft peaks and then add the sugar and continue to beat to a meringue stage. Whip the heavy cream to soft peaks and fold with the meringue into the puréed bananas. Pipe or spoon into glasses, leaving at least ½ in (1 cm) of space from the top for the sauce. Refrigerate to set.

For the chocolate sauce, melt the chocolate with the heavy cream in a bowl over warm water. Once melted, add the butter, remove from the heat and stir in. Once at a warm temperature, pour into the glasses and serve.

# Hot Chocolate 'Cappuccino'

*This isn't a dessert but an absolutely fabulous drink. It was made for me a little while ago. The flavor and smooth, silky consistency were so good I had to have the recipe! I've made a couple of changes and topped it with soft whipped cream. You can either dust with cocoa or scatter over lots of finely grated bittersweet chocolate.*

---

**Serves 4**

4 oz (100 g) semisweet chocolate, broken into pieces

1 oz (25 g) milk chocolate, broken into pieces

2½ cups (600 ml) milk

6 tablespoons heavy cream

A splash of coffee extract (optional)

4 mugs!

**For the Topping:**

⅔ cup (150 ml) heavy cream, lightly whipped

Cocoa powder or ¼–½ cup (25–50 g) finely grated semisweet or milk chocolate

Melt the chocolates in a bowl over a pan of simmering water. While melting, bring the milk to a boil. Add the 6 tablespoons of heavy cream to the chocolate and take it off the heat. Mix the hot milk and melted chocolate cream together, adding the coffee extract, if using. Pour into the mugs and spoon the whipped cream carefully on top. Dust with cocoa or grated chocolate and serve.

**Note:** This can become a strong liqueur chocolate by adding a few measures of Baileys, whisky, brandy, rum, Cointreau, Grand Marnier, Drambuie, or any other liqueur you like.

The recipe can be made entirely with bittersweet chocolate for a really rich chocolate flavor. However, this does make it quite bitter, so if you are going to use this chocolate, add 2 tablespoons (25 g) of packed, light brown sugar to the milk.

# Homemade Brioche

*Brioche is a buttery loaf that can be used in or to accompany many courses: a toasted slice with pâté, stuffed with cheese, fried and topped with sweet peppers and olives, or made into brioche bread and butter dessert. This recipe makes quite a large amount – three loaves – but I think it is very practical because you can freeze two loaves for later. Perhaps you could make them go even further by cutting all three loaves in half and freezing five halves.*

---

**Makes 2lb (3 x 1 kg) Loaves**
2 cups (500 ml) milk, warmed
4½ oz (120 g) fresh yeast
4 cups (500 g) cake flour
12 eggs

½ cup (120 g) sugar
2 tablespoons (30 g) salt
3¾ lb (1.7 kg) butter, melted

Preheat the oven to 350°F/180°C. Butter three 2 lb (1 kg) (9 x 5 x 3 inches) loaf pans and line the bottoms with waxed paper.

Dissolve the yeast in the warm milk and leave it somewhere warm until it goes frothy. Add to the 4 cups (500 g) flour, cover with a cloth and leave to proof in a warm place until doubled in size.

Once doubled in volume, add the eggs, flour, sugar and salt and mix well. Beat the butter into the dough mix and then divide the mixture between the three pans. Let it rise in a warm place for 20 minutes.

Bake until golden for 30–40 minutes. Remove the loaves from the oven and let them cool for 10 minutes before lifting from the pans to cool completely.

**Note:** For a glossier finish, brush the loaves with beaten egg 5 minutes before the end of baking.

For a Prune and Walnut Brioche, add ¾ cup (225 g) chopped prunes and 1¼ cups (175g) chopped walnuts per loaf. Add the prunes with the eggs. This enables them to be broken into the mixture and the prune flavor to spread throughout. Add the walnuts along with the butter and the job is done.

If you wish to make only one of the loaves into a prune and walnut one, add both ingredients to a third of the dough once it's made and knead them in. The prune and walnut brioche goes very well creamy fried with fruit sauce, as on page 206. It is also a perfect accompaniment to cheese. The quantity of prunes and walnuts used for one loaf will give you a very rich taste of prune and nuts. For a slightly less rich finish, simply halve the quantity of both these ingredients.

The number of loaves can be changed in various ways:
1. Make 1 lb (6 x 450 g) (8 x 3 x 2½ inch) loaves
2. Cut the recipe in half for 1 lb (3 x 450 g) (8 x 3 x 2½ inch) loaves
3. Make a third of the recipe for 2 lb (1 x 1 kg) (9 x 5 x 3 inches) or 1 lb (2 x 450 g) (8 x 3 x 2½ inch) loaves.

# Fruity Ravioli

*It's dessert time for pasta! These homemade ravioli, filled with fresh or canned fruits, can also be topped with Crisp 'Parmesan' Lemon Crumbs (page 231), or drizzled with a fruity syrup and served with custard, ice cream or cream: a fun dessert with fun flavors.*

**Serves 4**

⅔ cup (150 ml) Basic Stock Syrup (page 227)

Cream, sour cream or Anglaise Sauce (page 223), to serve

**For the Ravioli:**

3 cups (350 g) fine semolina

2 eggs

1 scraped vanilla pod or 1 teaspoon of strong vanilla extract

The finely grated zest of 1 lemon, lime or orange (optional)

Powdered sugar, sifted, for rolling

**For the Filling:**

1½–2 lb (750–900 g) soft fruits e.g. apricots, peaches, mangoes or Summer fruits (canned fruits can be used)

A pat of butter

¼ cup (25–50 g) sugar

Soft fruits, mint leaves and lemon or orange zest, to garnish

Work the egg into the semolina with the vanilla and zest. Once worked into a dough, cover and let rest for 15–20 minutes.

Meanwhile, to cook the filling, halve or chop any of the soft fruits that need it (berries can be left whole). Melt the butter, add the fruits and 2 tablespoons (25 g) of sugar. Cook until pulpy but still with some texture left in the fruit. Taste for sweetness – if it's too sharp, add the remaining sugar. Let cool. If using canned fruits, just drain and chop them.

The pasta can now be rolled out very thinly (about ⅛ in/3 mm thick) with a pasta machine, if you have one, or by hand on plenty of powdered sugar. Cut the pasta into 4 in (10 cm) discs with a plain biscuit cutter, allowing 2–3 ravioli (4–6 discs) per portion. Put a tablespoon or two of fruit in the center. Brush water around the outside rim and press a lid on top. Add any remaining fruits to the stock syrup and warm to make a purée. Push through a sieve to get a rich, thick, fruity syrup.

Cook the ravioli in boiling water for 3–4 minutes. This will cook the ravioli pasta and warm the fruits through. Remove from the water with a slotted spoon.

Drizzle some cream, sour cream or Anglaise sauce across the base of the serving bowls with some fruit syrup. Place the ravioli on top, dust with powdered sugar and spoon more fruity syrup on top. Garnish with some of the fruits used in the filling and mint leaves or shreds of citrus zest.

**Note:** Liqueurs such as Cointreau, Grand Marnier, cognac and rum can be added to the syrup.

Water can be used in place of the stock syrup to purée any remaining fruits. Simply add water and simmer until a good, thick consistency is reached and push through a sieve.

# Molasses Loaf

*I am sure we all do the same thing – find a recipe and then play with it, making adjustments to improve (we hope!) the results. Well, here's an example of this. I love the rich flavor of molasses but I did find the original recipe a little too dry. This loaf has a texture very similar to malt loaf, with a moist finish. With these changes, the result is rich and delicious!*

**Makes a 500 g (1 lb) Loaf**

¼ cup (75 g) molasses

¼ cup (50 g) packed brown sugar

1 egg

2 cups (225 g) flour

1 teaspoon ground allspice

¼ cup (50 g) currants

⅓ cup (50 g) golden raisins

4 tablespoons (50 g) butter

⅓ cup (65 ml) milk

Preheat the oven to 350°F/180°C. Butter a 1 lb (500 g) loaf pan and line the base with waxed paper.

Cream the molasses with the sugar and egg. Sift together the flour and allspice and mix into the molasses mixture. Add the currants and golden raisins. Melt the butter with the milk and add to the mixture. Mix well. Spoon the mix into the pan and bake for 30–40 minutes.

After 30 minutes, check the loaf by piercing with a skewer or small knife. The skewer should come out clean but moist. Once it's cooked, remove the loaf from the oven and let stand for 10 minutes. Turn out the loaf, peel off the paper and slice once cool.

**Note:** This molasses loaf mix does not really rise like bread in the pan, but becomes quite dense in texture, giving a richer, almost chewy taste.

# Homemade Eccles Cakes

*Eccles cakes are a classic for British corner shop bakers and for us to eat! So, why not have a go at making your own? They really are very simple and easy to make and even more delicious to eat.*

*To lift the basic flavors of currants, sugar and butter, I have added some grated orange zest and a dusting of cinnamon.*

---

**Makes 4 Cakes**

8 oz (225 g) Quick Puff Pastry
   (page 225) or frozen bought
   puff pastry, thawed
¼ cup (50 g) currants
2 tablespoons (25 g) packed light
   brown sugar

2 tablespoons (25 g) butter, softened
A pinch of ground cinnamon
The finely grated zest of 1 orange
1 egg white
Granulated sugar

Preheat the oven to 400°F/200°C.

Roll out the pastry to about ⅛ in (2 mm) thick. Mix together the currants, brown sugar, butter, cinnamon and grated zest of orange.

Cut four 6 in (15 cm) discs of pastry. Divide the filling between each of the discs, placing a dome of mix in the center of each one. Brush the edges of the pastry with water and gather all together, creating a 'bag' effect. Press the pastry together, cutting off any excess. The 'bag' can now be turned over onto a lightly floured board and softly rolled so that the pastry thins a little to reveal the currants, keeping a good circular shape. Repeat this simple process for the remaining three.

Brush each cake with egg white and sprinkle with granulated sugar. Score the tops with a sharp knife, making three or four lines. Let the cakes rest in the refrigerator for 15–20 minutes. Bake on buttered waxed paper for 25 minutes until rich, golden and crisp.

The eccles cakes can be eaten as a pastry cake, warm or cold. However, they can also be served as a dessert with custard, lightly whipped cream, vanilla ice cream.

# Golden Ginger 'Flapjack' Cake

*This is a rich afternoon tea cake, flavored with a lot of corn syrup and ginger to spice it up.*

**Makes about 12 Slices**

12 tablesoons (175 g) butter
1 cup (100 g) flour
4 cups (450 g) oatmeal
½ cup (100 g) packed light brown
  sugar
1 tablespoon (15 g) ground ginger
1 tablespoon (25 g) baking soda
1¼ cups (450 g) corn syrup
¼ cup (50 ml) milk

Preheat the oven to 350°F/180°C. Butter a 8 in (20 cm) round cake pan and line the base with waxed paper.

Rub the butter into the all-purpose flour and then add the oatmeal, sugar, ginger and baking soda.

Warm the syrup with the milk and pour into the dry ingredients, mixing well, to give quite a thick consistency. Spoon into the cake pan and bake for 45–50 minutes. The mix will rise slightly, giving a 1½–2 in (3–5 cm) deep cake.

Once cooked, let stand for 10–15 minutes to cool a little and turn out while still warm and peel off the paper. Slice into wedges and serve as a dessert with pouring or lightly whipped cream, or leave to serve cold as an afternoon tea cake.

# Homemade Crumpets

*I love having afternoon tea cakes, hot-cross buns, and scones. They are treats the British enjoy and they are so easy to get hold of in Britain – almost every shop sells them. Crumpets warmed and served toasted with lots of butter and jam are also a favorite. So, when a friend of mine passed on this recipe to me, I just had to try it. They do work and, with lots of butter, are delicious.*

**Makes about 20**
4 cups (450 g) all-purpose flour
2 tablespoons (15 g) salt

½ oz (15 g) cake yeast
2½ cups (15 g) warm water

Sift together the flour and salt. Mix the yeast with a few tablespoons of the warm water. Whisk three-quarters of the remaining warm water into the flour and then add the yeasty liquid. Cover and leave in a warm place until the mixture has risen. Once risen, check the consistency. If the batter is very thick, loosen with the remaining water. The batter should now be left to stand for 8–10 minutes.

Warm a non-stick frying pan on a low heat. Butter some crumpet rings or small tartlet rings.

Place the rings into the frying pan and pour in some of the batter until half-full (¼–½ in deep/5 mm–1 cm). Cook on a low heat until small holes appear and the top has started to dry. The bottom of the crumpet will now be golden and it can be turned over and cooked for another minute. The crumpets are now ready for lots of melting butter!

**Note:** The crumpets can be cooked without turning: simply cook until the tops are completely dry.

The finely grated zest of 1 lemon can also be added to the batter to give a lemon bite.

# Lemon Genoise Cake

*This cake base can be used for many things: cakes, gâteaux, or trifles. If you keep a couple of vanilla pods in an air-tight jar with your sugar, you will have vanilla sugar ready whenever you need it.*

---

**Makes 6–8 in (1 x 15–20 cm) Cake**

3 eggs

¾ cup (75 g) sugar flavored with a vanilla pod

¾ cup (75 g) flour

2 tablespoons (25 g) unsalted butter, melted

Juice and zest of 1 lemon

Preheat the oven to 400°F/200°C. Butter a 6–8 in (15–20 cm) round cake pan and dust with flour.

Whisk the eggs and sugar together in a bowl over a pan of hot water. Continue to whisk until the mixture has doubled in volume and is light and creamy. Remove from the heat and continue to whisk until cold and thick. This is called the ribbon stage because the mixture will trail off the whisk in ribbons when you lift it out of the mixture. Lightly fold in the flour, melted butter, the juice and lemon zest. Gently pour the mix into the prepared pan and bake in the Preheated oven for about 30 minutes. The easiest way to test is with a skewer, which will come out clean when the cake is ready.

Allow to cool for 10 minutes in the pan, then turn out onto a wire rack and leave to go cold.

**Note:** To make a Chocolate Lemon Genoise Cake, replace ¼ cup (25 g) of the flour with 2 tablespoons of cocoa.

# Anglaise (Fresh Custard) Sauce

*This recipe is for a fresh custard or anglaise sauce which can act as a base for so many different flavors. You must only serve it warm, not boiled, or you will scramble the egg yolks in the cream mix. The fresh vanilla is optional and can be omitted when using other flavors.*

---

**Makes 5 cups (750 ml)**
8 egg yolks
¾ cup (75 g) sugar

1 vanilla pod (optional)
1¼ cup (300 ml) milk
1¼ cup (300 ml) heavy cream

Beat the egg yolks and sugar together in a bowl until well blended. Split and scrape the insides of the vanilla pod, if using, into the milk and cream and bring to a boil. Place the bowl over a pan of hot water and whisk the cream into the egg mixture. As the egg yolks warm, the cream will thicken to create a custard. Keep stirring until it coats the back of a spoon. Remove the bowl from the heat. The custard can now be served warm or stirred occasionally until it cools. Serve warm or cold.

**Variations:** For Lemon Custard Sauce, add the rind, not the pith, of two lemons to the milk and cream when heating, then leave it in the mix throughout the cooking process. Once the custard has thickened, add the juice of one lemon and taste. If the lemon flavor is not strong enough, simply add more lemon juice to taste. Strain the custard through a sieve to serve.

For Orange Custard Sauce, add the rind of two oranges to the milk and cream when heating, then cook as for the basic recipe. Orange juice will not be used in this recipe. To lift the flavor of the sauce, try adding a few drops of Cointreau or Grand Marnier.

For Rum Custard Sauce, add some rum to taste at the end of cooking the vanilla custard. Shredded coconut could also be added to this recipe during the cooking process and/or coconut milk added at the end.

Coffee Custard Sauce can be made by replacing the vanilla pod with 2 teaspoons of freshly ground coffee and made as for the vanilla recipe. Once the coffee custard has completely cooled, strain to remove any excess granules.

# Short Crust and Sweet Short Crust Pastry

*Both of these pastries have the same method; the difference is the sugar. Other recipe ideas that give the pastry different flavors follow (below and page 225) and can be used with the different fillings given on page 176.*

| **Makes 12 oz (350 g)** | **For Sweet Short Crust Pastry** |
|---|---|
| 2 cups (225 g) flour | 1 quantity Shortcrust Pastry |
| 10 tablespoons (150 g) butter, chopped | ¼ cup (50 g) powdered sugar or regular sugar, |
| 1 egg (an extra egg yolk can be added for a stronger flavor) | |

For the basic short crust pastry, rub the flour and butter together to a crumbly texture. Add the egg and mix briefly to a smooth dough. Wrap in plastic wrap and refrigerate for 20 minutes before rolling and using.

To make the sweet pastry, add the sugar to the flour and butter mixture.

**Note:** When pre-baking any pastry shell, line with waxed paper or foil and fill with baking beans or rice. This applies to all the pastry recipes.

For a Sweet Lemon and Raisin Short Crust Pastry, add the finely grated zest of 2 lemons and ⅓ cup (50 g) chopped raisins to the sweet short crust pastry mix. These flavors give the pastry a completely different finish. The pastry works well with fruit, especially with the Gooseberry Tart (see Note on page 177).

# Rich Short Crust Pepper Pastry

*The only pepper that really works in this pastry is the black variety. Once it has been milled, I strain it through a sieve, taking out any coarse lumps. I use this recipe for savory tarts and quiches.*

| **Makes 14 oz (400 g)** | 1 teaspoon freshly ground black pepper (heaping, if you are a real pepper fan!) |
|---|---|
| 2¼ cups (250 g) flour | |
| 10 tablespoons (150 g) salted butter | |
| 1 egg, beaten | |

Rub the butter into the flour with the black pepper until it resembles breadcrumbs. Add the egg and 1–2 tablespoons of very cold water to give a good pastry texture. Wrap in plastic wrap and let rest in the fridge before rolling.

# Sweet Black Pepper and Crunchy Sugar Pastry

*Black pepper can be added to unsweetened short crust pastry for savory tarts and quiches to give an extra bite (see page 224). The pepper flavor also works well in the sweet pastry: it spices up the tart without being overpowering. The crunchy texture of light brown granulated sugar helps balance the 'hot' flavor.*

---

**Makes 14 oz (400 g)**
1 quantity of Sweet Short Crust
   Pastry (page 224)

1 teaspoon cracked black
   peppercorns
¼–¾ cup (50–75 g) light brown
   granulated sugar

---

Cracked black pepper can be found in most supermarkets. This guarantees that the coarse pepper is totally even in size. Add the pepper to the flour and then complete the sweet short crust pastry recipe. Once rested, roll out and sprinkle half with the sugar. Fold the other half over and reroll. The sugar will keep its crunchy texture inside the pastry.

**Note:** This pastry works very well with strawberries, especially peppered strawberries and with the crunchy sugar they will taste even better! Some Pastry Cream (page 231) can be spooned into the cooked pastry shell before covering with strawberries. These can now be heavily dusted with powdered sugar and glazed (and burned slightly) under the broiler or with a gas gun.

# Quick Puff Pastry

*Making puff pastry the traditional way cannot really be matched. But here's a recipe that gets you very close to it. Of course the quickest puff pastry is bought frozen!*

---

**Makes about 1½ lb (750 g)**
4 cups (450 g) flour
20 tablespoons (275 g) butter,
   chilled

1 teaspoon salt
1¼ cups (300 ml) water

---

Cut the butter into small pieces. Sift the flour with the salt. Mix together all of the ingredients without totally breaking down the butter. This will enable the butter to work its way into the pastry while it's being rolled. Once the dough is made, roll as for classic puff pastry, into a rectangle (approximately 18 × 6 in/45 × 15 cm). Fold in the right-hand one-third and then fold in the left-hand side on top. Leave to rest for 20 minutes. The pastry needs to be rolled three times in the same way, resting it for 20 minutes between each turn.

# Shortbread Pastry

*This recipe is for a basic shortbread dough. Shortbreads normally finish up as cookies or cakes. With this recipe, I am using the dough to line tart shells. A good fresh raspberry tart, or strawberries, peaches or summer fruits on a shortbread pastry shell is delicious. Put the raw fruits directly on the shortbread or spread extra-thick heavy cream on the base and arrange all the fruits on top.*

---

**Makes 12 oz (350 g)**
8 tablespoons (100 g) butter
¼ cup (50 g) sugar

The grated zest of 1 lemon
1⅓ cup (175 g) flour

Cream the butter and sugar together. Add the zest and flour and work to a dough. Once completely mixed, wrap in plastic wrap and rest for 20 minutes before rerolling and baking.

# Hazelnut Pastry

*This pastry is virtually impossible to roll! Don't be put off, though, because this mixture can be just pressed by hand into a tart shell. It is important to work the ground hazelnuts and flour into the sugar and butter mixture for some time, preferably using a food processor or electric mixer. This technique will release the natural hazelnut oils which in turn will help bind the pastry.*

---

**Makes 500 g (1 lb 2 oz)**
8 tablespoons (100 g) butter
¼ cup (50 g) sugar
1¼ cups (150 g) ground hazelnuts

1¾ cups (200 g) flour
1 egg yolk

Preheat the oven to 400°F/200°C.

Cream the butter and sugar together. Add the ground hazelnuts and flour and leave to work well in the processor or mixer. Add the egg yolk and bind together. It will have a very dry texture. Press the mixture evenly into a buttered tart ring. Line with waxed paper or foil and fill with baking beans or rice. Leave to rest in the fridge for 20 minutes.

Bake for approximately 30 minutes. The pastry shell will now be crisp and, when eaten, quite crumbly and packed with hazelnut taste.

**Note:** This is the perfect base for the Raspberry Meringue Pie (page 182).

# Basic Stock Syrup

*Stock syrups are used mostly for poaching fresh fruits and as sorbet bases. This recipe gives you the quantities needed.*

*The basic recipe is usually 1lb (450 g) sugar to 2½ cups (600 ml) of water. This quantity will give you at least 3¾ cups (900 ml) of finished, very thick syrup. For a less sweet and thick syrup, use 1⅔ cups (350 g) of sugar to 2½ cups (600 ml) of water. Here are the quantities to give you approximately 2 cups (450 ml) of sweet, thick syrup.*

---

**Makes about 2 cups (450 ml)**

1⅓ cups (225 g) sugar
1¼ cups (300 ml) water

Bring both ingredients to a boil and simmer for 8–10 minutes. The syrup will now have thickened and is ready to use.

**Note:** Other flavors can be added, such as grated fruit zests or liqueurs.

# Blood Orange Syrup

*The rich, red color from blood oranges makes this syrup even more exciting but if blood oranges are unavailable, just use another variety.*

---

**Makes 1¼ cups (300 ml)**

2½ cups (600 ml) blood-orange juice
1⅛ cups (225 g) sugar
The juice of 2 lemons
¼ cup (50–75 ml) Cointreau (optional)

Bring all the ingredients to a boil and reduce to 1¼ cups (300 ml). Strain through a sieve and the syrup is ready.

**Note:** This recipe can also be made into an orange and rum syrup with the addition of 2-3 tablespoons – or more! – of good rum.

# Madeira Syrup

*Madeira was always served with Madeira cake. This syrup can be served warm over Mini Madeira Prune Cakes (page 205), and it will keep the cake, taste and tradition very much alive.*

**Makes about 1 cup (250 ml)**
½ bottle Madeira

¾ cup (175 g) sugar
⅔ cup (150 ml) water

Simply boil all the ingredients together and simmer to a thick, syrupy consistency.

**Note:** This syrup will also liven up ice creams, meringues and sponge cakes.

# Golden Raisins Syrup Sauce

*I made this syrup originally to serve around the Lemon and Sultana Savarin on page 196. I have used it since with many other desserts, ranging from hot steamed desserts to ice-creams.*

**Makes 1–1¼ cups (250–300 ml)**
⅔ cup (100 g) golden raisins

⅔ cup (150 ml) water
¼ cup (50 g) sugar
The juice of 1 lemon

Mix all the ingredients together and bring to a simmer. Cook for 10 minutes and then purée in a food processor. Push through a sieve and the sauce is ready.

**Note:** The lemon juice can be replaced with rum, Madeira, cognac and more!

# Mint Syrup

*Here's another syrup to finish many dishes. It's a great alternative to use with a simple fruit salad, giving the dish a completely different taste. It can also be used as a garnish for almost any chocolate dessert. The flavor is immense and the color just as strong. The quantity of mint seems high, but is needed to achieve the right strength of flavor.*

---

**Makes about 8 cups (250 ml)**
8 oz (225 g) fresh mint leaves

¾ cup (175 g) sugar
½ cup (120 ml) water

Blanch the mint leaves in boiling water and then refresh in ice water. Once cold, drain off all the water and chop the mint.

Bring the sugar and water to a simmer and cook for 10 minutes until it has reached a thick syrup. Remove from the heat and leave to cool.

Add the mint to the cold syrup and purée to a smooth paste in the food processor. Let infuse for at least 8 hours and preferably overnight. Once infused, pass through a sieve. The syrup is ready and is best kept refrigerated before using.

# Strawberry (or Raspberry) Syrup

*This syrup will also work with other red or black berries. The strawberry version is featured in the Crème Chiboust on page 202 and the raspberry with the Roast Peach Melba (see Note on page 198).*

---

**Makes 1¼ cups (300 ml)**
1¾ cups (225 g) red, ripe
    strawberries, chopped

⅓–½ cup (85–120 ml) water
¼ cup (50 g) sugar

Simmer all the ingredients together until the strawberries are tender. Remove from the heat, cover the saucepan with plastic wrap and let cool. Once cooled, push the strawberries and syrup through a sieve. Return to the heat and reduce to a thick syrup.

# Coffee Syrup

*This syrup can be made with freshly brewed or instant coffee. The brewed coffee will obviously give you a fuller taste, but the instant a quicker result. The only other ingredient is sugar.*

---

**Makes ²/₃ cup (150 ml)**
1¼ cups (300 ml) strong freshly brewed or instant coffee

²/₃ cup (150 g) sugar

Boil the coffee and sugar together and reduce by half. You now have a rich coffee syrup that is best served at room temperature or cold.

**Note:** For a liqueur coffee syrup, simply add a splash of Tia Maria.

# Fruit Jam Sauce

*This is really a recipe for homemade, syrupy jam. It has a double use; once you've made it for a dessert, use it the next morning to spread on your toast! The sauce goes very well with the Creamy Fried Slice on page 206 or spooned into baking dishes for your next steamed dessert. Various fruits can be used, for example, blackberries, blackcurrants, rhubarb, raspberries, loganberries, apricots, strawberries, gooseberries, or peaches.*

---

**Makes 450–750 g (1–1½ lb)**
1 lb (450 g) blackberries, washed

4 tablespoons water
1 cup (225 g) sugar

Place all the ingredients in a saucepan and bring to a simmer. Increase the heat to boiling, skimming off any impurities. Return to simmer and cook for 4–5 minutes. Remove the pan from the heat and allow to cool. You now have the rich fruit jam sauce. You can keep it refrigerated in sterilized jars for several weeks. This sauce is best served warm, rather than hot, due to its high sugar content.

**Note:** For jam increase the sugar to the same quantity as the fruit.

When making jams, the longer the cooking time the smoother the jam becomes; simmering it for 4–5 minutes will give you a chunky finish, and increasing the time to 10–15 minutes or longer will leave you with a fruit jelly consistency.

# Crisp 'Parmesan' Lemon Crumbs

*Whenever pasta is made, I always think about freshly grated 'Parmesan'. It seems to be a natural companion. Here's a recipe for crispy 'Parmesan' for any pasta desserts, especially the fruity Raviolis on page 216.*

---

**Serves 4**

4 slices of white bread, crusts removed, quartered

The finely grated zest of 1 large lemon or orange

A pat of butter

1 teaspoon chopped fresh mint (optional)

A good pinch of powdered sugar (optional)

Blend the bread to crumbs in a food processor with the grated zest. Melt the butter, and fry the crumbs until golden and crisp. The crumbs are now ready to sprinkle over the pasta. Chopped fresh mint can be added to the food processor at the last minute along with a good pinch of powdered sugar to balance the acidity with sweetness.

# Pastry Cream

*This is a wonderful base for fruit tarts. It is spooned into baked tart shells and then covered with fresh fruits. Quickly cooked rhubarb and gooseberries or raspberries and strawberries, topping a good pastry cream, in a crisp pastry – how does that sound?*

---

**Makes about 2½ cup (600 ml)**

4 egg yolks

¼ cup (50 g) sugar

1½ tablespoons cornstarch

2 cups (450 ml) milk

1 vanilla pod, split and scraped, or 2 teaspoons vanilla extract

2 tablespoons heavy cream

1 tablespoon butter

Cream together the egg yolks and sugar in a bowl. Add the cornstarch. Bring the milk to a boil with the vanilla and pour onto the egg yolk mixture. Return the mixture to the pan, bring back to a simmer and cook for a few minutes, making sure it doesn't boil. Add the cream and butter and then pass through a sieve. Press a piece of waxed paper or plastic wrap onto the surface to prevent a skin from forming. Let cool. The fresh, vanilla-tasting pastry cream is ready to use.

**Note:** Grated fruit zests can be added to the milk for a different flavor.

# stocks, sauces and basics

*t*his is a chapter for basics and extras. The stocks and recipes haven't really changed from the previous books. One or two have been tweaked here and there, but basics are basic and shouldn't really need a change.

However, making stocks and sauces doesn't have to become a chore. Good-quality stock cubes or packet bases can be found quite easily and will give very good results. The rarebit recipe has reappeared but this time it is flavoured with Gorgonzola. The flavour is immense and goes well with green vegetables. The Gorgonzola can be replaced with almost any other blue cheese; Stilton, Roquefort and so on, or just make it the classic way with Cheddar.

There are combinations of the Butter Sauce recipe (page 236), some flavoured oils, chutneys and relishes. The flavour of the Macerated Grapes (page 239) is quite sensational, working equally well hot or cold with *foie gras*, pâtés and salads.

A basic chapter that finishes the rest of the book – in every sense!

# Gorgonzola Rarebit

*Here's another rarebit alternative, others having been featured in the* Rhodes Around Britain *trilogy. I find this goes very well melted over green vegetables such as cabbage, greens, broccoli and leeks. It also tastes lovely with cauliflower or as a topping for the vegetarian Roast Mushroom and Leek Shepherd's Pie (page 125).*

*Gorgonzola is an Italian cow's milk blue cheese with a mild creamy texture and not too overpowering in flavor. The cheddar is still needed to balance the strength of the gorgonzola; half and half seems to be the right proportion.*

---

**Makes 14 oz (400 g)**

1 ½ cups (175 g) cheddar, grated
⅓ cup (85 ml) milk
1 ½ cups (175 g) gorgonzola, chopped
¼ cup (25 g) all-purpose flour
⅓ cup (25 g) white breadcrumbs
½ tablespoon English mustard powder
1–2 shakes of Worcestershire sauce
1 egg
1 egg yolk
Salt and pepper

Melt the cheddar with the milk over a low heat. Once melted, add the gorgonzola and stir it in until it melts. Bring the mixture to a soft bubble on the stove and add the flour, crumbs, mustard and season with salt and pepper. Cook for a few minutes until the mixture comes away from the sides of the pan and begins to form a ball shape. Add the Worcestershire sauce and let cool.

When cold, beat in the egg and egg yolk (this can be done easily in a food processor). Once totally mixed, chill for a few hours before using. The rarebit mix is ready to use.

# Homemade Pasta

*This pasta recipe can be used for so many different pasta dishes: lasagne, ravioli, fettucine, spaghetti, and others. It is simple to make and can be put together in an electric mixer, food processor, or best of all, by hand. When working the dough by hand, you will be able to feel the texture you are looking for – it should have a slightly elastic finish. The pasta dough can be rolled either by hand, or if you have one, with a pasta machine.*

---

**Makes about 9 oz (250 g)**

2 ¼ cups (250 g) fine
   semolina flour
A pinch of salt

½ teaspoon olive oil
2 eggs, beaten
3 egg yolks, beaten

Add the semolina flour to the salt and olive oil and mix well. Add the eggs and egg yolks and work to a dough. On a clean, lightly floured board, work the dough for 10 minutes until you have a good, slightly elastic, smooth dough. Wrap the dough in plastic wrap and let rest for 30 minutes.

For whatever pasta you are making, it will first need to be rolled by hand to approximately ⅛ in (3 mm) thick.

The choice of pasta shapes is yours!

**Note:** For a better taste, use Italian or French 00 flour if you can get it.

# Quick Hollandaise Sauce

*This is a quick way of making a Hollandaise sauce, without having to make a flavored reduction. I use this as a base for the Confit of Sea Trout on page 70 with the addition of a tablespoon or two of Dijon mustard to fire up the flavor. I originally included the recipe in* More Rhodes Around Britain, *but I'm repeating it here for convenience.*

**Makes about 1 ¼ cups (300 ml)**
½ lb. (225 g) unsalted butter
2 egg yolks

1 tablespoon warm water
The juice of ½ lemon
Salt and cayenne pepper or freshly ground white pepper

Melt the butter in a pan and then leave it to cool slightly, so that it is just warm when added to the sauce; if it is too hot, the sauce will curdle. The butter should have separated, so you will only be adding the butter oil to the sauce, not the buttermilk that will have collected at the bottom of the pan. This is clarified butter.

Add the egg yolks to the water in a bowl and whisk over a pan of hot water until lighter in color and thickened. Remove from the heat and slowly add the clarified butter, whisking until the sauce is thick. Add the lemon juice and season with salt and cayenne or pepper.

# Maltaise Sauce

*This is also a fairly quick recipe, following the Hollandaise method above but replacing the lemon juice and water with a reduction of white wine vinegar and blood orange juice. The chopped blood-orange segments give the sauce a lot more texture.*

**Makes about 1 ¼ cups (300 ml)**
⅓–½ cup (85–120 ml) white wine vinegar
4 blood oranges, juiced

1 blood orange, segmented and diced
Ingredients for 1 quantity of Quick Hollandaise Sauce (above)

Boil the vinegar and orange juice and reduce by three-quarters. Allow to cool slightly and then mix with the egg yolks and follow the method for Hollandaise sauce. Season with salt and pepper and add the diced blood orange segments to finish.

# butter sauces
*The sauce is better known among chefs as* beurre blanc. *It is a very simple and very buttery sauce that works with many dishes, whether they're fish, meat or vegetarian. The basic ingredients are, normally, white wine vinegar, water, chopped shallots and butter. I have added a few more ingredients to this recipe to add a lot more flavor.*

*I have also given four 'stocks' as alternatives, starting with water and running through fish, chicken and vegetarian. It will really depend on which dish you are serving the sauce with. Three alternative ideas for flavorings follow the basic recipe.*

## Basic Butter Sauce

**Makes about 1 ¼ cups (300 ml)**

1 cup (250 g) butter, chilled, and cubed
2 shallots or 1 small onion, finely chopped
½ star anise (optional)
2–3 cardamom pods (optional)
1 bay leaf (optional)
Freshly ground black pepper

⅓ cup (85 ml) white wine vinegar
¾ cup (175 ml) white wine
⅔ cup (150 ml) water or Fish, Chicken or Vegetable Stock (page 240/1) or alternative (page 243)
2 tablespoons heavy cream (optional)
Salt and pepper

Melt a small pat of the butter and add the shallots or onion, star anise, cardamom pods, bay leaf, if using, and a twist of black pepper. Cook for a few minutes, without letting the vegetables brown, until softened. Add the vinegar and reduce by three-quarters. Add the wine and reduce by three-quarters. Pour in the water or stock of your choice and reduce again by three-quarters. If using the heavy cream to help emulsify the butter, pour it in at this stage.

Bring the reduction to a simmer and whisk in all of the butter, a few pieces at a time. Season with salt and pepper and strain through a sieve. If the sauce is too thick, loosen it with a few drops of water or lemon juice. The basic butter sauce is now ready to use.

# Cilantro Butter Sauce

**Makes about 1 ¼ cups (300 ml)**
1 quantity Basic Butter Sauce (opposite)

1 bunch of fresh cilantro
1 teaspoon lightly crushed coriander seeds

Reserve a quarter of the cilantro leaves for chopping and adding to the finished sauce. Roughly chop the remaining leaves and stalks and add to the basic butter sauce reduction with the crushed cilantro seeds. Once the sauce has been cooked and strained, add the chopped cilantro just before serving.

# Carrot Butter Sauce

**Makes about 1 ¼ cups (300 ml)**
1 quantity Basic Butter Sauce (opposite)

3 carrots, peeled
The juice of 1 orange

Grate 2 of the carrots and add to the chopped shallots at the start of the cooking period. This will release a lot of sweet carrot flavor and color. Cut the remaining carrot into very small dice and then cook in salted water for a few minutes until tender. The carrot dice will be used to garnish the sauce before serving. Add the orange juice to the sauce once the white wine has reduced. Finish as for the basic recipe and the carrot butter sauce is made.

# Mustard Butter Sauce

**Makes about 1 ¼ cups (300 ml)**

1 quantity Basic Butter Sauce (opposite)
2 tablespoons whole grain mustard

Push the butter sauce through a sieve and then add the mustard. I like the sauce to have a fairly strong flavor and 2 tablespoons of whole grain mustard will give you just that. Add more if you like it stronger.

# Orange Oil

*This flavored oil works well as a dressing for many dishes. A tasty duck à l'orange summer salad would go very well with this dressing. I use it to help flavor the Seared Scallops with Homemade Pasta on page 66.*

**Makes 2 ½ cups (600 ml)**

1 ¼ cups (300 ml) olive oil,
   preferably extra virgin
1 ¼ cups (300 ml) peanut oil
2 garlic cloves, sliced
3–4 cardamom pods, lightly crushed
1 bay leaf

1 star anise
The finely grated zest and juice of
   4 oranges (blood oranges can also
   be used)
Salt and pepper

Place all the ingredients, except the orange juice, in a saucepan and bring to a simmer. Remove the pan from the heat and leave to stand for a few hours to help all the flavors infuse.

Boil the orange juice and reduce by three-quarters, giving you a very strongly orange-flavored reduction.

Once the oil has infused, season with salt and pepper and strain through a sieve, squeezing out all of the oil. Add the orange juice and store in a tightly closed jar. The oil, without the juice, will keep almost indefinitely. With the juice, it is best to keep it refrigerated for up to 10 days.

# Macerated Grapes

*These grapes can be used to help flavor so many dishes. In this book they are featured with Roast Foie Gras on Potato Pancakes (page 42), but I also like to use them as a warm salad dressing. They keep very well, refrigerated and in an air-tight jar, for a few weeks; although the grapes become softer and start to break down, the flavor just keeps getting better.*

**Makes about 1 1/4 cups (300 ml)**

1 lb (450 g) seedless white grapes, washed
1 tablespoon peanut oil
A pat of butter
1 heaping teaspoon packed light brown sugar
1 tablespoon brandy
2 tablespoons sherry vinegar
1 teaspoon strong balsamic vinegar
1 ¼ cups (150 ml) sweet white wine or white wine with ½ teaspoon packed light brown sugar
Salt and pepper

Heat a frying pan with the peanut oil. Add the grapes and pan-fry for 2–3 minutes until golden. Add a pat of butter and continue to fry for another minute. Add the brown sugar, which will start to caramelize, with the butter. Add the brandy, which can be flambéed and reduced. Add the sherry vinegar and reduce by half and then follow with the balsamic vinegar and sweet white wine. Reduce by half and lightly season with salt and a twist of pepper.

Remove the grapes from the heat and leave to cool. They are now ready to use and will improve in flavor after a few days of marinating. The grapes are best kept in a jar or other air-tight container.

# Chicken Stock

**Makes 10 cups (2.25 liters)**

2 onions, chopped

2 celery sticks, chopped

2 leeks, chopped

2 tbs (25 g) unsalted buttter

1 garlic clove, crushed

1 bay leaf

1 fresh thyme sprig

A few black peppercorns

4 lb (1.75 kg) chicken carcasses, chopped

14 cups (3.4 liters) water

Salt

In a large stock pot, lightly soften the vegetables in the butter, without letting them brown. Add the garlic, bay leaf, thyme, peppercorns and chopped carcasses. Cover with the cold water, season with salt and bring to the simmer, skimming off the impurities all the time. Allow the stock to simmer for 2–3 hours.

Drain through a sieve. The stock is now ready to use and will keep well, chilled or frozen.

# Vegetable Stock

**Makes about 5 cups (1.2 liters)**

1 ¼ cups (225 g) carrots (optional)

2 onions

4 celery sticks

2 leeks, white part only

1 fennel bulb

1–2 zucchini

1 bay leaf

1 sprig fresh thyme

1 teaspoon coriander seeds

1 teaspoon pink peppercorns

½ lemon, sliced

3 ½ cups (1.5 liters) water

A pinch of salt

Vegetable oil

Cut all the vegetables roughly into ½ in (1 cm) dice. Warm the vegetable oil in a pan, then add all the diced vegetables, the herbs, coriander, peppercorns and lemon. Cook without browning for 8–10 minutes, allowing them to soften slightly. Add the water with a good pinch of salt and bring to a simmer. Once at simmering point, cook for 30 minutes without a lid. During this time the stock should have reduced, increasing the flavor and depth.

The stock can now be strained through a sieve, leaving you with about 3 cups (1.2 liters). If you find there is more than this quantity, simply boil rapidly to reduce. You can also reduce it if you find that the flavor is not full enough.

STOCKS, SAUCES, AND BASICS

# Fish Stock

**Makes about 8 cups (2 liters)**

1 large onion, sliced
1 leek, sliced
2 celery sticks, sliced
4 tbs (50 g) unsalted butter
A few fresh parsley stalks
1 bay leaf
6 black peppercorns
2 lb (1 kg) turbot or sole bones, washed
1 ¼ cups (300 ml) dry white wine
16 cups (2.25 liters) water
Salt

Sweat the sliced vegetables in the butter, without letting them brown. Add the parsley stalks, bay leaf and peppercorns. Chop the fish bones, making sure there are no blood clots left on them. Add to the vegetables and continue to cook for a few minutes. Add the wine and boil to reduce until almost dry. Add the water, season with salt and bring to the simmer. Allow to simmer for 20 minutes, then drain through a sieve. The stock is now ready to use, or you can store it in the refridgerator for a few days.

# Veal or Beef Stock and *Jus*/Gravy

**Makes 19 cups (4.5–6 liters) stock or 5 cups (600 ml–1.2 liters) *jus*/gravy**

3 onions, halved
2–3 tablespoons water
5 lb (2.25 kg) veal or beef bones
8 oz (225 g) veal or beef trimmings from the butcher

1 ¼ cups, (225 g) carrots, coarsely chopped
3 celery sticks, coarsely chopped
1 leek, chopped
3–4 tomatoes, chopped
1 garlic clove, halved
1 bay leaf
1 fresh thyme sprig
Salt

Preheat the oven to 250°F/120°C. Lay the onion halves flat in a roasting tray with the water. Place the onions in the oven and allow to caramelize slowly until they have totally softened and browned. This process will take 1–2 hours. The sugars in the onions will cook slowly and give a wonderful taste.

Pop the onions into a large stock pot and leave on one side. Increase the oven temperature to 400°F/200°C. Place all the bones and trimmings in a roasting tray and roast for about 30 minutes until well browned. Roast the chopped carrots and celery in another roasting tray for about 20 minutes until lightly browned.

When ready, add the roasted bones, trimmings and vegetables to the onions in the pot, along with the leek, tomatoes, garlic, bay leaf and thyme. Fill the pot with cold water – you'll need about 10–12 pints (6–7.2 liters). Bring the stock to the simmer, season with salt and skim off any impurities. Allow to cook for 6–8 hours for the maximum flavor. If it seems to be reducing too quickly, top up with cold water.

When ready, drain and discard the bones and vegetables. This is now your veal stock, and you can cool it and freeze it in convenient quantitites.

Alternatively, make a veal *jus*/gravy with the stock. Allow the liquid to boil and reduce to 5 cups (600 ml–1.2 liters), skimming all the time. The stock should be thick and of a sauce-like consistency. Make sure that you taste all the time during reduction. If the sauce tastes right but is not thick enough, thicken it slightly with cornstarch. (Of course, I do hope that won't be necessary!) You now have a veal *jus*/gravy, a classic sauce.

# Alternative Stocks and Sauces

## Fish and Chicken Stocks

Alternatives to these can be found in the frozen food section of most quality supermarkets. They are sold in plastic tubs, each containing about 1¼ cups (284ml). The beauty of these is they taste great, they have a good color and jelly texture and they are sold as stocks ready to use. They really are the best I've found but, if you can't get hold of them, there are also some good quality bouillon cubes.

## Beef and Veal *Jus*/Gravy

In the basic recipe, the beef and veal *jus* start out as stock and are then reduced to a sauce consistency for other recipes. I've found a sauce which will cut out all of this and is an instant *jus* to use as a base sauce in many of the recipes that need veal or beef *jus*. Madeira Wine Gravy or White Wine Gravy are both made by Crosse & Blackwell in their Bonne Cuisine range, and should be available in just about every supermarket or grocery shop. The Madeira flavor gives good body and, when made, has a lovely, glossy finish. My only advice is to mix them with 2 cups (450 ml) of water instead of 1 ¼ cups (300 ml). This way, when slow-braising or stewing, there's room for reducing without them becoming too thick.

## Other Sauces and Ingredients

Another sauce I found, also in the Bonne Cuisine range, is Hollandaise Sauce. If you are unsure about making Hollandaise, give this version a try: it's so easy.

As for dried pastas and ready-made pastry, all varieties can be found in local shops. If you're lucky enough to have a good delicatessen nearby, then buy your pasta there; it's often made on the premises.

# Mustard Dressing

*This is a basic recipe for a simple dressing that I have used in many recipes. It's so versatile and has a creamy texture. If you have a favorite mustard – such as English, French, or grain – then simply use the one of your choice.*

**Makes 1 ¼ cups (300 ml)**

4 teaspoons Dijon mustard
2 tablespoons white wine vinegar
8 tablespoons walnut oil
8 tablespoons peanut oil
Salt and freshly ground black pepper

Whisk the mustard with the vinegar. Mix together the two oils and gradually add to the mustard, whisking all the time as you would if making mayonnaise. Once everything is thoroughly mixed, season with salt and pepper.

**Note:** This can also be made into a herb dressing by adding a choice of chopped mixed fresh herbs, or perhaps just chopped fresh tarragon to give you a mustard and tarragon dressing that will go well with fish or poultry.

The addition of 1–2 egg yolks, mixed with the mustard and white wine vinegar, will guarantee a creamy texture, almost like mayonnaise.

# Mustard Seed Butter

*This isn't so much a recipe as a flavoring. Melting this butter over fish or roasted pork or chicken dishes gives the finished result a much fuller flavor, with the crunch from the mustard seeds adding a new texture.*

**Makes 4 oz (100 g)**

2 tb (50 g) unsalted butter, softened
2 tb (50 g) whole grain mustard

Simply mix the two ingredients together. This can now be kept chilled or used immediately.

# Onion Gravy (1)

*Making this onion gravy with chopped onions gives you a completely different result in terms of consistency from the recipe below. This onion gravy can be cooked and reduced to an almost hot onion chutney/relish stage. Thick, rich, and tasty!*

**Makes 2 –4 cups (450–600 ml)**

4 large onions, finely chopped
2 tablespoons water

1 ¼–2 cups (300–450 ml) Veal or Beef Jus/Gravy (page 242) or alternative (page 243)

To make the onion gravy, place the chopped onions in a pan with the water. They must now be cooked on a very low heat, which will slowly draw the natural sugar content from the onions; together with its juices, the two will caramelize. This is a slow process, possibly taking up to 2 hours. It is very important that the onions do not burn or it will create a bitter taste. Once a caramel flavor has been achieved, add the gravy. By adding just 1¼ cups (300 ml) you will have a thick onion marmalade. This goes very well just spooned into cooked Yorkshire puddings. For a thinner sauce consistency, use 2 cups (450 ml) of *jus*.

For a quicker caramelizing method, cook the onions to a golden brown in a pat of butter. Add a teaspoon of light brown granulated sugar and cook for 1–2 minutes. Taste the onions for sweetness. If you feel they need more, add more sugar until the flavor you are after is achieved. Now just add the gravy and cook for 6–8 minutes before serving.

# Onion Gravy (2)

**Makes 2 ½ cups (600 ml)**

8 onions, thinly sliced
2 tablespoons water

2 ½ (600ml) Veal or Beef Jus/Gravy (page 242) or alternative (page 243)

Place the onions in a pan with the water and cook very slowly, stirring all the time. The sugar from the onions will slowly caramelize and become brown and sweet tasting. The process will take 1½–2 hours.

Add the *jus*/gravy and simmer for a further 30 minutes. The gravy will now be even richer in taste and color with a lovely shiny finish.

# Hot Mustard Shallot Sauce

*This sauce is, in fact, a French classic called* sauce diable – *'deviled sauce'. It is traditionally served with grilled or fried fish or meats. I've taken the sauce and played with the basic flavors. It is sweet, sharp, and has a good bite. I also like to use it as a dip for cocktail sausages, chicken or grilled shrimp on sticks.*

*The shallots can be replaced with onions but they don't quite give you the same result.*

---

**Makes about ½ pint**

1 ¼ cups (300 ml) finely diced
    shallots or onions
A small pat of butter
A good twist of freshly ground
    pepper
¼ cup (50 ml) red wine vinegar,
    preferably a thick, strong Cabernet
    Sauvignon variety

1 glass white wine
⅔ cup (150 ml) Jus/Gravy
    (page 242) or alternative
    (page 243) (it must have a good
    coating consistency)
1 teaspoon (or more) of English
    mustard (not powder)
Salt and pepper

Melt the butter in a small pan and add the chopped shallots or onions. Cook on a medium heat until they have started to take on a good golden brown color for about 4–5 minutes. Season with a twist of pepper and add the vinegar. Reduce the vinegar until almost dry, about 2–3 minutes. Add the wine and continue to reduce, again until almost dry. Add the *jus*/gravy and bring to the simmer. Lightly simmer for 5–10 minutes and then add the mustard. Season with salt and pepper, if needed, and taste. The sauce will now have a sharp, sweet flavor with a bite from the pepper and mustard. The taste can be strengthened with a little more mustard.

**Note:** The shallots have to be measured by volume to take into account the various sizes of shallot. The 1 ¼ cups (300 ml) listed in the ingredients guarantees the right quantity.

A small pinch of cayenne pepper can be added to the shallots while they are cooking in the butter to lift the 'bite'. Also,1 tablespoon of brandy can be added before the red wine vinegar to give a fuller flavor.

# Homemade Redcurrant Jelly

*Redcurrant jelly and mint sauce are two flavors and accompaniments usually offered with lamb. A good roast cut of lamb helped along with either (or both) is delicious to eat. So, I thought I would feature a recipe for the red one. The green one – the mint sauce – has already been featured in one of my previous books and I didn't want the redcurrants to feel left out.*

**Makes 1 ½ cups (750–900 g)**     About 2 cups or more of sugar
3 lb (1.5 kg) freshly picked
    redcurrants

Place the picked redcurrants in a saucepan and barely cover with water. Bring to the boil and then reduce the heat and simmer for 25–30 minutes until the currants have become overcooked and mushy.

Leave to strain through a fine sieve or muslin bag and allow to drain naturally. This will take all of the flavor and color from the fruit. After several hours, when the dripping has stopped, measure the quantity of juice. For every 2 ½ cups (600 ml) of juice, add 1 ⅔ cups (350 g) of sugar. (Normally, the quantity is 1 lb/450 g sugar to 2 ½ cups/600 ml of juice but I find this too sweet. Redcurrants have a high pectin level, and with preserving sugar, 1 ⅔ cups/350 g will be plenty.) Boil the sugar with the juices and simmer for 10 minutes. The jelly is now ready to pour into sterilized, hot jars. Once cold, the jelly will set.

**Note:** The flavor can be changed slightly with the addition of the grated zest of 1 orange and 2–3 tablespoons of port. This will give you an even richer jelly with an orange tang.

# Mango Chutney

*This is a chutney I love to spoon on to a good spicy curry dish. "Curries" have become a way of British life, so I thought I would include this recipe. Normally, the mango chutney is the thing you buy and quite often the curry is the thing that you make. Next time you order a take-out, at least part of it will be homemade!*

**Makes about 4 lb (1.75 kg)**

6 mangoes, not too ripe

1 lb (450 g) packed light brown sugar

2 teaspoons ground allspice

A good pinch of ground turmeric

½ teaspoon cayenne pepper

3 cooking apples, peeled, cored and chopped

2 onions, finely chopped

4 garlic cloves, finely crushed with 1 teaspoon salt

3 cups (750 ml) malt vinegar

½ pinch (50 g) finely grated fresh ginger

Peel the mangoes and then cut either side of the pit, giving you two thick slices of the fruit. Cut the opposite ends of the mango away from the edge of the pits. Any remaining fruit should be scraped off into a bowl. Cut the large fruit slices into thick strips.

Stir the sugar, mixed spice, turmeric, and cayenne into the mango. This is now best left for a good few hours to 'marinate'.

Next place all the ingredients together in a large saucepan. Bring to a simmer and cook for 1½ hours, stirring from time to time, for even cooking and to prevent it from sticking. The mango will have become soft and cooked through, leaving a thick syrup. If the chutney seems to be too thin, simply increase the heat, reduce and stir to a 'drier' consistency. Leave to rest for 20–30 minutes, before ladling into sterilized preserving jars.

These can now be cooled and kept in a cool area. The chutney can be eaten just days after cooking, but is best left for several weeks to mature.

# Pear Chutney

*A chutney that can be served with a variety of cold foods, this is at its best with a plate of cheese.*

**Makes 2–2½ lb**
**(900 g–1.25 kg)**

2 lb (1 kg) pears, peeled, cored and
  cut into ½ in (1 cm) dice
1 complete head of celery, peeled
  and cut into ½ in (1 cm) dice
1 ¼ cups (275 g) packed light brown
  or white sugar

1 onion, diced
1 teaspoon finely grated fresh ginger
  or ½ teaspoon ground ginger
1 teaspoon coriander seeds
2 garlic cloves, crushed
1 ¼ cups (300 ml) cider vinegar

Cook all the ingredients together for 20–25 minutes or until tender but still retaining their shape. Strain off the liquid and reduce to a syrup consistency (10–15 minutes). Pour the syrup back on to the pears and celery. Mix well, spoon into warm, sterilized jars and cover.

**Note:** This chutney will eat well after just 24 hours but obviously improves with time.

# Apple and Mustard Chutney

*This is a combination of flavors that goes particularly well with slices of good ham or cold roast pork; apples are the classic accompaniment to pork, and mustard puts fire in the combination.*

**Makes 1–1½ lb (450–750 g)**

10 green apples
4 tablespoons yellow or black mustard seeds
1 cup (250 ml) white wine vinegar
¾ cup (225 g) sugar
The finely grated zest of 1 lemon
2 onions, finely chopped
A pinch of salt

Peel, core and dice the apples. Place all the ingredients together in a pan and cook until the apples have become tender, about an hour. The liquid can now be drained and reduced to a syrupy consistency and then poured over the apple mixture and transferred to air-tight jars. This will give you a chunky chutney. Or just continue to cook to a more 'mashed' texture, cooking all the ingredients to a thick consistency.

# Apple, Prune, and Lime Chutney

*This is a very quick and easy chutney recipe. It goes well with pâtés, terrines and cold meats.*

---

**Makes 1–1½ lb (450–750 g)**

6 Granny Smith apples, peeled, cored, and cut into eighths
2 limes, peeled and segmented
½ onion, finely chopped
¼ cup (50 g) prunes, chopped
4 tablespoons red wine vinegar
1 glass of red wine
¼ cup (50 g) sugar
¼ teaspoon ground mixed spice
Salt and pepper

Place all the ingredients in a saucepan, bring to the simmer, cover and cook to a thick pickle consistency, about 30 minutes. Season with salt and pepper and the pickle is ready. Place in warm, sterilized jars and seal.

**Note:** The preserving sugar gives the chutney a longer life and helps it to hold a better consistency. The apple will break down to a chunky purée during the cooking.

# index

INDEX

INDEX